IN THE ADOPTED LAND

Recent titles in
Criminal Justice, Delinquency, and Corrections

The Fragmentation of Policing in American Cities: Toward an Ecological Theory
of Police-Citizen Relations
Hung-En Sung

Profiles from Prison: Adjusting to Life Behind Bars
Michael Santos

Racial Issues in Criminal Justice: The Case of African Americans
Marvin D. Free, Jr.

IN THE ADOPTED LAND

ABUSED IMMIGRANT WOMEN AND THE CRIMINAL JUSTICE SYSTEM

~

Hoan N. Bui

Foreword by Merry Morash

Criminal Justice, Delinquency, and Corrections
Marilyn D. McShane and Frank Williams, Series Editors

Westport, Connecticut
London

Library of Congress Cataloging-in-Publication Data

Bui, Hoan N., 1950–
    In the adopted land : abused immigrant women and the criminal justice system / Hoan N.
Bui ; foreword by Merry Morash.
        p.   cm.—(Criminal justice, delinquency, and corrections, ISSN 1535–0371)
    Includes bibliographical references and index.
    ISBN 0–275–97708–0 (alk. paper)
    1. Victims of family violence—United States—Case studies.   2. Abused women—United
States—Case studies.   3. Vietnamese American women—Abuse of.   4. Women
immigrants—Abuse of—United States.   5. Criminal justice, Administration of—United
States.   6. Police services for minorities—United States.   I. Title.   II. Series.
HV6626.2.B85   2004
362.82′92′0899592073—dc22   2003062430

British Library Cataloguing in Publication Data is available.

Library of Congress Catalog Card Number: 2003062430
ISBN: 0–275–97708–0
ISSN: 1535–0371

First published in 2004

Praeger Publishers, 88 Post Road West, Westport, CT 06881
An imprint of Greenwood Publishing Group, Inc.
www.praeger.com

Printed in the United States of America

The paper used in this book complies with the
Permanent Paper Standard issued by the National
Information Standards Organization (Z39.48–1984).

10 9 8 7 6 5 4 3 2

CONTENTS

Series Foreword		vii
Foreword		ix
Acknowledgments		xiii
1	Introduction	1
2	Family Lives in Transition	17
3	Contacts with Criminal Justice Agencies	45
4	When Victims Become Offenders	71
5	Women's Safety and Family Life	93
6	Women's Differences and Social Policies	113
	Appendix A: About the Study	127
	Appendix B: Attitudes of Vietnamese Americans Toward Intimate Violence Policies	137
Bibliography		139
Index		151

SERIES FOREWORD

Over the past two decades domestic violence research has come of age. As evidenced by the well-funded Minneapolis experiment and its replications, much of the energy in this arena has been directed at police operations and court processing options. Researchers have made significant progress in clarifying the issues surrounding the complex dynamics of mandatory arrest and treatment policies.

At the same time, insightful qualitative pieces have attempted to explain the perspectives of perpetrators and victims who live out these often misunderstood violent domestic relationships (e.g., Neil Websdale's 1997 research on rural women battering). Some works use a feminist approach that places events in the context of power, poverty, learned helplessness and gendered roles. However, the degree to which these "truths" are generalizable beyond our immediate cultural and social venues is best explained perhaps with a comparative investigation.

Dr. Bui's descriptions of the domestic violence experiences of her Vietnamese subjects are a fascinating look into the realities of cultural conflict, dysfunctional immigration, and adaptive politics. From the accounts that follow, the reader is able to see how the unique background of these women, their histories and ethnic values influence their expectations of the criminal justice system and, ultimately, their reactions to it. Hoan Bui has masterfully woven the tales of battered women and their families into a realistic look at the limits of the system. We are a diverse and multicultural nation, yet we seem to settle for homogenous policy responses that deny the very specific needs of individuals as they face their own personal crises and decision points. Most significantly, this work addresses questions about the universality of the immigrant experience, as well as the similarities in our responses to domestic violence across groups of women whose powerlessness seems to exponentially increase the hopelessness of their plight.

Marilyn McShane and Frank Williams

FOREWORD

In the past two decades, feminist theory has alerted practitioners and scholars to the tremendous force that the distribution of resources according to gender, race, class, and ethnicity has on people's social locations, actions, and well-being. At the same time, postmodern and other critical theorists (including feminists) have expressed growing concern with the extension of criminal justice controls into the community, the family, and, indeed, the very person. Community oriented police are now responsible for building community capacity to problem solve about everything from broken windows to the threats of school violence and international terrorism. Community prosecution, incredibly high rates of incarceration, and various courts that handle family, drug, and other human problems bring many, many people into the formal criminal justice system. Monitoring technologies, programs to restructure thinking processes, and the use of persistent drug testing put large numbers of people under the scrutiny of formal agents of social control and punishment. Pushing forward critical feminist work, Hoan Bui's book, *In the Adopted Land: Abused Immigrant Women and the Criminal Justice System*, documents the effects of the growing apparatus of criminal justice intervention on abused women who have immigrated to the United States from Vietnam. This criminal justice apparatus is the result of the transformation of domestic violence from a private family matter to a social problem, and the concomitant push for police, prosecutors, and judges to bring people into the justice system and arrange for their punishment.

The book is based on lengthy interviews with 34 Vietnamese women in four communities in the United States. The communities are located in Boston (Massachusetts), Houston (Texas), Orange County (California), and Lansing (Michigan). The analysis of the interview data reveals how gender affects women's resources, their goals, and the available strategies for achieving these goals; and the analysis also fully contextualizes women's accounts of their lives. Many contemporary theorists have noted the interplay of one or more slices of social reality: historical context, cultural traditions, the nature of law, social movements, criminal justice and INS policies and practices, individuals' life courses, and particular people's thinking, feelings, dreams, aspirations, and motivations. It is much easier to call attention to the need for research to reveal multilevel complexity than to actually capture this complexity. By embedding women's poignant accounts of their lives into dynamic and inconsistent multicultural, multinational and multihistorical contexts, Bui accomplishes this feat. She goes beyond women's own accounts and assessments of their situation to reveal how gender, class, and the experience of immigration intertwine in the lives of women who are abused by their husbands.

The examination of women's accounts reveals much about men. For many Vietnamese men, historical events and immigration translated into a loss of social standing and power. Military men found themselves with opportunities for only menial jobs, but with wives who could be breadwinners. Professional men could not break the language barrier. Some men gave up and did not work much or at all, were criticized by disappointed wives, and responded with anger and abuse. Others resented their wives' changing gender ideologies, which typically involved greater resistance to being dominated, and they responded with abuse. Some of the men seem frozen in time, unable to adapt to changing gender expectations and the realities of living as an immigrant in the United States.

Globalization is stamped all over the research results. Through a series of military occupations, Vietnamese history is affected by a variety of Asian and Western cultures. The United States' war in Vietnam created the need and the opportunity for women and men, including children, to immigrate to the United States. Men came as political refugees, and women followed their men. Amerasians came because American soldiers had been in Vietnam. Because of global inequities, women immigrated to join abusive husbands; they found no other way to ensure medical care for their children or to secure other necessities for family survival and well-being. Once in the United States, women and men drew from and were influenced by alternative gender ideologies and expectations; as Bui puts it, the norm of women's subordination that was derived from Confucianism had to compete with American culture. Inside of the broad effects of globalization, Vietnamese immigrant women use complex and varied approaches to work things out for themselves and their families.

In the end, this volume provides a clear picture of the lack of fit of Vietnamese women's desires and realities with inflexibly designed laws and policies. State power over families creates havoc in some women's lives. Women fear that noncitizen husbands will be deported, leaving them without financial and social support. The inability of most people in the United States to speak more than one language coupled with the fact that bilingual criminal justice system employees and translators are unavailable from initial police contact to court, means that what people say in Vietnamese can be misunderstood, or distorted by purposeful mistranslation. Police, prosecutors, and judges are sometimes oblivious to the fact that bystanders, neighbors, husbands, and other relatives purposely translate what women say incorrectly in order to protect the abuser, the family, or the reputation of the Vietnamese community. Police intervention sometimes results in extreme emotional abuse and family breakups, which magnifies the devastating impact on women because of cultural beliefs about the importance of marriage.

Despite the research that supports or criticizes one or another response to domestic violence, despite social movements and resulting program pressures on women to leave their abusers, and despite being hurt and unhappy, some women stay with abusive men. Others seek alternatives in order to meet their goals of giving their children a good life, or living their own lives without abuse. Shelter programs and the criminal justice system do support some women's aims. All of the women, no matter what they do, have rationales that make sense in the context that is described so well in this book. What does not make sense are inflexible laws, policies, and practices that ignore the increasingly diverse group of women and men in the United States. This book raises troubling questions about how American institutions can be helpful and effective for the increasingly diverse population, and provides descriptions and analyses that policy makers, law writers, practitioners, students, and scholars should consider when they ponder "What next?" in response to domestic violence in America.

                                                                            Merry Morash

Acknowledgments

The completion of this book was made possible by the support of numerous people. My greatest debt is to all of the women who had the courage to share their personal experiences. Thanks also go to Hai Nguyen, Tuy-An Ngo, Thanh Thuy, Kathy Thuy Pham, Vietnamese Community of Orange County Inc., Thai Ha, Thanh Thao, Tam Nguyen, Lan Nguyen, Thien Cao, Quynh Dang, Katherine Nguyen, Tuong Nguyen, Oanh Tran, and Truong Tran for their help during the data collection process.

I would like to express my sincere gratitude to Merry Morash, Katherine See, and Christopher Smith for their guidance and unwavering support throughout the study. I would like to thank Suzanne Statszak-Silva, my acquisition editor, for her faith in the project; Steven Gold, Joanne Belknap, and Claire Renzetti for their reviews of the manuscript and their comments. This book could not have been complete without the invaluable assistance from my series editor, Marilyn McShane, and her tremendous patience.

INTRODUCTION

Phuong[1] began to experience physical abuse by her husband shortly after they were married; he often beat her when she did not satisfy his demand for sex. Facing economic hardship under the new communist regime that took over South Vietnam at end of the Vietnam War, Phuong and her husband fled the country in 1990, just a few months after their wedding, hoping to find a better life. After arriving in Malaysia, the couple spent seven years in a refugee camp where Phuong gave birth to her daughter. Eventually, they were repatriated because they did not meet the criteria for refugee status. Because the abuse became more and more severe over time, Phuong planned to file for divorce. However, when her husband applied for resettlement in the United States under the Resettlement Opportunities for Vietnamese Returnees (ROVR) program, she decided to remain in the relationship to complete the paperwork for immigration. Her daughter was paralyzed shortly after birth, and Phuong wanted to go to the United States in order to receive better medical treatment and care for her child. Two years later, Phuong, her daughter, and her husband were allowed to resettle in the United States.

Phuong had received little education in Vietnam, and even less training in English in the United States. She did not work and spent most of her time at home taking care of her disabled daughter. When Phuong learned that spousal abuse was prohibited in the United States and supportive services were available for domestic violence victims, she wanted to report the incidents to deter her husband. However, fearing the brutal retaliation that she had experienced several times in the refugee camp, she did not call the police. Because she needed her husband to work and support the family, she did not want him involved with the law. She believed that his arrest would endanger his immigrant status and his employment. Phuong sought help from a women's shelter, but she was not admitted because the shelter could not accommodate her daughter's disability. When the abuse became unbearable, Phuong decided to call the police not only to save her life but also to teach her husband a lesson. However, she still did not want her husband to be arrested, and she even lied to the police that she had attacked her husband to help him avoid arrest. Because the relationship did not improve after that brief police intervention, Phuong followed the advice of a Vietnamese police liaison and requested a restraining order and filed for a divorce. Protected by the restraining order, Phuong no longer experienced physical attacks, but her difficulties increased when her husband stopped providing financial support for her daughter after he was required to move out.

For Diep, criminal justice interventions in intimate violence can do more harm than good. Escaping Vietnam with her parents and arriving in the United States at the age of 16, Diep was resettled on the East Coast where she went to school and earned a degree in business. Several years later, she moved to the Midwest to attend a professional education program and started a relationship with a highly educated professional who was an Asian immigrant. Two years later when the couple had a son, Diep moved in with him and depended on his financial support while going to school. To help Diep concentrate on her studies and complete the program as soon as possible, Diep's boyfriend decided to place their son under the care of his parents who lived outside the United States. Three weeks before Diep went to retrieve her son, an argument took place. Diep angrily smashed two or three glasses on the floor. Considering her behavior provocative and disrespectful, her boyfriend kicked her in the back several times. A few hours later, he took Diep to the hospital to check for internal injuries. The nurse at the hospital called the police. Despite Diep's opposition, her boyfriend was arrested.

After Diep was released from the hospital, she devoted all her time and energy to helping her boyfriend avoid involvement with the law. Because her boyfriend did not have permanent residency, Diep was afraid that his involvement with the law would affect his immigration status. More importantly, Diep feared that the arrest would hurt the relationship and the couple's plan for an official marriage and the reunion with their son. Despite Diep's explanation to the police that he was a good and responsible person, that she had provoked him, and that his violent behavior was the first in their relationship, her boyfriend was charged with domestic assault and was released from jail pending trial under the no-contact condition.[2] Diep was embarrassed and worried about her boyfriend having difficulties maintaining his professional career when the no-contact bond made their neighbors, friends, and colleagues aware of the problem. She asked the prosecutor to dismiss the case, and as a result, her boyfriend was placed in a diversion program that required him to complete a treatment program for batterers. To Diep's disappointment, their relationship deteriorated after her boyfriend attended counseling. Humiliated by the criminal justice process and activities in the treatment program, he blamed Diep for what had happened to him and decided to end the relationship. Unable to reconcile with her boyfriend, Diep had no choice but to move out with her son after he completed the paperwork for child support.

When Dung decided to marry her boyfriend and followed him to the United States, she expected to have a better life, not the arrest and jail time she actually experienced. Growing up in a rural area near Saigon with only an elementary education, Dung met a man, who later became her husband, after he was repatriated from a refugee camp in Thailand. Because his parents and siblings already left the country, he had no place to stay and decided to move in with Dung. After they were married, Dung's husband applied and was approved for resettlement in the United States under the ROVR program. Dung and their newborn son were allowed to accompany her husband to the United States as his dependents. After arriving in this country, Dung began experiencing family problems. Her husband's parents and siblings did not welcome her to the family, and they even attempted to separate the couple because of her rural background. Staying home to take care of her baby, and having no other relatives in the new country, Dung became totally dependent on her husband for emotional and financial support. When Dung realized that her husband paid more attention to his parents and siblings than her, she feared that she would be abandoned. Conflicts and arguments occurred when Dung complained about the time her husband spent at his parents' and siblings' houses, leaving her at home alone.

One day, depressed and fed up with her husband's neglect, Dung held a kitchen knife to her belly, threatening to commit suicide if he left to go gambling despite her opposition. Witnessing this, her parents-in-law intervened and took away the knife. However, her parents-in-law falsely reported to the police that she had threatened to stab her husband with the knife, and Dung was arrested and charged with a felony. Dung had to stay in jail waiting for trial because her husband would not post bail for her. Without legal counsel, Dung had to spend three weeks in jail until she agreed to plead guilty and was sentenced to three years on probation for an offense that she had not committed. Because of a restraining order, Dung had to move out and could not contact her son. One year later, Dung was notified that her husband had filed for divorce without her knowledge and had been granted the full custody of their son. Unfamiliar with the American legal system, speaking limited English, and lacking financial resources, Dung went to a refugee resettlement agency seeking help appealing the custody decision and applying for child visitation, but she was told that legal counsel was not available for domestic violence offenders.

This book relates the stories of abused Vietnamese immigrant women whose voices have not been heard and whose experiences with intimate violence and criminal justice interventions have not been included in the literature and discussions of domestic violence policies. For Vietnamese immigrants, domestic violence, especially wife beating, is not new as it occurs in both Vietnam and the United States, but the prohibition of domestic violence in the United States and criminal justice interventions represent new experiences. In Vietnam, abused women had no legal recourse because of the absence of government interventions or laws targeting domestic violence. Also, there were no social support systems or resource networks for women who wanted to leave abusive relationships.

EVOLVING DOMESTIC VIOLENCE POLICY AND RESEARCH

In the United States, efforts to change perceptions of domestic violence from a private family matter to a social problem have resulted in major changes in domestic violence policies. Feminists and advocates for battered women who first raised the issue of domestic violence as a social problem took a leadership role in initiating legislative change and altering criminal justice policies and procedures. With support from grassroots activists and professionals, new criminal justice interventions, including arrest and prosecution, along with various types of supportive services for abused women, have been established to improve women's safety and to help women escape domestic abuse. Gradually, mandatory arrest, mandatory prosecution, punitive sanctions, restraining orders, shelters and advocacy programs for battered women, and batterers' treatment programs have been institutionalized and become official domestic violence policies in the United States. Since the implementation of these initiatives, many abused women have sought refuge in women's shelters across the country, reported abuse incidents to the police, relied on the protection of restraining orders, or used victim services to cope with violence at home.

Over the two decades of policy changes, there have been discussions about the deterrent effects of arrest, prosecution, and treatment on batterers' behavior; the cooperation of battered women with the criminal justice process; and unintended consequences of new criminal justice interventions. Although new criminal justice responses to domestic violence have been perceived as effective weapons to combat domestic violence, there was no consistent scientific evidence of the rehabilitative effect of mandatory treatment and the deterrent effects of arrest and prosecution. While a number of studies found that arrests could reduce battering (Sherman & Berk, 1984; Dutton et al., 1992; Pate & Hamilton, 1992), other studies indicated that arrests were not effective in deterring subsequent assaults or had no long term effects (Hirschel, Hutchinson & Dean, 1992; Berk et al., 1992; Dunford, Huizinga & Elliot, 1990; Sherman et al., 1992). Some studies showed that an arrest could increase hostilities, especially when the offender was quickly released from custody (Goolkasian, 1986). Although research found that prosecution could reduce subsequent violence, there was no consistent evidence that no-drop-charge policies could have greater deterrent effects than the drop-permitted policy (Ford & Regoli, 1993). Despite the popularity of court-mandated treatment for domestic violence, research findings on the effectiveness of batterers' treatment programs were inconclusive (Ford & Regoli, 1993; Dutton et al., 1992; Davis & Taylor, 1999).

Effects of new criminal justice responses on women's help-seeking behavior have been an important topic for research and discussions. In fact, the legal approach to domestic violence depends on not only the action of criminal justice agencies but also the action of victims who report abuse incidents to the authorities and work with criminal justice agencies as witnesses for successful prosecutions. Traditionally, the enforcement of domestic violence laws, especially the prosecution of domestic violence offenders, was often difficult because victims of domestic violence were unlikely to cooperate with the criminal justice process. Scholars have charged that the police's discriminatory treatment of women which is reflected in inadequate protection from batterers, and prosecutors' lack of interest in domestic violence cases; posed a major obstacle to women's empowerment and discouraged women from seeking legal actions against domestic violence and working with the criminal justice process (Stark, 1993; Ford, 1983). Changes have been made with the expectation that new policies would promote the use of criminal justice approaches among domestic violence victims and their cooperation with the criminal justice process to end domestic violence. Stark (1993) has argued that mandatory arrest policies have been designed to control police behavior and reduce women's sense of powerlessness by requiring the police to intervene. Similarly, no-drop-charge policies have been established with an expectation that they would effectively reduce high rates of case attrition and facilitate victims' cooperation with the criminal justice process. Research, however, indicated that not all victims of domestic violence embraced these new criminal justice responses. Many victims were still reluctant to call the police, and if they called the police, they did not want arrests (Dutton, 1995; Rimonte, 1989; Hackler, 1991; Kantor & Straus, 1990; Smith & Klein, 1984). Although research found that women victims of domestic violence reported abuse incidents to the police half of the time when injuries were involved, they were less likely to report when they did not sustain injury (Bureau of Justice Statistics, 1995). With regard to new prosecutorial practices, there was no scientific evidence that no-drop-charge policies could increase victims' cooperation with the judicial process (Davis & Smith, 1995).

Scholars and practitioners have also been concerned about unintended consequences of criminal justice interventions (Corsilles, 1994; Miller, 2001; Walsh, 1995; Wanless, 1996). After the implementation of mandatory arrest policies, there has been an increase in arrests of women in conjunction with their abusers, or women arrested alone as the sole aggressors. The arrests of women who use force to defend themselves have been viewed as not only failing to deter the abusers and protect the victims but also as discouraging abused women from calling the police in the future (E. Buzawa & C. Buzawa, 1993; Wanless, 1996). No-drop-charge policies can also have negative side effects when they expose abused women to retaliation by their abusers. Because prosecutors cannot guarantee the victim's safety, policies that require the victim to testify against her abuser can subject her to further victimization (Corsilles, 1994). Victims' safety may be further endangered when no-drop-charge policies inadvertently prevent abused women who do not want to go to court from calling the police for help (E. Buzawa & C. Buzawa, 1993). Contrary to the view of proponents of new criminal justice interventions, no-drop-charge policies can undermine women's efforts toward achieving self-empowerment by denying domestic violence victims the ability to make choices for themselves and their children (Ford & Regoli, 1993). In fact, many victims who turn to the criminal justice system for help to end domestic violence want to continue the relationship with their partners. Requiring the victim to testify against the offender in a domestic violence case and the subsequent imposition of a jail sentence can produce results contrary to the wishes of the victim (Carlson & Nidey, 1995).

The proliferation of research on criminal justice responses to domestic violence, however, has largely neglected the experiences of abused immigrant women and the effects of criminal justice interventions on the safety and family lives of these women. Abused women are different from most crime victims because of their relations to the assailant. Not only is there a direct emotional bond between the woman and her abusive husband or lover, but they are also tied in a myriad of connections, including children, finances, legal status, and community (E. Buzawa & C. Buzawa, 1993; Ferraro & Pope, 1993). Depending on their particular experiences and situations, women's responses to abuse vary; treating all abused women as a common group ignores their many differences and, at the same time, creates a conceptual error of assuming that all batterers respond similarly to a given approach. Social scientists have emphasized the importance of knowledge on culture, race/ethnicity, and social contexts for understanding women's experiences of and responses to domestic violence (Abraham, 2000; Crowell & Burgess, 1996; Kanuha, 1996; Morash, Bui & Santiago, 2000). Immigrant women can have different experiences of abuse and seeking help because of their unique situations caused by immigration and the resettlement process. For example, problems faced by many immigrant families, such as stress from unemployment, role changes between spouses and between parents and children, and conflicts arising from the breakdown of the extended family system, can contribute to the likelihood of domestic violence (Jang, Lee & Morello-Frosch, 1990; Morash et al., 2000). Social, economic, and cultural isolation resulting from the process of immigration can negatively affect immigrant women's help-seeking behavior; lack of economic and emotional support from the network of friends and the extended family left behind in the countries of origin can force immigrant women to stay in abusive relationships (Dasgupta & Warrier, 1996; Mehrotra, 1999; Preisser, 1999). Language barriers can prevent meaningful communication between abused immigrant women and helping agencies (Orloff, Jang & Klein, 1995); cultural perceptions about the role of legal and criminal justice agencies in solving family problems can impede immigrant women's efforts to seek help from outside the family (Rimonte, 1989; Jang et al., 1990; Rasche, 1988). Immigration status also plays an important role in women's help-seeking behavior. Women who are not legal residents and whose immigration status depends on the sponsorship of their partners are isolated by the power dynamics that can thwart any effort to reach out to the legal system for help (Orloff et al., 1995, Abraham, 2000); undocumented women may fear being reported to immigration authorities by law enforcement or victim service agencies.

DOCUMENTING THE IMMIGRANT EXPERIENCE

While it is important to understand why immigrant women do not seek help from outside the family, by focusing only on impediments to immigrant women's efforts to reach out, we ignore the fact that many immigrant women have contacted agencies in the mainstream society for help and that many other immigrant women have been charged with domestic offenses under new criminal justice polices. A lack of research on these women limits our knowledge about women's experiences with criminal justice policies on domestic violence. The number of immigrants coming to the United States has increased substantially over the past three decades as a result of the 1965 Immigration Act that dismantled the national quota system and opened the door to renewed migration to this country. For this reason, it is important to understand how criminal justice interventions can become a resource for abused immigrant women to deal with domestic abuse; how they can respond to the needs of abused immigrant women for personal safety and improved family relationships; and when arrests, prosecutions and restraining orders are effective in protecting the safety of the immigrant women.

This book focuses on the Vietnamese immigrant group to draw attention to the diversity of women's responses to abuse, the various needs of abused women, and their different experiences with criminal justice and victim service agencies. Immigrants, regardless of their racial/ethnic backgrounds, share common dilemmas such as language barriers, cultural differences, and unfamiliarity with American legal systems; but each immigrant group possesses different human capital and resources and has distinctive experiences with the labor market, the legal system, racial/ethnic relations, and adaptation. By focusing on the experiences of Vietnamese immigrant women, this book seeks to explain how women's experiences with criminal justice interventions in domestic violence are deeply affected by gender practices pervasive in culture as well as in social and organizational structures. This book highlights the stories of 34 Vietnamese immigrant women who talk about constraints and impediments caused by the complex interactions of gender, race/ethnicity, cultural traditions, acculturation, socioeconomic conditions, social policies, and institutional practices that they faced when seeking help and/or contacting the criminal justice system. As such, they make clear that subjective and objective realities of women's experiences must be situated and understood within larger social, economic, cultural, and political contexts of immigration and adaptation.

The analysis of these women's narratives points to the need for reconceptualizing women's needs, including safety. Discussions of criminal justice interventions have emphasized the deterrence aspect of arrest and prosecution measured by the absence of physical reoffending, but they have ignored other forms of emotional and psychological abuse occurring after criminal justice interventions that can cause the same or even more devastating effects than the original physical attacks. In addition, preserving and improving family relationships are often ignored in the agenda of domestic violence policies. In fact, the adversarial nature of prosecution and the separation required by restraining orders cannot help improve family relationships (E. Buzawa & C. Buzawa, 1993). Furthermore, many advocates for battered women have considered the relationship between a woman and her abuser as dangerous and pathological—one that should be ended. Therefore, various social and legal services have been established to assist abused women to leave the relationship through separation or divorce. While it is indisputable that abused women want to avoid abuse, many may not want to end violence at all costs. Women who reach out to criminal justice agencies for help can have different expectations and needs. Some may want to end violence by leaving their abusive partners, but others may want both personal safety and family relationships. While the family may not be as important for middle-class professional women in mainstream society, it is important in helping immigrant women cope with the social isolation that occurs during immigration.

WOMEN'S VOICES AND THE INTERPLAY AMONG GENDER, RACE/ETHNICITY, AND CLASS

The feminist standpoint, a defining characteristic of feminist research, is rooted in the Marxist view that social being determines consciousness. It emphasizes the social location of research subjects and individuals involved in social problems (Hartsock, 1983). The feminist standpoint approach uses women's experiences as a starting point for the analysis of social problems and focuses on gender differences as well as differences between men and women in social situations (Harding, 1991). Because the production of social knowledge has been traditionally grounded in men's experiences and relationships, the opening up of women's experiences allows social scientists to access social realities of women's lives that have previously been repressed and unavailable (Smith, 1990; Harding, 1991). By taking up the standpoint of women, beginning from women's ordinary, everyday experiences, the standpoint approach discredits the claim that it is possible to constitute an objective knowledge independent of the researcher's social situations (Smith, 1990).

An important characteristic of the standpoint approach is to "give voice" to the silenced group and facilitate their own discoveries (Gorelick, 1991). Rooted in the symbolic interactionist tradition that recognizes the hierarchy of credibility in the creation and dissemination of knowledge, "giving voice" emphasizes the actor's interpretation and understanding of the situation (Gorelick, 1991; McCall & Wittner, 1990). For symbolic interactionists, subjectivity is central to the understanding of social phenomena because people interpret their situations and act in terms of the meanings or perspectives they develop within a particular context and from a specific position within an organization or group (McCall & Wittner, 1990). For example, studying racism must begin from the standpoints of minority groups, classism from the standpoint of lower class people, and sexism from the standpoint of women. For feminists, women are authoritative speakers of their own experiences. Thus, "giving voice" has been considered a progressive development of feminist research and theory (Gorelick, 1991).

Direct experience, however, has its limitations. When gendered practices permeate social activities across time and places, making sexism deeply internalized and buried beneath the conscious level, there are hidden aspects of women's oppression that women may not be able to reveal by themselves (McKinnon, 1987;

Maguire, 1987; Harding, 1991). A lack of cumulative knowledge on the part of research participants makes the role of the researcher different from that of the research subject. Dorothy Smith (1987) has recognized the important role of social scientists in producing knowledge of the sources of women's oppression. In addition, knowledge production and theory making must go beyond the notion of fragmentary sciences and the hierarchy of standpoints of different social groups (Harding, 1986). Differences within and between diverse groups of women and the process of sexism, classism, and racism that create these differences must be discovered in order to understand how they connect to each other (Gorelick, 1991). Because the structure of women's oppression is multifaceted, knowledge of the conflicts constructed within the hidden oppression must be based on both experience and theory.

Feminist scholarship suggests that women's experiences are products of social interaction and unequal gender relations (Scott, 1986). In a gender-stratified society, women and men are assigned different kinds of activities and, consequently, have different experiences. Early feminist theories relied on the concept of patriarchy to understand women's behavior and experiences. The patriarchy has been viewed as causing women's subordination through its social structure and ideologies that favor men's domination (R. E. Dobash & R. P. Dobash, 1979). The structure of the patriarchy consists of a hierarchical organization of social institutions and social relations regarding power and privileges that places women in an inferior status; the ideological aspect reinforces the acceptance of this hierarchy and the rationalization of inequality. The concept of patriarchy assumes a universal, trans-historical, and transcultural phenomenon and, therefore, fails to recognize differences in the various forms of gender inequality, the variation in the construction of gender relations among different ethnic groups within a society, and the diversity of women's experiences caused by women's different social locations (Acker, 1989; Walby, 1989; Messerschmidt, 1993). Critics of early feminist theories have challenged the concept of patriarchy, arguing that it tends to universalize the experience of mainly middle-class white women and downplay the diversity of male dominance and women's agency (Morash et al., 2000).

Recent feminist scholarship has emphasized the importance of understanding women's experiences from a situated perspective and recognizing the diversity of women's experiences (hooks, 1984; Collins, 1991; Chow, 1987; Mohanty, 1991). Because human beings, social organizations, and social practices are gendered, the notion of gender as a system of social practices provides a theoretical framework for understanding the complex connections among various forms of human interactions (Connell, 1987, 1996). In other words, the structures and operations of the economy, the labor market, the state, social and global institutions, and human patterns of emotional relationships have been established and functioning on the basis of the gendered division of labor and power. As a foundation for social practices and social relations, gender is conceptualized as far more than an individual trait somehow connected with bodily differences between men and women. Rather, gender is considered as a constitutive element of social practices and social relations based on perceived differences between the sexes (Connell, 1996; Scott, 1986).

Although gender permeates all social practices, women's lives are not influenced by gender alone. Feminist scholars have long recognized the interrelation of race, class, and gender that creates a matrix of domination and shapes women's lives (Spelman, 1988; Alexander & Mohanty, 1997; hooks, 1984; Zinn & Dill, 1994). With racism, classism, and compulsory heterosexuality in American society, the oppression faced by white middle-class women is not the same as the oppression faced by women from different social classes and racial/ethnic backgrounds (Alexander & Mohanty, 1997). Lamphere, Zavella, and Gonzales (1993) have used the term "social locations" to specify the ways in which economic structure and the labor market interact with class, ethnicity, culture, and sexual preference to shape women's various experiences. Harding (1991, p. 179) has asserted, "There are no gender relations per se, but only gender relations as constructed by and between classes, races, and cultures." In the area of domestic violence, the conceptualization of gender as the primary foundation of battering as a social problem can mitigate the significant role of other factors in the analysis and understanding of women's experiences of and responses to domestic abuse (Kanuha, 1996).

A benefit of considering the interaction among gender, class, race/ethnicity, and culture in the study of women's experiences, including their experiences with criminal justice interventions, lies in its ability to recognize the interweaving of women's personal lives with social structure, institutional power, race relations, and culture. The gendered structure of economic production that tends to exclude women from opportunities to accumulate wealth and gain economic power can directly impact women's responses to domestic violence and their experiences with criminal justice interventions. Women have been traditionally assigned to unpaid housework and, as a consequence, often financially depend on men. When women participate in the labor market, they tend to work in low-paying jobs and possess low occupational statuses relative to those of men (Connell, 1987). Furthermore, immigrant women, by virtue of their gender, birthplace, and class status, are likely to occupy the lowest level in the labor force hierarchy and work primarily in poorly paying jobs that offer little security and few benefits (Brettell & Simon, 1986). For women who depend on their husbands/partners for financial support, arrest and prosecution of their husbands/partners can lead to the imprisonment of their providers, thus eliminating or reducing the women's financial resources. Women victims who seek the prosecution of their abusers but have few financial resources may find participation in the criminal justice process costly because of their absence from work, childcare expenses, and transportation fees for multiple trips to the courthouse (Hart, 1993). Women who depend on their husbands'/partners' economic support and are charged with domestic assaults may not have financial resources to obtain pretrial release and retain quality defense lawyers to fight for justice. If they are convicted and separated by restraining orders or divorce, they may lose financial support from their husbands/partners and, subsequently, the custody of their children.

Although domestic violence occurs within the context of unbalanced power relationships, women's experiences of and responses to violence are not solely affected by the power dynamics within the family because gendered practices in
other institutions also interfere with family life (Connell, 1987). By formulating
ideals, defining morality, and establishing policies to sustain the power of men, the
state and various social, political, and religious institutions form a system of social
power that reinforces gendered practices and shapes women's behaviors and experiences. For example, some religious institutions assign a secondary status to
women, encourage women to obey their husbands and stay in family relationships,
or discourage women from testifying against their abusive husbands (Ferraro &
Pope, 1993). The normative definition of femininity, which is based on the general
inferior status of women and emphasizes women's compliance with subordination
to and accommodation of the interests and desires of men, can prevent women victims of domestic violence from taking legal actions against their intimate partners.
The cultural image of women as docile and submissive that has been used to con-
struct the "battered woman" stereotype and guide mandatory arrest practices can
influence women's responses to domestic abuse. Under the dual concepts of
agency and victimization, the victim is seen as helpless and deserving of protection.
As a result, women who use force to fight against their abuser are not considered as
helpless and, therefore, do not fit the cultural profile of domestic violence victims
(Mahoney, 1994). Women who use self-defense are often arrested along with their
abusers and charged with a domestic offense. Consequently, they may be discouraged from participating in the prosecution of their abusers because they may feel
guilty for deviating from the gender norms of women's appropriate behavior (Bui,
2001). They may also receive harsher treatment for violating the socially-con-
structed image of women.

As part of the system of social power, the practices of criminal justice agencies
that fail to protect women or take the needs of abused women seriously can discourage women from using criminal justice approaches to prevent future violence.
In fact, battered women are much more likely than other victims to be revictimized
after the assaults that gave rise to criminal justice interventions. Research found
that a majority of protection orders were violated by the abusers, and the number
of calls to the police to report violations was high, but arrests were rare (Hart, 1993;
Harrell & Smith, 1996). Many abused women were also dissatisfied with criminal
justice interventions because the system did not provide them with meaningful relief from their abusers (Erez & Belknap, 1998a). Pressure from abusers, fear of reprisal, and a lack of trust in the protective abilities of criminal justice agencies can
cause battered women to drop charges, prevent them from testifying in court, or
discourage them from requesting a personal protection order.

Women's experiences with criminal justice interventions can be affected by the
goals and interests of criminal justice agencies. By pursuing organizational goals,
criminal justice officials may disregard and ignore the needs of abused women, especially when they are inconsistent with organizational interests. Manning (1993)
has commented that despite the rhetoric about police commitment to maintaining

the collective good and serving with honor, law enforcement practices in domestic violence have been guided by pragmatic obligations, budgetary constraints, and concerns with how to avoid legal liabilities and civil suits. Organizational characteristics of the court also influence case-processing practices because case outcomes are determined by the structural context of legal decision making (Fagan, 1988). For example, the "going rate" for an offense that judicial officials expect offenders to receive is influenced by organizational factors independent of case-specific variables (Casper & Brereton, 1984).

Public welfare and immigration policies can create further barriers to abused women's efforts to seek help. Welfare has been considered a main opportunity for women to rely on the state and break their dependency on men (Piven, 1990). Changes in welfare policies that limit financial support for women may increase women's dependency on their husbands/partners and, consequently, the threat of harm caused by domestic violence (Pearson, Thoennes & Griswold, 1999). Similarly, strict immigration laws and policies regarding legal residency in the United States can affect the response to domestic abuse among alien women who are married to American legal residents or citizens. In recent years, the United States government has toughened immigration laws, making it more difficult for aliens who are married to American citizens to gain permanent residency (Thompson, 1999). When a woman has to rely on her husband to complete the paperwork for legal residency, threats of abuse may become more potent, and the chance to leave the abusive relationship may be substantially reduced (Chin, 1994).

The system of social power, combined with the division of labor, creates and supports the heterosexual culture (Connell, 1987). The culturally constructed pattern of heterosexual attachment dictates social norms that govern men's and women's roles and defines within a given social context behaviors considered appropriate and socially acceptable for individuals in different social roles, such as husband and wife, male/female partner, father, and mother (Raj et al., 1999). For many women, relationships and family units are important because marrying and maintaining intimacy are highly valued by the state and religious institutions, and because divorce and separation are considered a failure that should be avoided (Ferraro & Pope, 1993; Schechter, 1982; Corsilles, 1994). When violence occurs, these women may avoid leaving and would rather stay in the relationship. Influenced by the ideology of romantic love, they tend to embrace a cultural image of intimate relationships as havens of shared love and commitment, especially when their husbands/partners can fulfill some aspects of the image, adding to these women's hope for change (Ferraro & Pope, 1993). For women who do not want or who are not ready to leave their intimate partners, criminal justice interventions may be considered a threat that can disrupt family relationships.

Unlike women in the mainstream society, immigrant women experience both traditional culture of their country of origin and American culture. The process of cultural and economic adaptation, however, is not the same for all immigrants, but it is largely determined by human capital and the socioeconomic and political contexts of immigration resettlement that shape the meaning of the family. For immigrant women, the family can be an arena of patriarchal oppression and, at the same time, a site of resistance to the dominant society. The interaction among gender, race/ethnicity, and culture means that immigrant women experience oppression not only as women in a society dominated by men but also as minorities facing various forms of racism (Dill, 1988; Glenn, 1986; hooks, 1984). Women of color and immigrant women tend to share an understanding of cultural distinctiveness with men of similar class and ethnic backgrounds and to view family ties as resources for ethnic solidarity against racism (Chow, 1987; Gabaccia, 1994). In the midst of changes resulting from immigration, racism combined with loneliness caused by the loss of women's traditional sources of support and power, including the support of the extended family and the power of parents over children, can promote family and community solidarity and prevent abused immigrant women from seeking help in the mainstream society (Hart, 1993; Rasche, 1988; Huisman, 1996).

QUALITATIVE ASSESSMENT OF EXPERIENCES

Besides theories, research methods for understanding human experiences also affect the way human beings are viewed. When human beings are studied in a statistically aggregated fashion, there is a danger that the conclusions may not fit the reality (Mills, 1959). Studies on legal responses to domestic violence have been criticized for failing to examine the process of legal intervention from the victim's perspective. Critics have pointed to the absence of abused women's voices and their assessments of the impact of criminal justice interventions on their lives, their relationships, and changes in the behavior of their partners (Lewis et al., 2000). In addition, debates concerning criminal justice responses to domestic violence are limited to the outcomes, to the exclusion of the process, and tend to view women survivors of abuse as passive recipients of legal intervention, but not active agents who constantly negotiate for their personal safety and family lives.

As a form of inquiry, the qualitative method emphasizes the importance of understanding the meanings of human behavior within its situational and structural contexts and places social interactions, processes, and changes at the center of analysis (Merriam, 1998; Strauss, 1987). Thus, qualitative research is highly appropriate for studying women's experiences with criminal justice interventions to improve knowledge about the effects of domestic violence policies on women's lives. Because meanings, which are constructed through human interactions and personal experiences, are difficult to quantify, qualitative research provides a way to access unquantifiable facts about people. Rooted in symbolic interactionism, qualitative research recognizes the importance of subjective interpretations of human experiences and allows not only an understanding of multiple realities of women's experiences but also the construction of a holistic reality based on women's differences (Blumer 1969; Lincoln & Guba, 1985). By relying on abused women's perspectives and women's interpretations of their own experiences, this method is consistent with the feminist standpoint approach of "giving voice."

Women's experiences of and responses to male domination are not uniform because men and women hold different social positions in terms of race, class, and gender. The recognition of the interplay among class, race/ethnicity, and culture within the context of immigration facilitates an understanding of how Vietnamese immigrant women's experiences with criminal justice interventions are shaped by not only their gender, but also by their social class, race/ethnicity, and two conflicting sets of values from traditional Vietnamese culture and American culture. Within this theoretical framework, the feminist standpoint approach and a qualitative method help produce a holistic understanding of Vietnamese immigrant women as active agents who engage in a complex process of adaptation, negotiation, and strategic resistance to both their intimate partners and the range of helping agencies in their struggle for safety and justice.

ORGANIZATION OF THE BOOK

The voices of abused Vietnamese immigrant women are at the center of this book. Their narratives are included in each chapter, highlighting their different experiences with abuse, seeking help, and criminal justice interventions in domestic violence. Chapter 2 provides an overview of the immigration context that shapes the Vietnamese immigrant women's experiences with and responses to intimate violence. The process of immigration and adaptation has changed the structure of Vietnamese families and gender dynamics in this country. Two competing cultural values, economic and cultural isolation, and the availability of the personal support network all influence Vietnamese immigrant women's help-seeking behavior and their decision to reach out to criminal justice agencies. Chapter 3 describes the problems faced by Vietnamese immigrant women when they contact criminal justice agencies, including the police, prosecutors, and the court, as victims of intimate violence. It highlights the important effects of traditional culture, acculturation, economic adaptation, the practices of criminal justice agencies, and victim services on the participation of Vietnamese immigrant women in the criminal justice process of their abusive husbands/partners. Chapter 4 examines the criminal justice process and its consequences faced by abused Vietnamese immigrant women who are charged with domestic violence offenses. The chapter focuses on the importance of gender, socioeconomic conditions, legal status, and the organizational structure of criminal justice agencies in shaping these women's experiences. It also reveals how gender biases embedded in social and criminal justice practices as well as legal culture can inadvertently allow domestic violence laws to reinforce male domination. Chapter 5 explores the effects of criminal justice interventions on women's safety and women's family lives. The experiences of Vietnamese immigrant women expose the limitations of criminal justice approaches to domestic violence such as when they fail to provide abused women with long-term protection and force women to choose between personal safety and family life. Chapter 6 discusses factors contributing to the limitations of criminal justice interventions. It highlights the importance of recognizing women's different experiences in the design of intervention strategies. The chapter concludes that effective interventions must address the issue of gender inequality as the root cause of the problem and respond to abused women's needs of both personal safety and family life.

NOTES

1. In order to protect the anonymity of the study participants, all names used in this book are pseudonyms, unless indicated otherwise.

2. The no-contact bond, whose purpose is to protect victims of domestic violence, prohibits defendants in domestic violence cases from making contact with their victims before final court decisions.

2

FAMILY LIVES IN TRANSITION

When I talked with my mother about the abuse by my husband, she told me not to call the police. She was afraid that when the police came, everybody in the neighborhood would know about the problem. She said that a woman's life belonged to her husband, and that a woman should accept her fate and be patient to avoid family conflicts.[1]

(Interview with Hue)

The situation that Hue faced reflects those of many abused Vietnamese immigrant women. As first-generation immigrants, Hue and many other Vietnamese in the United States tend to conform to Vietnamese cultural values and practices. However, the legacy of war that caused their journey to the United States and the process of resettlement and adaptation also have had important impacts on their experiences with life in the new land. This chapter presents a history of the Vietnamese in the United States, some background on Vietnamese culture and family traditions, and the immigration context of women's experiences of and responses to abuse.

HISTORY OF IMMIGRATION TO THE UNITED STATES

The intense involvement of the United States in the Vietnam War led to the immigration of almost a million Vietnamese to America in the 25 years following the end of the Vietnam War and the victory of Vietnamese communists in 1975. Beginning with the first major group of 125,000 Vietnamese refugees coming to the United States in early 1975, the Vietnamese-American population has increased substantially over time and has become one of the fastest growing ethnic groups in the United States (H. Nguyen & Haines, 1996). By the time of the 1990 Census, more than 600,000 Vietnamese had resettled in the United States (U.S. Census Bureau, 1993). By 2000, the number of Vietnamese in the United States had reached more than 1.2 million, of which almost a million Vietnamese Americans were foreign born, making the Vietnamese-American group the third-largest foreign-born Asian-American population (U.S. Census Bureau, 2000; 2002).

Vietnamese came to the United States from a variety of social, religious, and ethnic backgrounds. They also came in different periods, each of which had its unique features. The first major exodus of Vietnamese to the United States occurred in 1975 after the collapse of South Vietnam and included many South Vietnamese military officers, government officials, and professionals who, along with their families, were evacuated by airplanes or boats during the communist takeover. Members of this group tended to be well educated and have more exposure to Western culture than those who migrated later (Do, 1999; Gold, 1992). Most of the first-wave immigrants left Vietnam because of their fear of communism and their concerns about their fates under the new regime, such as possible imprisonment or even execution and expected loss of social status and political freedom (H. Nguyen & Haines, 1996).[2]

The second-wave Vietnamese refugee exodus began in 1978 and continued sporadically throughout the 1980s. Racial, economic, and religious discrimination by the new communist government fueled this second wave of emigration. Many of this group were ethnic Chinese who had lived in Vietnam for generations and were forced or "asked" to leave by the communist government after the Sino-Vietnamese conflict and the border war of 1979 occurred (Gold, 1992). Religious leaders and their followers (Christians and Buddhists) also escaped to avoid religious persecutions. Others left Vietnam because life had become hard and unbearable to them and held no future for their children. Particularly, those who had been associated with the South Vietnam government and those who had been released from re-education camps suffered severe discrimination. Many were forced to go to the "new economic zones" located in rural areas where their lives became so hard and hopeless that they had to come back to the cities as illegal residents. They could not get jobs, and their children were deprived of opportunities for college education. Because many Vietnamese parents helped their children escape to avoid discrimination, children and young people formed a major segment of those escaping on boat in the late 1970s (H. Nguyen & Haines, 1996).

Second-wave refugees were termed "boat people" because they escaped Vietnam by boats. Most ethnic Chinese left Vietnam through "unofficial departure" by paying a certain amount of gold for a place in overcrowded boats unofficially organized by Vietnamese local authorities (Gold, 1992). For those who were not ethnic Chinese, clandestine escapes by sea in small, unsafe boats were often their routes out of Vietnam. In both cases, female refugees tended to be at high risk for "boat rapes" committed by Thai pirates who frequently attacked refugee boats that were trying to escape Vietnam via the South China Sea (C. Tran, 1997). After leaving Vietnam, these refugees often spent many years in overcrowded refugee camps in

Thailand, Hong Kong, the Philippines, Indonesia, or Singapore while waiting for permission to enter the United States. The situation in most of these camps was very bad with poor sanitary conditions, overcrowding, a lack of food, and no schools for children. In addition, there were also high incidents of sexual violence against women (rape) in these refugee camps.

The third wave of Vietnamese immigration resulted from the Orderly Departure Program (ODP) established in 1979 to provide a safe and legal route of exit for Vietnamese who wanted to leave Vietnam. The goal of the ODP was to halt the flow of refugees leaving Vietnam illegally and dangerously on small boats. The program was initially established for those having family ties to people who live in the United States. It was later extended to Vietnamese-Amerasian children who had been subjected to both official and popular abuse in Vietnam, and to former employees of American missions in Vietnam during the Vietnam War (H. Nguyen & Haines, 1996).[3] More recently, the fourth wave of Vietnamese immigrants came to the United States through the Humanitarian Operation (HO) program established in 1989 to allow the resettlement of re-education camp survivors and their families in the United States. These South Vietnamese veterans had faced years of debilitating life in re-education camps and severe discrimination after their release (H. Nguyen & Haines, 1996).

After 25 years of immigration and resettlement, more than a million Vietnamese Americans, including American-born and foreign-born, have their presence in every state in the United States. Despite the initial government attempt to disperse them throughout the country, secondary migration has led to heavy concentrations of Vietnamese refugees and immigrants in a few states on the West Coast and in the South, including California, Oregon, Washington, Texas, and Louisiana, where the climate is more moderate and Asian culture is more prevalent than in other places.

VIETNAMESE CULTURAL BACKGROUNDS

Religious beliefs have exercised the most powerful influence in the formation of Vietnamese society. Vietnam's religious outlook, called *Tam Giao* (Three Religions), actually consists of three faiths: Buddhism, Confucianism, and Taoism. Despite the existence of Christianity that was introduced into Vietnam in the sixteenth century, these three schools of philosophy coalesced to form the core of the Vietnamese religious-cultural tradition (Gold, 1992; Kibria, 1993; L. Nguyen, 1987). In contrast to monotheistic Westerners, most Vietnamese find no contradiction in combining multiple belief systems. For example, Vietnamese Catholicism has been treated as a form of "Confucianized Christianity" because it has been deeply influenced by cultural traditions derived from centuries of Buddhist, Taoist, and Confucianist practices (Zhou & Bankston, 1998). The essence of Buddha's teaching is contained in the concept of Karma (the law of causality) according to which the vicious circle of existence is renewal in the course of endless reincarnations, and the present existence is conditioned by earlier existence and will condition those that follow (L. Nguyen, 1987). As such, Buddhism emphasizes the principle of "good works" toward all living things, arguing for detachment from the material world, and viewing wealth, power, and status as corrupting forces causing suffering (Gold, 1992). Taoism, which was founded by Lao Tse in China around 600 BC, emphasizes humility and renunciation of the material world (Gold, 1992). Although Taoism is currently regarded as a religion, Lao Tse thought of himself as a philosopher. His philosophy focused on the idea of a human being's oneness with the universe, thus emphasizing harmonious relationships between human beings and nature (Do, 1999). On the other hand, Confucianism, which is a philosophy of life rather than a religion, posits the patriarchal family as the ideal human institution (Gold, 1992). For hundreds of years, teachings of Confucius have been practiced in Vietnam and have become a code of conduct. Confucianism requires the sacrifice of the individual to the family and the state as well as each man's and woman's obedience to higher authorities, including rulers, parents, husbands, and older male siblings (Gold, 1992; T. Tran, 1959).

The influences of Confucianism, Buddhism, and Taoism are reflected in many social practices and traditions. In the ancient Vietnamese society, there was a prescribed social hierarchy reflected in the amount of respect given to different classes. In this hierarchy, the scholar class was at the top, followed by farmers, manual workers (artisans or laborers), and merchants (Do, 1999). The importance of the scholar class is reflected in an old saying "*Mot nguoi lam quan, ca ho duoc nho*" (A mandarin can help all his relatives). The merchant or business class was often looked down on and was considered undesirable because business transactions were generally seen as involving dishonesty. On the other hand, education was revered because it was the only means for upward mobility and achieving a high social status (Do, 1999). Vietnamese also place high values on the art of peacefulness and living in harmony. In any social interactions, open disagreements disturb the harmony of the group. As a result, Vietnamese tend to seek out peaceful resolutions and avoid confrontations. The importance of harmony and peacefulness is reflected in the Five Cardinal Virtues that all people are expected to practice. These include: 1) benevolence; 2) equity and justice; 3) politeness and civility; 4) wisdom; and 5) truthfulness (Do, 1999). The Vietnamese lifestyle that is orientated toward the family and the group makes a fundamental distinction between Vietnamese traditions and Western culture. Vietnamese religious faiths, especially Confucianism, that emphasize collectivism and hierarchy in social interaction, have had a major role in shaping the Vietnamese family institution.

VIETNAMESE FAMILY TRADITIONS AND WOMEN'S STATUS

The traditional Vietnamese family has been considered the most basic, enduring, and self-consciously acknowledged form of national culture among Vietnamese refugees and immigrants (Gold, 1992). Unlike the typical "nuclear" family in the United States, the traditional Vietnamese family, which was seen as the most important of all social units in Vietnam, was a large, patriarchal, extended unit where people from three or four generations lived under the same roof and acted as a source of mutual support. The family was also an institution where individual problems and social conflicts were to be resolved. The collectivist orientation of the traditional Vietnamese family stemmed from the influence of the Confucian philosophy that emphasized close family ties, hierarchy, and order in interpersonal relationships. Within the family, collective obligations and decision making were encouraged, but independence and autonomy of the individual were de-emphasized. Because the needs of the family took precedent over those of the individual, each family member was expected to promote harmony, adhere to specified hierarchical positions, and comply with familial and social roles (Gold, 1992; Kibria, 1993).

Even though Confucianism stresses the obedience of females to males (e.g., the Three Obediences), traditional women in Vietnam had a relatively favorable economic position in comparison with their Chinese counterparts whose culture also incorporates the norms and values of Confucianism (Ta, 1981). Vietnamese women commonly handled the financial affairs of the household, acted as conservers of the family wealth, and were often jokingly referred to as "*Noi Tuong*" (Chief of Domestic Affairs) (Gold, 1992). The relative independence and autonomy of Vietnamese women resulted from their right of inheritance granted by Vietnamese ancient laws in the fifteenth century and their participation in economic activities when men spent time studying, trying to move up to the scholar class, or fighting in the battlefield during wars.

Despite the fact that women in Vietnamese society enjoyed some economic and property rights, their subordination to men was embedded across kinship, political, legal as well as economic institutions, and reflected in various traditional ideals and practices (Kibria, 1993; C. Tran, 1997). Traditionally, the birth of a boy was given greater importance than that of a girl as reflected in an old saying "One hundred girls are not worth a single testicle." Women who produced sons could increase a status in society and their husbands' families, but those who were unable to bear sons were considered "defective," were stigmatized, and suffered great shame and maltreatment by their husbands and in-laws.

In traditional Vietnamese society, men's and women's behaviors were bound by different sets of rules and precedents derived from Confucian teachings that basically dictated the subordination of women to men (T. Tran, 1959). Men were to work outside the home and serve the community, but women's lives were oriented toward the family and motherhood. A typical woman was expected to be married and educated as a good housewife who performed her productive duty of carrying on the lineage and devoted her life to her husband and children. Most marriages were prearranged, and most women had little to say about the choice of their mates (Jamieson, 1993). Because marriages usually involved the exchange of money and gifts from the man's family to the woman's family, the wife was often considered to be property paid for by the husband and his family.

Various rules and ideologies were used to legitimate the inferior status of women by glorifying passivity and submission to male authority. For example, a model woman should possess the Four Virtues, including good working habits, attractive appearance, polite speech, and exemplary conduct. She should also follow the principle of Three Obediences, which says that a woman should obey and submit to her father when young, to her husbands when married, and to her oldest son when widowed (L. Nguyen, 1987). In addition to the Three Obediences and Four Virtues, suffering and persevering were also valued virtues for traditional Vietnamese women (C. Tran, 1997). The emphasis on enduring, suffering, and persevering, which was in accord with the Buddhist belief in the acceptance of one's fate, was adaptive in Vietnamese traditional culture because it served to preserve harmony and order in the family. Vietnamese folklore often dramatizes and glorifies the ideal wife as someone who is completely devoted to her husband, her children, and her two sets of parents; her primary mission in life is to be completely selfless and to care for everyone but herself. Her complete devotion is measured by her numerous self-sacrifices as well as her ability to endure and persevere under the worst mistreatments and circumstances.

The idealized image of a "good woman," which was used to create double standards for judging the sexual conduct of men and women, conveyed to Vietnamese women a message that their submission to men would have positive results and was a good thing that they should strive to attain. Embedded in the Four Virtues was the unwritten rule that women must "retain their purity" before marriage (C. Tran, 1997). At the same time, such a standard was not expected of men because, traditionally, Vietnamese men were allowed to be sexually promiscuous before and within marriage. It was not uncommon for Vietnamese men to have open and/or frequent affairs with more than one woman. In fact, traditional legal codes sanctioned polygamy, which was held as a mark of affluence and prestige and was usually practiced by wealthy men (Kibria, 1993). However, nonwealthy men also had affairs that were used to demonstrate their manly prowess and superior male status in society. Such a double standard for sexual conduct is reflected in the popular old saying, "*Trai nam the bay thiep, gai chinh chuyen mot chong*" (A man could have five wives and seven concubines, but a woman should have one husband). Women were completely absent from all political and leadership positions because only men could be heads of towns and family groups (Kibria, 1993). While Vietnamese women could participate in ancestral rituals, they were not given the authority to be ritual heads, who were responsible for maintaining the lineage assets, making entries in the family genealogies, approving major decisions such as marriages or divorce, and arbitrating various disputes that might occur among members within the lineage.

The subordination of women to men is also reflected in ancient Vietnamese laws that treated women more harshly than men. The laws punished offenses committed by the wife against the husband with the same severity as crimes committed by children or grandchildren against parents or grandparents, or as offenses committed by slaves or serfs against masters (Ta, 1981). When men and women committed the same crime, women were punished more severely than men. Particularly, wife beating was legally sanctioned as long as no injuries resulted, but husband beating was severely punished. Exile was often the penalty for women who struck their husbands. The dominant position of the husband was also evident in the stipulation in ancient laws that a man could repudiate his wife on several grounds, such as childlessness, lasciviousness, refusal to serve and obey parents-in-law, jealousy, or incurable diseases (Ta, 1981; Vu, 1971).

Vietnamese culture and family traditions, however, underwent tremendous changes during the nineteenth and twentieth centuries. The long history of multiple wars, urbanization, and contacts with western cultures during the French colonization and the Vietnam War altered the basic structure of the Vietnamese traditional family and undermined some old manners and customs in Vietnamese family traditions. For example, various aspects of life during the French colonial period facilitated the involvement of women in the public domain (Haines, 1986). In urban areas, education was opened to women to some extent, offering them access to certain economic skills, and causing less social resistance to explicitly economic activities by women. A new literary school of thought (*Tu Luc Van Doan*), which emerged in the 1930s and devoted itself to the liberation of women, also contributed to changes in the social norms regarding gender-role expectations (Ta, 1981). Members of *Tu Luc Van Doan* demanded the emancipation of women from the yoke of the extended family, their freedom of marriage and education, and their participation in new careers on an equal footing with men. In addition, wars caused deaths or the absence from home of many men, making it difficult to maintain the expected ancient family traditions and practices. Women who were left alone to support themselves, their children, and elderly relatives became more involved in social and economic activities, taking the men's position of the family provider and caretaker. In families with two parents, women often worked to supplement their husbands' income. The involvement of women in all aspects of social activities increased sharply during the Vietnam War. Many women participated in the military and fought along men in battlefields, and many more took civilian positions in educational, economic, and health care institutions.

IMMIGRANT FAMILY LIFE

Most Vietnamese in the United States are first-generation immigrants who came to the United States after 1975. Growing up in a country with a culture very much different from that in the United States, Vietnamese immigrants have brought their cultural traditions and practices to the new land. Thus, it is not surprising that many of these immigrants continue to uphold the traditional Vietnamese family as the preferred basis of social organization in the United States (Gold, 1992). The process of resettlement and adaptation has further altered the traditional Vietnamese family, which had experienced many changes before migration. Immigration resettlement not only requires new arrivals to learn a different language and new customs, but it also disrupts the continuity of family life and traditional norms. Besides new values that ultimately affect how family members relate to each other, economic, political, and social resources available for Vietnamese immigrant men and women also contribute to the shaping of power dynamics in Vietnamese immigrant families that in turn affect women's experiences with and responses to abuse.

Men's Downward Mobility and Changes in Family Dynamics

Resettlement in the United States has changed Vietnamese family dynamics mostly in terms of the loss of economic and social status among men and increased opportunities for the growth of women's power. Limited English proficiency and occupational skills, the requirement of professional experience and certifications in the United States, and an ethnic minority status have prevented many Vietnamese immigrants from obtaining employment commensurate with their education and training in Vietnam, causing a tremendous loss of status for many Vietnamese immigrants. The loss of status is particularly acute among former Vietnamese military officers who have skills that are not marketable in the United States and, therefore, have to hold jobs at low levels in the occupational structure. It is not uncommon for former colonels, captains, and lieutenants to work in manual, temporary, and low-status jobs, such as janitors, factory assemblers, warehouse stockers, and security guards. Those who worked as professionals in Vietnam but cannot update their professional credentials in the United States often hold jobs at the levels of technician, secretary, clerk, and even manual laborer.

Besides a lack of language and occupational skills, Vietnamese immigrant men who felt betrayed by the United States when South Vietnam was lost to the communists also experience a "Vietnam syndrome" similar to the one experienced by American veterans of the Vietnam War (see H. Nguyen & Haines, 1996). The syndrome, which is found most acutely among those who were heavily involved in the Vietnam War, including former military officers and soldiers in the South Vietnamese government, causes withdrawal, a pessimistic outlook, and a negative attitude toward social participation. As a result, many members of this group have lost their motivation to improve their own adjustment to American society.

Men's downward mobility is often accompanied by a role reversal and a shift of power in many Vietnamese immigrant families. In most cases, when the husbands' salaries alone are not sufficient to meet the high cost of living, the wives have to work to contribute to the family economy. As in Vietnam, women often engage in a variety of income-generating activities, but different from traditional Vietnam, economic contributions of Vietnamese immigrant women to the family budget has risen relative to, or even more than, those of Vietnamese immigrant men. Women can make more money because unskilled jobs, such as house cleaning as well as hotel and food services, are common while unskilled male-oriented occupations are not (Gold, 1992). In addition, traditionally charged with the responsibility to take care of household "internal affairs," Vietnamese immigrant women used to find ways to provide enough food and clothes for everyone in the household. Therefore, they are willing to work in menial jobs to support the family. Men, on the other hand, are more concerned with their social status and often try to find high-status jobs that are less available for new immigrants. It is not uncommon for Vietnamese immigrant women to work in two jobs while their husbands hold a part-time job or are unemployed. Educational opportunities in the United States also help many women become professionals and work in jobs that have the same status as, or even higher than, those of their husbands. In these cases, women's ability to earn and provide more to the family than their husbands often shifts the roles of the husband and the wife, with the wife taking on the role of the primary wage earner.

Cultural and Gender Norms: Continuity and Change

Central to the experience of disorder that accompanies the settlement of Vietnamese in the United States is the challenge to the integrity of Vietnamese culture and identity and changes in the relations of men and women. Because the traditional role of the Vietnamese woman and her relationship with her husband, shaped by Confucian norms and values, clashes with American culture, which supports the ideal of gender equality, Vietnamese immigrants, especially the elderly, often consider American culture extremely corrosive to traditional Vietnamese patterns of gender relations (Kibria, 1993). While they praise individual liberties, they also find that the young in America have too much freedom (Tran, 2000).

Vietnamese immigrants of the first generation still retain strong ties to the language and culture of their homeland. Like other immigrant groups (Gold, 1992), language has been used to conserve the Vietnamese cultural identity. A substantial majority of Vietnamese immigrants in Little Saigon, the largest Vietnamese community in the United States, read Vietnamese newspapers or magazines and listen to Vietnamese-language radio everyday. Vietnamese videos are also a major source of entertainment for young Vietnamese Americans (Martell & Tran, 2000b). Ethnic-based religious congregations offer another set of key institutions among Vietnamese immigrants. According to Gold (1992), traditional religious leaders can use the culture and religion of the old country to build communities in the United States. Not only in large Vietnamese communities, but also in small ones with a few thousand residents, Vietnamese immigrants often have their own Buddhist temples as well as Catholic and Protestant churches where they can meet together and participate in different kinds of religious and cultural activities. There are almost twenty Buddhist temples and more than twenty Christian churches in Little Saigon; sixteen Buddhist temples, and the same number of Catholic and Protestant churches are found in Houston, the third-largest Vietnamese community in the United States. While tolerating the assimilation of American customs to different extents, Vietnamese religious leaders usually assert the need for the preservation of a Vietnamese past to avoid assimilation and to re-create an authentic community ethnic identity in the United States (Gold, 1992).

Despite efforts to retain Vietnamese culture and traditions, adaptation to new cultural and social conditions is an important, or even a necessary, part of making a new life in the United States. Under the economic conditions of immigration resettlement in which the earnings of many Vietnamese men are not enough to support the family, Vietnamese women have quickly moved into the work force and made money. Although in Vietnam women often worked to supplement family incomes during war times when their husbands fought in the battlefields, women's position in the family and society was still subordinate to men's under the traditional gender norms shaped by Confucian teachings. Things, however, are somewhat different in the United States where the norm of women's subordination derived from Confucianism has to compete with American culture. Women's economic contributions combined with the ideal of gender equality have helped women gain some power in the family and created a shift in power in many families. For many Vietnamese immigrant women, household decisions and housework should be shared fairly between the husband and the wife, especially when women work and contribute income to the family. Women's changing power in the family is also reflected in family budget management. Unlike in Vietnam where the housewife often received a sum of money from her husband to spend for the household needs without knowledge of his actual wage or income, most Vietnamese immigrant women have joint bank accounts with their husbands and can control, to some extent, earnings and spending. Gold (1992) also found that Vietnamese-American women were less enthusiastic about patriarchal Vietnamese traditions; many denounced the rule of Three-Obediences and questioned their husbands' control over their behavior. Xuan, a middle-aged woman who had been a secretary-clerk in Vietnam but worked as a waitress in the United States, was excited when talking about how she defied her husband's effort to control her behavior. "You know, he often tried to force me to follow his demand, but he was not often successful [laughed]. 'America is not Vietnam,' I often told him. . . . He was jealous and didn't want me to wear make-ups or fashionable clothes, but I just ignored his unreasonable demand."

While Vietnamese immigrant women have adapted a view toward gender equality, many Vietnamese immigrant men have not changed their views about gender-role expectations; instead, they see a woman's request for a fair share of family decision making as arrogant and even disrespectful to her husband. Besides efforts to control women's behavior, many Vietnamese immigrant men have tried to retain the power of the head of the family, as men in Vietnam used to hold, and caused family conflicts by ignoring or putting down their wives' opinions in major family decisions. The story of Lan, who spoke at length about her frustration over her husband's efforts to control the family, is an example of how many Vietnamese immigrant men still maintain a traditional view of male domination and female subordination in the family. Lan, who migrated to the United States in 1973 as a student and became a professional five years later, identified herself as "very Americanized" because, as she explained, she did not accept the definition of femininity under Vietnamese traditions. Lan's husband, who was also a college graduate in Vietnam and migrated to the United States in 1975 right after the fall of Saigon, however, still valued Vietnamese family traditions. As Lan told her story, her voice was filled with anger:

My husband lived here but his mind was in Vietnam. He often talked about his "golden years" back there and complained about Vietnamese women in America having too much freedom and power, and becoming disrespectful to their husbands. He always told me that I talked back to him too much, that his mother had never talked back to his father, that his mother always deferred to his father's desires and wills. . . . I encouraged him to go back to college, but he didn't want to. So, he had to work in manual jobs. . . . After I helped him get a loan, he became an owner of a car repair shop. The business went well, and with his income combined with my income, we bought a nice house far away from the city. I didn't want to live in the rural area, but he wanted to have a farm he had dreamed of back in Vietnam. He raised several goats, chickens, and a couple of cows for fun. He also built a pond in the backyard to raise fish. By deferring to his desire, I have to drive 40 miles one way to work in the city, while his shop is just less than 10 miles from home. He was also authoritarian in many ways: like he rarely discussed with me what he was going to do, whom he was going to invite to party at our house, and when he would have a party. He usually spent large amounts of money, sending it to his family and friends in Vietnam, without my consent.[4]

Although immigration resettlement has created a shift of power in many Vietnamese immigrant families, the change still remains conservative. According to Rimonte (1989), Asian men, who see women's working outside the home as threatening and describe these changes as the "Americanization" of their Asian wives, often resist the changes and insist on their accustomed privileges and esteemed place. Besides men's resistance to the ideal of gender equality, women's economic conditions and cultural isolation also have important impacts on family dynamics. Vietnamese immigrant women may not be very enthusiastic about patriarchal family traditions, but they also view economic protection from men as necessary, especially when they work in temporary, low-paying jobs, to sustain a decent life. Moreover, isolation from mainstream society has created a need in many Vietnamese immigrants to rely on their families and to turn to the Vietnamese community for emotional support. Communities with a large concentration of Vietnamese immigrants often provide a social context for the reinforcement of Vietnamese family traditions and gender practices. The Four Virtues and Three Obediences, which dictate the subordination of women to men, continue to be promoted in Vietnamese books, newspapers, magazines, as well as radio and TV programs; Vietnamese family values are also often mentioned in religious and social events. This context has limited Vietnamese immigrant women's efforts to challenge male authority.

Experiences of Intimate Violence

Abused Vietnamese immigrant women have suffered different forms of violence by their husbands/partners. Most abused women have experienced both physical and emotional abuse. Violence often began in Vietnam and continued in the United States. Some women even experienced abuse in refugee camps where they were waiting for permission to enter the United States, as illustrated by the story of Phuong. Raised in a family with a rural background, Phuong did not fall in love with her husband, but she still married him because she thought that, as a woman, she needed to have a husband, especially in her late twenties. Her marriage of almost ten years was a nightmare filled with violence and humiliation.

When we were in Vietnam, I mean before we escaped, he often slapped and kicked me when I didn't follow his commands. This continued in the [refugee] camp. . . . You couldn't imagine how life was hard there. We lacked everything, from food, medicines, to clothes. Life became harder for me after I gave birth to my daughter [in the camp] because she was sick and became paralyzed right after birth. . . . He often beat me when I refused to have sex with him. You know, I usually felt very tired because I had to take care of my daughter all day and night. . . . He didn't do anything, just hanging around with other men in the camp. He also beat me when I felt frustrated and swore at him because he didn't help me. . . . The most severe incident happened when I discovered that he had borrowed money from a person in the camp to buy cigarettes but lied that he would use the money to buy medicines for my daughter. When he learned that I had told the truth to the lender, I almost died because of his retaliation. I can still recall that day. . . . He stormed into the community kitchen where I was preparing food for my daughter, grasped my hair and kicked very hard at my back many times. I couldn't breath and almost passed out. I was taken to the hospital in the camp and couldn't stand up and walked for several days. . . . I was told that I might suffer internal injuries in the lung, but Malaysia nurses, after learning that I was hit by my husband, refused to do a X-ray for me because, as they said, we caused troubles at the camp. When the Red Cross delegation came to visit, one lady ask whether I agreed to sign the paperwork allowing the camp to arrest and detain my husband. I refused to sign because I was afraid that when he was released, he would hit me harder. . . . We were repatriated after staying in the camp for seven years. Back in Vietnam I left him and lived with my sister, but I still had contacts with him to complete the paperwork for resettlement in the Unites States because I needed medical treatment for my daughter. He continued beating me after we arrived in the United States for the same reason: because I refused to have sex with him, especially when he was drunk.[5]

Physical abuse could range from throwing and destroying things in the home or things belonging to wives/partners, to threats of physical attacks (threats to hit and/or to kill wives/partners or wives'/partners' relatives), and actual physical attacks (slapping, kicking, choking, punching, whipping, pushing, and forcing wives/ partners to have sex). In some situations, weapons, including guns, knives hammers, wooden sticks, and electric cords, were also involved. The most frequent forms of emotional abuse by husbands/partners included swearing and yelling at wives/partners, calling them names or calling them stupid and crazy in front of other people. Some men hurt themselves or threatened to commit suicide to force their wives/partners to satisfy their demands. Some women also experienced harassment and stalking by their ex-husbands/partners after separation and divorce.

Migration to the United States has changed women's experiences of abuse in many ways. A number of women were abused in Vietnam but experienced less physical abuse after they arrived in the United States. The prohibition of domestic violence in the United States has been part of the reason for the change. Unlike in the United States, wife beating was sanctioned explicitly in traditional Vietnamese societies and implicitly in contemporary Vietnam because of women's inferior status and the absence of law against domestic violence. Awareness of the prohibition of domestic violence in American society and fear of being involved with the law has caused many Vietnamese-American men to stop or reduce the use of force against their wives/partners. A survey of Vietnamese Americans in the United States found that a substantial majority of respondents were aware of the illegality of wife beating in the United States (97%) and understood that spouse beating could lead to arrest (80%) (see Appendix B). Lien, who experienced abuse less frequently in the United States, attributed the change to domestic violence laws. "He [her husband] began physically abusing me after he was released from the re-education camp. Once we arrived in the United States, he did not beat me as often as he had done in Vietnam. Probably he learned from his friends that wife beating was illegal in the United States and he was afraid of the law." A counselor who worked with Vietnamese men in a batterers' program confirmed that view. As he explained,

Many men in Vietnam felt that they were entitled to beat their wives. So, a man could beat his wife whenever he didn't feel satisfied with her behavior, or when he felt angry with her. Because of the law [against domestic violence] in the United States, Vietnamese men now often have to think more carefully before using force at home, either against their wives or their children. To make it easier to understand, just consider an anger scale with ten levels, from one to ten. . . . For example, a man in Vietnam might beat his wife when he felt angry at levels one or two, but he may use force in the United States only when he feels very angry, say at levels nine or ten.

One of my informants who was affiliated with an association of former Vietnamese military officers also confirmed that members of his organization often bitterly reminded each other not to use force against children or wives because "there will be a good chance to go to jail."

In other situations, however, physical abuse got worse or only began after the couples came to the United States. Immigration and adaptation have created a unique context of intimate violence among Vietnamese immigrants. Although the core dynamics of spouse abuse are male dominance as well as the quest for control and power in intimate relationships, the ways those power dynamics are constructed and manifested are influenced by economic, cultural, and political contexts (Lee & Au, 1998). The inversion of elements of the traditional gender order in the family due to men's downward mobility and women's increased economic power often causes family conflicts leading to men's use of violence to restate their authority. The humiliating conditions of working in menial jobs and status inconsistency also causes distress and provokes hostility and resentment among many Vietnamese immigrant men. Some men escape their economic failure and family distress through alcoholism and gambling that can trigger family conflicts. Other men use force against their wives/partners who complain about their gambling and alcohol problems, or who refuse to give them money needed for their gambling and drinking habits.

Violence also occurs within the context of unfulfilled expectations. Raised in family traditions in which men are expected to take the role of the breadwinner, Vietnamese immigrant women continue to value men's meeting the obligation of the family provider despite a decline in the ability of many Vietnamese immigrant men to perform this task. Women, like Xuan, who have to shoulder the burden of making money for the family often feel disappointed about their husbands' lack of responsibility as the breadwinner. Xuan's husband, who had been a captain in the South Vietnam military during the Vietnam War, lacked English fluency and vocational skills and had to hold a packaging job in a garment factory. Xuan's husband did not like the job and only worked part time because it was not consistent with his status as a former military captain.[6] His lack of interest in making money has forced Xuan to work two jobs as a waitress to support the family. Xuan's frustration over her husband's failure to meet her expectations is not uncommon among Vietnamese immigrant women.

He [Xuan's husband] didn't want to learn English or a vocation to find a better job and make more money to support the family. While other people worked two or three jobs to make ends meet, he worked less than one job. Instead, he spent most of his time to meet with his former military fellows and discuss politics. I wish if his politics could bring home some money to buy food for our children. I don't know what made them [her husband and his friends] change so much; they don't act like [good] men and husbands any more.[7]

Women's complaints about their husbands' failure to fulfill the norms of masculine behavior often make things worse because they cut deep into men's insecurities, and force is often used to express men's power.

Women's changing views of gender roles clash with those of their husbands and cause family conflicts and subsequent violence by the men. Traditionally, Vietnamese women were compelled to work while still bearing the major burden in the domestic realm. Many women who silently accepted their double-days in Vietnam—working to support the family, doing housework, as well as taking care of children and the elderly—began to demand a fair share of family responsibilities on the part of their husbands after arriving in the United States. Wives' complaints about husbands' failure to do housework can hurt men's feelings and cause them to use violence, such as in the case of Huyen:

I also worked to make money like him [Huyen's husband]. . . . I even worked over time, but I had to do all housework and take care of our [two] children. I didn't have time to watch TV or read newspapers, but he never thought about how hard my work was. . . . He never gave me a hand to help me, so that I can take a break. . . . He came home from work and watch TV until dinner was served. He often ignored the division of household chores we had agreed upon. When I complained, he became angry and said that I wanted to be the boss. . . . In one incident, he said that because I wanted to be the boss, he would let me know who was the boss at home. He hit [slapped] me to make me shut up.[8]

Wives' resistance to husbands' control over their lives can lead to men's use of force to reinstate male authority. Oanh, a successful career woman in her late thirties, recounted how her ex-husband attacked her because she protested his attempt to prevent her from pursuing a career goal.

I married him when I just graduated from high school, and he was a college graduate. He made good money and wanted me to stay home, take care of children, and do housework. I thought he loved me and wanted to protect me, as he usually said. After my son and daughter started going to school, I also wanted to go to college and have my own career. All my brothers and sisters had college degrees, and I wanted to become a lawyer. So, I decided to enroll in a college program. . . . He didn't like the idea but let me do it. A few years later, I was accepted to a law school. I was very happy and I thought he would be happy, too. However, he didn't welcome the news. He said that my study would be useless because I couldn't become a lawyer, that I should spend more time with my children. . . . We argued for several days. When he finally said, "No more school. Period," I felt furious and told him, "You can't prohibit me from pursuing my career. If you want to stop me from going to school, you have to step over my dead body." He, then, beat me up because I didn't follow his command to shut up.[9]

Jealousy among Vietnamese immigrant men can also lead to family conflicts and violence. The literature suggests that men's ability to control women's sexuality is a major feature of masculinity, and men's jealousy and subsequent violence against women are expressions of masculinity, sexual possessiveness, and control (J. C. Campbell, 1992; R. E. Dobash & R. P. Dobash, 1979; Messerschmidt, 1993). Jealousy among Vietnamese immigrant men is often caused by women's changing status and behavior as a result of adaptation to American culture. According to Lin, Tazuma & Masuda (1979), the fact that young Vietnamese immigrant men are more distressed than women of the same age may be explained by gender-role expectations and the stereotypes of American society that are more favorable to Asian female subjects, who are often viewed as feminine and adorable, than to the young Asian men, who are frequently seen as weak and nonmasculine. In addition, Vietnamese immigrant men's fear of losing their wives or partners are also based on their perception that women in the United States, including Vietnamese women, have more freedom to engage in intimate relationships, contrary to the Vietnamese norm of feminine behavior. There has been an inverse situation with regard to sexual jealousy among Vietnamese immigrant men and women. As a social worker who had contact with both Vietnamese men and women explained,

In Vietnam, married women were often worried about their husbands' disloyalty because most married men had either girlfriends, mistresses, or concubines at some point in their marriages. In the United States, [Vietnamese] men have become very jealous and been usually worried about their wives or partners leaving them to go with "American" men. . . . Many [Vietnamese] men have become paranoid because they think they are less attractive than their "American" counterparts and [Vietnamese] women have more freedom to engage in intimate relationships in the United States than they did in Vietnam.[10]

Vietnamese men who lost social standing and power in the family often fear losing their wives or partners to other, more successful, men. Adapting to the new ideology of gender equality in the United States, many Vietnamese immigrant women have come to doubt their husbands' right to dominate them; violence occurs when these women disregard their husbands'/partners' controlling efforts, as in the case of Ly. A businessperson in her early forties, Ly came to the United States with her husband and three children under the sponsorship of her husband's family. Because Ly had prepared by learning English in Vietnam, she quickly adapted to the new life, went to college, and became a successful real-estate agent. Her husband, however, had limited English proficiency and worked as a courtesy clerk. He felt jealous when Ly wore fashionable clothes, worked after hours, and went out with male customers. However, because of the job requirement, Ly usually disregard and sometimes opposed her husband's jealousy and criticisms of her mode of dressing and "Americanized" gestures. Violence was often preceded by arguments occurring after a male customer called Ly and asked her to go out to show him a house. As Ly explained:

Because my job required me to go out often even beyond business hours, he couldn't control my schedule and became suspicious and jealous. . . . When he learned that someone had called me at home, he became suspicious. When we argued against each other, he usually repeated his unreasonable accusations that I lacked chastity, was arrogant, and lacked of respect for him. He often slapped me when I did not shut up at his order. One day, I became very angry and couldn't bear his insult anymore. So, I told him that if he continued to say bad about me, I would act this way to make his accusations become true. Enraged by my provocation, he reached out to grasp me, push me into the wall, choked me, and said that he would not let me live to see my children the next morning. The children were terrified and called the police.

Some jobs that require a woman to work at night and in certain work environments also arouse a husband's suspicions. Factory and restaurant jobs that require night shifts, and hotel services, such as cleaners and chambermaids, are among the few jobs available for immigrant women who do not have vocational skills and English proficiency. On the other hand, under Vietnamese gender norms, women are not expected to go out alone at night, and hotels are not a suitable workplace for women because of possible prostitution activities. Many Vietnamese men do not want their wives to work night shifts, but due to the demand of the family economy, especially when men do not have jobs or do not earn enough to support the family, many women still have to work night shifts. Women's work schedules, however, often cause family conflicts that can lead to men's use of violence against them. A misperception about some jobs in the United States can cause men to suspect their wives' loyalty and beat them out of jealousy. This was the experience of Xuan:

We got married in Vietnam, but I had never seen him become so jealous . . . only after we came to the United States. . . . I was almost 50 years old, but he usually thought I acted like a

20-year-old girl who was trying to "get" other men. I was working at two hotels in downtown, but he didn't like it. He told me to change my job many times because under his view only prostitutes worked in hotels. . . . I did try to move to other jobs, but none could help me earned the same amount of money to support our five children while he worked only part time, and sometimes he even didn't work. He got mad when I brought home pretty large amount of money from tips. Then, he started scrutinizing the way I dressed. He even prohibited me from wearing make-ups and certain kinds of clothes. When I disregard his unreasonable demands, he beat me and even threatened to kill me.[11]

Awareness of the prohibition of domestic violence in the United States has caused many husbands to change attack strategies to prevent outsiders from learning about the abuse. For example, instead of slapping the face of the victims where injuries can be seen by outsiders (the third party), many men hit their wives/partners in parts of the body where signs of injuries can be covered by clothes. Many men also carefully disconnect the phone line or lock the door to prevent their victims from calling the police and running out of the house. As Cuc, a young woman in her late twenties, told her story,

He used to slapped and punched into my face. One time he kicked into my mouth and caused me two broken teeth and bleeding lips. This happened in the street . . . because I ran out of the house and he chased me. One passenger saw the incident, stopped his car and came to rescue me. The passenger attempted to call the police but I asked him not to call. . . . After that incident, my husband didn't hit me in the face. Instead, he punched me in my chest and my back, or used a stick to hit me at my legs.

Hien, who dated and lived with a Caucasian man, had a more horrible experience. After Hien's boyfriend discovered that she had a sexual relationship with another man, he prepared a plan to punish her. Because Hien felt guilty about her behavior, she thought that she deserved some sort of punishment, but she never thought it would be so cruel.

He ordered me to take off my clothes. Then, he tied me on the bed, face down, and whipped me with an electric cord. He whipped me in the buttock, so that no signs of injuries could be seen by others, even by his mother who lived with us in the same house. . . . I got bleeding, but I had to keep silent because he said he would kill me if I let other people know about the problem. He also took away the phone. . . . He prohibited me from leaving the room, and he continued whipping me the next day, and the next day until I couldn't walk. When I couldn't bear the pain anymore, I talked with his mother and asked to use her phone to call the police.

A majority of abused women have suffered injuries from physical attacks. The most common forms of injury are bruises, scratches, black eyes, and swelling, but many women also have had more severe injuries, including dislocated joints, broken teeth, bleeding, and internal injuries. In many situations, severely injured women do not seek medical attention because they do not want other people to know about the problems. Abused women are taken to the hospital or the emergency room only in extreme cases where they have passed out or had heavy bleeding. Most women have also experienced stress and depressive symptoms resulting from physical and emotional abuse, including loss of appetite, insomnia, and constant headaches. For some women, unbearable stress caused by abuse can lead to suicide attempts, such as in the case of Tram whose husband often destroyed kitchenware and small household appliances when the couple had conflicts. Tram learned about my study from a Vietnamese radio broadcasting program, and called me to tell her story. As Tram explained:

He never hit me. He only threw dishes, books, and other small things against the walls, or smashed flower pots on the floor.... This happened almost every month, sometimes several times a month, making home like the hell. I didn't get [physical] injuries, but my mental and physical health gradually deteriorated.... I couldn't sleep and eat; I lost concentration to my work. His violence became so unbearable that I attempted to commit suicide several times. I told him [her husband] if he wanted me to die to satisfy him, I would die, but I couldn't see him turn our home like the hell.

Seeking Help

Personal Support Networks. For most Vietnamese immigrant women, the personal support network is often the first place they reach out for help. This tendency is found among those raised in the tradition that requires the individual to turn first to her immediate family and then beyond in widening concentric circles to the extended family, the community, and to an agency that is perceived as culturally hospitable and linguistically accessible (Rimonte, 1989). When abused Vietnamese women need emotional support and/or advice for a solution to the problem, they tend to talk with their relatives, friends, and/or religious leaders about their experiences of intimate abuse.

Shame, fear of the abuser, and racial prejudice, however, often prevent abused Vietnamese women from disclosing their experiences of intimate violence. Within the cultural milieu that emphasizes one's obligation to the family, many abused women would rather remain silent than admit to a problem that might disgrace their families (Rimonte, 1989). Moreover, Vietnamese Amerasians tend not to contact people outside the family who, they think, may look down on them. Racial prejudice against Amerasians, which stems from the view of some Vietnamese that Amerasians are children of prostitutes who sold their bodies to American GIs to make a living, often turns off the attempt of Vietnamese Amerasians to reach out to people in their own ethnic community for help. Women who married members of other racial groups often do not contact people outside the family because of negative attitudes toward interracial marriages among many in the Vietnamese population. Le married an Iraqi man despite the opposition of her parents and siblings. Le did not want her family to learn about the abuse, nor did she talk with her friends or co-workers. As she explained,

I felt ashamed with my parents. They did advise me not to marry him. How could I talk with them [her parents] about the abuse. . . . I didn't want to talk with my friends either. You know, Vietnamese don't want to see [Vietnamese] women marry Americans. If they learn that a woman was abused by her American husband, they will laugh and say something like, "Hey, you think American men are nice, don't you. But they beat you anyway."[12]

When Vietnamese immigrant women talk about their experiences of intimate abuse with members of their personal network, they often receive mixed responses. In some cases, siblings, parents, relatives, or friends encourage and help abused women contact victim service agencies. Some also give shelter to women who have left home to escape abuse. More often than not, however, women who talk with friends and relatives do not receive helpful responses. Relatives who believe in the traditional role of women often discourage a battered woman from taking steps toward safety and rescue. Although friends and relatives may feel sympathetic toward victims of intimate abuse, those who view domestic violence as a private matter do not want to intervene. Others who still conform to Vietnamese family traditions even advise the victim to accept abuse, or to try not to make her husband/partner angry. Hoa had talked with her parents and siblings about the abuse many times before she decided to seek help from the police. However, her relatives refused to intervene because under Vietnamese family traditions, women were seen as outsiders from their own families, and married women were viewed as belonging to their husbands' family, as reflected in the old saying, "My daughters are other people's children, but my daughters-in-law are my true children." "My mother and siblings told me they couldn't do anything about it [the abuse] because I was a married woman. . . . I belonged to my husband and his family. My mother advised me not to make my husband angry, not to up set him." (Hoa)[13]

Barriers to Agency Social Services. For Vietnamese immigrants, the prohibition of domestic violence is one of the special features of American life. Unlike in Vietnam, where women had no legal recourse to deal with abuse at home, women in the United States can rely on the law to fight against their abusive husbands/partners, or seek help from other victim service agencies, including women's shelters. However, abused Vietnamese women tend to be reluctant to call the police to report abuse incidents, regardless of the availability of criminal justice services. Social isolation often has a major impact on women's decisions not to seek help from the mainstream society. Social isolation is defined as being emotionally and socially alone, economically confined, and culturally disconnected. It creates a sense of not belonging or not having meaningful relationships in terms of the frequency and quality of social interactions in informal networks of friends, relatives, and co-workers, and access to and participation in formal economic, political, and legal organizations (Abraham, 2000).

Economic isolation often leads to economic dependency and a fear of criminal justice interventions among immigrant women. Although most Vietnamese immigrant women participate in the labor force, they are likely to work in low-paying jobs due to their low levels of education, limited English proficiency, and few vocational skills. According to Rumbaut (1996), Vietnamese immigrants had an average of 9.9 years of schooling, but those who arrived in the United States after 1980 had only five or six years. In addition, a majority of Vietnamese immigrants do not speak English very well. Besides women who do not work and are totally dependent on their husbands/partners for financial support, women who work in low-paying jobs also need their husbands'/partners' incomes to make ends meet. The lack of a support network of extended family members often left behind in Vietnam and welfare reforms further contribute to economic dependency among Vietnamese immigrant women. Anti-immigrant sentiment has led to discriminatory policies in the 1996 welfare reform legislation that denies legal immigrants access to most federal, state, and local welfare programs, and has forced thousands of battered immigrant women to remain in abusive relationships (Abraham, 2000). Because most immigrants who entered the country after August 22, 1996, are not eligible for federal assistance during their first five years in the United States, economic isolation is one of the biggest problems for new immigrants (Capellaro, 1999). Vietnamese immigrant women's decision not to seek help from the criminal justice system often stems from their fear that police intervention may cause their husbands/partners to be arrested, prosecuted, and sentenced to jail, and that their family income may be lost. Mandatory arrest policies further reinforce their unwillingness to report abuse. Quyen and Nguyet, who did not work but stayed home to take care of their children, stopped calling the police for help after new policies requiring mandatory arrests in domestic violence cases were implemented. As they explained,

Since the new law [mandatory arrest], I didn't call the police because I depended on him [financially] and I didn't want him to be arrested. . . . After I gave birth to my first child, I gained a lot of weight and couldn't work in the cafeteria any more. . . . You know, they only hired women with slim bodies because they looked more attractive. . . . I didn't have any vocational skills, and I didn't want to work in assembly jobs. The pay was low, but day care cost was high and could consume all of my salary. . . . I'd rather stay home with my baby. (Quyen)[14]

After I began having children with him, I didn't call the police because nothing could be solved. I had to depend on him to survive. . . . I had three children, and you can see, I had no other choice. Some of my friends also told me to forget about his violence and not to call the police. They said it would be a shame if I called the police and continued to sleep with him. (Nguyet)[15]

Economic dependency, however, does not need to be absolute.[16] Women with high levels of education and a career are also reluctant to call the police to report abuse. With the growing need for dual incomes to sustain urban family life, professional women still fear that police interventions will strain the relationship, cause family breakups, and negatively affect their living standards. Lan, who was a college graduate, worked in a high-tech industry, and lived in a middle-class neighborhood, but she had tried to avoid a separation that might affect not only the emotional but also the financial aspects of her life. Oanh, who had her own business, also shared this view.

Although I work and can support myself, my financial situation will be worse without his income. When we live together, costs of housing and food for each person are cheaper. If we had a divorce, we would have to sell the house, and I wouldn't be able to buy another one. (Lan)

Without his income, I can still survive because I have my own career. However, things would be different if we had a divorce or separation. We would have to sell the house, and I would probably not be able to live in another house like this but instead in an apartment. (Oanh)

Women who temporarily depend on their husbands' financial support while pursuing an education for self-improvement also fear family breakups and the loss of income. Diep, a young woman who had a college degree and was pursuing a professional education, explained why she needed her husband's financial support, "I have a college degree and I can support myself. However, I also have a small child, and I'm pursuing a professional degree [MBA]. It will be very hard for me if I don't have his income during this time and have to work to support my child and myself while in school."[17] Economic dependency affects not only the decision to seek help from the criminal justice system among women who want to stay with their abusers but also among women who have decided to leave the abusive relationship. Because separated or divorced women still need child support from their husbands/partners to raise their children, they do not want their ex-husbands/partners to be arrested.

Cultural isolation reflected by a lack of English proficiency and understanding of the American legal system is another barrier to women's efforts to seek help from the mainstream society. While a large proportion of Vietnamese immigrants have limited English proficiency, interpretation assistance for Vietnamese immigrants by criminal justice and victim service agencies is severely inadequate, especially in small Vietnamese communities. In addition, when a woman wants to talk with an interpreter, she has to first communicate with the dispatcher in English to ask for assistance, or she has to ask other people to talk with the dispatcher on her behalf. For women who speak limited English but do not want others to know about the problem, reporting abuse to the authorities is extremely difficult. Moreover, many are reluctant to contact law enforcement agencies because they do not understand the law and do not know what will happen once the police arrive. Isolation also keeps immigrant women unaware of the availability of support services that may help them, and the lack of English fluency and social networks add to their isolation. Many Vietnamese immigrant women are unaware of the availability of women's shelters and other victim services in their local areas because they have few social connections with people who could tell them about the services, or because bilingual materials are not available.

Immigration status is another barrier for immigrant women attempting to use the criminal justice system to escape abuse. Since the 1930s, United States immigration policies have allowed American citizens to marry foreign nationals and sponsor their spouses into the United States (Houston, Kramer & Barrett, 1984). However, the process of obtaining a permanent residency in the United States through marriage has become harder and more complicated after the enactment of the Immigration Marriage Fraud Amendment (IMFA) in 1986. Although the main purpose of IMFA is to prevent marriage fraud, the new law has inadvertently become a power tool for abusive spouses to use against their alien partners and children (Abraham, 2000). Under the IMFA, the citizen spouse controls the initiation and the withdrawal of a petition for the sponsored spouse's permanent residency. The requirement that the sponsoring spouse must initiate the petition makes these immigrant women totally dependent on their husbands for legal status. Despite the fact that the law has changed to provide relief for battered spouses by creating a special "waiver" for battered immigrants and allowing them to finish the process of gaining permanent resident status without the participation of their abusers, immigrant women are still often intimidated by their abusers due to their lack of understanding of the law (Chin, 1994).

The legal dependency created by IMFA has prevented many Vietnamese women who married American citizens and came to the United States under the sponsorship of their husbands from leaving the abusive relationship or calling the police to report abuse. They are afraid that their husbands would retaliate and refuse to file a petition for their permanent residency, and they would be deported. Duyen's story is typical among Vietnamese women who came to the United States as "sponsored brides." Back in Vietnam, Duyen was a schoolteacher in a small town in South Vietnam. Like many Vietnamese who found life very hard under the communist regime, Duyen wanted to immigrate to the United States. Because it would take more than 10 years for Duyen to come to the United States under the sponsorship of her sister, Duyen agreed to marry a Vietnamese-American man to whom her sister introduced her and entered the United States under his sponsorship. As Duyen talked about her experience,

After a few months in the United States, I began to experience his violence.... He controlled me every moment, keeping me at home, prohibiting me from going out alone, and checking on every phone call I made. He hit me when I talked back to him, or when I didn't do what he wanted me to do. For example, he hit me when he discovered that I had called my sister because he didn't want me to contact my sister more often. . . . He made me feel like I was his prisoner. His violence increased over time, and he continued hitting me during my pregnancy of the first baby and caused me a miscarriage. When my sister learned about his violent behavior, she told me to call the police, but I didn't follow her advice. I didn't understand English very much because he didn't allow me to study English. I didn't have money either.... I had to ask him for money when I needed. But most of all, I was afraid that he would divorce me and wouldn't help me with the paperwork to get a green card. . . . He had told me that if he was arrested and jailed, I would be deported back to Vietnam and would lose my son.

Besides women who are concerned with their own legal status, many other Vietnamese immigrant women are also concerned about negative effects of police interventions on the immigration status of their husbands/partners. The 1996 Illegal Immigration Reform and Responsibility Act includes domestic violence offenses in the list of crimes that serve as grounds for the deportation of alien offenders. Therefore, abused women whose husbands/partners do not have American citizenship are afraid that police interventions may lead to the deportation of their husbands/partners or make it difficult for them to obtain American citizenship.

The legacy of Vietnamese family traditions, which emphasized collectivism, close family ties, family privacy, paternal piety, and women's subordination to men, also contributes to women's reluctance to use the criminal justice system to deal with abuse. The ideology of marriage, women's Four Virtues and Three Obediences, which were derived from Confucian teachings and have become an integral part of the definition of femininity in Vietnam,[18] have made many Vietnamese immigrant women feel ashamed for being beaten and have prevented them from talking with people outside the family about the abuse. By not calling the police, they can avoid making their family problems public and subject to criticism. They also fear that police interventions may cause more strain to the family relationship and lead to divorce. Although divorce has become more acceptable among Vietnamese in the United States than in Vietnam, many women are still afraid of the negative consequences of divorce, including economic hardship and unfavorable views toward divorced women. As Tram explained, "I'm a devoted Catholic and want to keep Vietnamese family traditions. I don't want my children to live with separate parents, and I don't want to be criticized for learning the American way."[19] Trang, a woman of rural background, also said that she did not want to have a divorce despite being beaten frequently by her husband because she was afraid that "other people would look at me and say that I was a 'husbandless' woman." Moreover, the importance of the father in children's lives and the traditional authority of parents over children also make many women concerned about the possible diminishment of the father's authority over the children resulting from police intervention.

The Decision to Seek Help from the Criminal Justice System. Despite the influence of Vietnamese family traditions, American culture also exerts its impacts on the family lives of many Vietnamese Americans through the process of adaptation and acculturation. The ideal of gender equality and the prohibition of wife beating in the United States give Vietnamese immigrant women an opportunity to express their agencies and fight against domestic violence. Because of numerous social, cultural, and legal barriers to using the legal approach, abused Vietnamese immigrant women often try other forms of assistance deemed more appropriate for their situations. When these approaches fail, government interventions become a resource for these women to deal with domestic violence.

Studies indicate that intimate violence tends to be a recurrent feature of the relationship (Straus, Gelles & Steinmetz, 1980). For many abused Vietnamese women, the need for safety becomes more urgent when violence continues and escalates in terms of severity and frequency. Fear for their safety and the safety of their close relatives often outweighs other cultural and economic concerns and causes many abused women to call the police to stop violence. Hue began to experience violence by her husband even before they were officially married. Hue was fully aware of police services for victims of domestic violence, but she did not call 911 because her mother, who feared that "the police car in front of the house would make everybody learn about the problem," advised her not to do so. Violence by Hue's husband, fueled by his jealousy, increased over time and caused her to become concerned with her safety. As Hue talked about her experience,

That day, he talked with my four-year-old son and he suspected that someone had come the night before. He began yelling and threatening to kill an imagined enemy and me. . . . He took a kitchen knife and placed it at my neck as if he was going to cut my throat. I was terrified. When I got loose from him, I reached the phone and called 911. . . . I had experienced his violence so many times and for so long . . . since the time we got married [five years ago], but he never scared me like this time. . . . I knew that my financial situation would get worse without his income because I didn't work at that time, but I was not afraid of poverty as much as of his violence.

Hien called the police after her boyfriend had beaten her for several days, causing her severe injuries. She returned, after leaving him for several months, and experienced more violence along with his threats of killing her, her father, and her siblings should she leave him again. She turned to the police for protection. "I called and asked the police to take me out of this situation. I was so scared of him. . . . [Two years later, he] threatened to kill my fathers, my brothers, and myself. Because I wanted to leave the relationship, I went to the police station and ask for the protection of my family and myself."

Besides safety issues, the desire to express agency and a feeling of being "fedup" with abuse also causes many women to call the police. The literature suggests that victims' determination not to put up with abuse any longer is an important factor for their cooperation with the criminal justice system to fight against domestic violence (Erez & Belknap, 1998a; Fischer & Rose, 1995). The availability of laws against domestic violence in the United States gives support to abused Vietnamese immigrant women who think that they can rely on government interventions to stop violence and protect their safety, the option they did not have in their home country. Trang, Hue, and Xuan explained their positions as follows,

I called the police to let him know that I could get him arrested for beating me. (Trang)[20]

I was fed up with his unreasonable jealousy and violence, and I wanted the police to arrest him to teach him a lesson. (Hue)[21]

He used to hit me in Vietnam and continued to hit me in the United States. Because he didn't change, I had to call the police to warn him. I called the police to let him know that he could not hit me as he used to in Vietnam. (Xuan)[22]

~

Resettlement in the United States has brought about changes in the family lives of many Vietnamese immigrants that, in turn, have a major impact on the likelihood of domestic violence and on women's responses to abuse. Men's downward mobility and failure to economically and culturally adjust to the new society often clash with women's new economic roles and elevated status. Feelings of powerlessness, depression, resentment, and jealousy among men as well as the inconsistency in gender-role expectations between men and women often cause family conflicts and subsequent violence by men. A variety of structural, cultural, and legal barriers have affected responses to abuse by Vietnamese immigrant women. Vietnamese cultural traditions still exert a strong influence on the lives of many Vietnamese Americans, especially those who grew up in Vietnam, but the process of resettlement and adaptation has also exposed them to American culture, the ideal of gender equality, and the legal norms that support the protection of women from domestic abuse. Economic and cultural isolations, as well as family traditions, have caused abused women to accept violence in exchange for economic security, legal status in the United States, emotional support from the family, or acceptance from the community. Concerns with consequences of criminal justice interventions, including the arrests of the abusers, the possibility of losing income, and criticisms from other family members and community, can also make abused women reluctant to use the criminal justice system to deal with abuse. Consequently, most abused Vietnamese women consider the personal support network as their first point of contact when they need help. However, when this approach does not work, and when violence continues and escalates, fear of violence and the desire to express agency have caused many women to rely on the criminal justice system for safety.

NOTES

1. All extractions from interview transcripts were originally in Vietnamese and were translated into English.

2. In this book, the term "immigrants" is used to indicate both immigrants and refugees. Although the United States government and immigration policies often treat refugees and immigrants as fundamentally different social groups, the literature shows that differences between the two groups are a matter of continuum (Gold, 1992). For the Vietnamese group, the difference in legal status (immigrants or refugees) is largely based on the means they used to get out of their home country (official departure or escape). However, there are many similarities between Vietnamese immigrants and refugees with regard to their experiences of political oppression in Vietnam as well as their experiences with resettlement and adaptation in the United States.

3. The term "Vietnamese Amerasian" is used to indicate a person whose mother is Vietnamese and whose father is an American who served in American missions in Vietnam. On December 22, 1987, the United States Congress passed into law the Amerasian Homecoming Act, allowing Vietnamese Amerasians who were born between 1962 and 1976 in Vietnam to enter the United States with their families and with full refugee benefits.

4. Part of this quote is from my article "Immigration Context of Wife Abuse: A Case of Vietnamese Immigrants in the United States," published in *It's a Crime: Women and Justice,*

3rd ed. (p. 402), edited by Roslyn Muraskin, copyright © 2002. Reprinted by permission of Pearson Education, Inc., Upper Saddle River, NJ.

5. Many Vietnamese who escaped Vietnam and arrived in Southeast Asian countries were repatriated in the late 1990s because they did not fall into the refugee category defined by the High Commission of Refugees and, therefore, were not allowed to resettle in Western countries. In the middle of 1995, the Resettlement Opportunity for Vietnamese Returnees (ROVR) program was created to allow resettlement in the United States of those who had voluntarily signed up for repatriation. Phuong and her family came to the United States under this program.

6. Many Vietnamese immigrants, especially those who held military and civilian positions in the South Vietnam government but experienced downward mobility in the United States, tend to live with their past. In social events or personal conversations, people often address each other by their old titles, such as Lieutenant, Captain, Professor, Doctor, and so on.

7. This quote is from my article "Immigration Context of Wife Abuse: A Case of Vietnamese Immigrants in the United States," published in *It's a Crime: Women and Justice,* 3rd ed. (p. 401), edited by Roslyn Muraskin, copyright © 2002. Reprinted by permission of Pearson Education, Inc., Upper Saddle River, NJ.

8. This quote is from my article "Immigration Context of Wife Abuse: A Case of Vietnamese Immigrants in the United States," published in *It's a Crime: Women and Justice,* 3rd ed. (p. 402), edited by Roslyn Muraskin, copyright © 2002. Reprinted by permission of Pearson Education, Inc., Upper Saddle River, NJ.

9. Part of this quote is from my article "Immigration Context of Wife Abuse: A Case of Vietnamese Immigrants in the United States," published in *It's a Crime: Women and Justice,* 3rd ed. (p. 403), edited by Roslyn Muraskin, copyright © 2002. Reprinted by permission of Pearson Education, Inc., Upper Saddle River, NJ.

10. This quote is from my article "Immigration Context of Wife Abuse: A Case of Vietnamese Immigrants in the United States," published in *It's a Crime: Women and Justice,* 3rd ed. (p. 402), edited by Roslyn Muraskin, copyright © 2002. Reprinted by permission of Pearson Education, Inc., Upper Saddle River, NJ.

11. This quote is from my article "Immigration Context of Wife Abuse: A Case of Vietnamese Immigrants in the United States," published in *It's a Crime: Women and Justice,* 3rd ed. (p. 403), edited by Roslyn Muraskin, copyright © 2002. Reprinted by permission of Pearson Education, Inc., Upper Saddle River, NJ.

12. The term "American" is informally used by Vietnamese immigrants to broadly indicate non-Asian Americans.

13. This quote is from my article "Help-seeking behavior among abused immigrant women: A case of Vietnamese American women," *Violence Against Women, 9,* (2), p. 218. Copyright © 2003 by Sage Publications. Reprinted by permission of Sage Publications, Inc.

14. This quote is from my article "Help-seeking behavior among abused immigrant women: A case of Vietnamese American women," *Violence Against Women, 9,* (2), p. 224. Copyright © 2003 by Sage Publications. Reprinted by permission of Sage Publications, Inc.

15. This quote is from my article "Help-seeking behavior among abused immigrant women: A case of Vietnamese American women," *Violence Against Women, 9,* (2), p. 224. Copyright © 2003 by Sage Publications. Reprinted by permission of Sage Publications, Inc.

16. According to Fernandez, Iwamoto and Muscat (1997), absolute dependency occurs when a woman is unemployed and totally dependent on her husband/partner for financial support. On the other hand, relative economic dependency happens when a combination of a woman's income and her husband's income puts her in a better financial situation and provides her with a better economic life.

17. This quote is from my article "Help-seeking behavior among abused immigrant women: A case of Vietnamese American women," *Violence Against Women*, 9, (2), p. 225. Copyright © 2003 by Sage Publications. Reprinted by permission of Sage Publications, Inc.

18. The women's Four Virtues include good work habits, an agreeable appearance, soft and polite speech, and exemplary conduct. The principle of Three Obediences says that a woman should obey and submit to her father when young, to her husband when married, and to her oldest son when widowed (Jamieson, 1993; L. Nguyen, 1987).

19. This quote is from my article "Help-seeking behavior among abused immigrant women: A case of Vietnamese American women," *Violence Against Women*, 9, (2), p. 232. Copyright © 2003 by Sage Publications. Reprinted by permission of Sage Publications, Inc.

20. This quote is from my article "Help-seeking behavior among abused immigrant women: A case of Vietnamese American women," *Violence Against Women*, 9, (2), p. 234. Copyright © 2003 by Sage Publications. Reprinted by permission of Sage Publications, Inc.

21. This quote is from my article "Help-seeking behavior among abused immigrant women: A case of Vietnamese American women," *Violence Against Women*, 9, (2), p. 232. Copyright © 2003 by Sage Publications. Reprinted by permission of Sage Publications, Inc.

22. This quote is from my article "Help-seeking behavior among abused immigrant women: A case of Vietnamese American women," *Violence Against Women*, 9, (2), p. 232. Copyright © 2003 by Sage Publications. Reprinted by permission of Sage Publications, Inc.

3

CONTACTS WITH
CRIMINAL JUSTICE AGENCIES

On the day of the pretrial, the victim advocate couldn't find a translator for me, and I had to ask my neighbor to help me at the court. . . . My husband accepted his fault and wanted me to ask the judge for leniency on his behalf. I had planned to say good things about him, but the judge didn't ask me or say anything to me as I had been told by the victim advocate. . . . The judge ordered my husband to come back two weeks later, but he didn't ask me to appear with my husband, and I didn't know why. I wanted to ask, but a woman official told me that the hearing was over, and I didn't need to return. . . . I didn't understand English and the law, and my neighbor wasn't much better than me. So, both of us didn't understand much of what was going on at the hearing.

(Interview with Hue)

American life provides many new experiences for Vietnamese immigrants. More specifically, resettlement in the United States opens new possibilities for Vietnamese women that have been previously unavailable or traditionally suppressed in their country of origin. Educational and employment opportunities have helped Vietnamese women gain economic power, increase their status in the family, and better balance relationships with their husbands/partners. Laws prohibiting child abuse and intimate violence in the United States are also new to Vietnamese immigrants whose family traditions sanctioned wife beating and the use of corporal punishment of children. Because law and individual behavior reflect social values, the view that domestic violence is a crime that should be handled by the criminal justice system seems to be at odds with Vietnamese cultural traditions and gender practices that emphasize family privacy and women's subordination to men. Yet, through the process of adaptation, Vietnamese immigrants have been made aware of new legal norms in the United States, and they have changed their views on domestic violence as well as approaches to the problem. Vietnamese immigrants often remind each other about the prohibition of using force against children and wife beating in the United States. A survey of more than four hundred Vietnamese immigrants in Orange County (CA), Houston (TX), Boston (MA), and Lansing (MI) in 2000 indicated that the majority of respondents (72%) considered domestic violence to be a problem requiring government intervention. Most respondents (83%) also believed that the police should be called when domestic violence occurs, but interventions through criminal prosecutions and jail terms for domestic violence offenders received lower levels of support.[1]

Despite the availability of legal recourse for abused women and the positive attitudes of Vietnamese immigrants toward government interventions to fight against intimate violence, abused Vietnamese immigrant women do not often contact the criminal justice system for help. Victim service providers in Boston and Houston estimated that about 10% to 15% of intimate abuse incidents among Vietnamese immigrants were reported to the police (Personal communications, November, 1999; March 19, 2000). Police records suggest even lower reporting rates among Vietnamese immigrants. For example, in 1999, the police in Houston received and responded to almost 24,000 domestic violence calls, of which 180 were made by Vietnamese immigrants. In addition, there were 3,600 to 4,800 walk-in reports made by abused women who did not call the police when violence happened, but wanted to press charges later; and of these, only three to five reports were made by Vietnamese immigrant women. Given that Houston has approximately 1,750,000 residents, including 60,000 Vietnamese immigrants, it appeared that the reporting rate of intimate violence among Vietnamese immigrants was disproportionately low. Vietnamese immigrants in Houston were five times less likely to call 911, and 40 times less likely to make walk-in reports than their American counterparts. Compared to the reporting rate of 50% in the general population (Bureau of Justice Statistics, 1995), the reporting rates among Vietnamese immigrants in Houston were minuscule. In Lansing where the entire population was about 100,000, and the Vietnamese immigrant population was more than 3,000, the police received and responded to more than 2,000 intimate violence calls in the year 2000; only 10 calls were from Vietnamese immigrant victims (Personal communication, March 2001).

Vietnamese immigrant women who have decided to reach out for help still face many difficulties in their contacts with criminal justice agencies. Coming from a country where there was no available legal recourse for victims of domestic violence, many want to take advantage of laws prohibiting domestic violence in the United States to protect their safety and avoid abuse. However, their desire to stop violence is often mixed with anxiety and fear of negative consequences from criminal justice interventions. The failures of criminal justice and victim advocacy agencies to provide adequate supportive services that meet the special needs of these women create further barriers to their participation in the criminal justice process.

REACTIONS TO CRIMINAL JUSTICE INTERVENTIONS

Opposition to Arrest

Early criminal justice approaches to domestic violence were criticized for not responding to domestic assaults in the same way they responded to assaultive behavior committed by strangers (R. E. Dobash & R. P. Dobash, 1979). The most noticeable aspect of police practices was the lack of arrests in domestic violence cases. Because police policies did not view domestic violence as a real crime unless it involved weapons and severe injuries, early police training tended to discourage arrests (R. E. Dobash & R. P. Dobash, 1979). Police officers responding to domestic calls often talked out the disputes, warned the disputants, or asked one of the parties to leave the premise (Parnas, 1967; Sherman & Berk, 1984). Police officers' decisions to arrest and press charges were often based on their assessment of the circumstances that, in turn, were affected not only by their training, but also by their individual beliefs and biases. The attitudes of male police officers toward arrests were influenced by their identification with the husband and the notion of the sanctity of the home (Websdale, 1995). Police officers who believe that "a man's home is his castle" might be less inclined to arrest and press charges against wife assaulters (Jaffe et al., 1993). Police responses to domestic violence victims were also related to their own approval or use of marital violence and their race and class biases. Officers who used violence at home tended to avoid intervening in domestic violence cases (Stith, 1990; Websdale, 1995); class and race biases also caused racial/ethnic minorities and lower class people to be arrested in disproportionately large numbers (Wanless, 1996).

In response to critics of the police's handling of domestic violence, pro-arrest and mandatory arrest policies have been created in an attempt to provide better protection for abused women. For proponents of mandatory arrest policies, the new approach has several positive features. First, the requirement to arrest when there is evidence that violence has occurred clarifies the role of the police and guarantees all victims of domestic violence appropriate protections and, at the same time, prevents police biases and prejudices (Wanless, 1996). Under this view, mandatory-arrest policies help remove the decision to arrest from the victim's control because victims of domestic violence, who are dominated by their abusers because of an inherent imbalance of power in the relationship, should not bear the burden of indicating their preference for arrest in front of their assailants (Wanless, 1996).

Although mandatory arrest policies were designed to protect battered women, Vietnamese immigrant women have different expectations for police interventions. Most Vietnamese immigrant women who have reported abuse incidents to the police do not want their abusers to be arrested and charged with a crime. Many understand that domestic abuse is illegal in the United States, but they are not aware of mandatory arrest policies and feel terrified when they learn that their husbands/partners are going to be arrested and treated like "bad guys" or "street criminals." Raised in a culture that emphasizes collectivism and respect for the authority, Vietnamese tend to consider committing crime and being arrested as very disgraceful and embarrassing, not only for those who violated the law, but also for other family members of the law violators. Moreover, many women do not want an arrest because it can diminish the authority of their husbands as the father and make the task of raising their children become more difficult. In many intimate violence cases, arrests can be traumatic for both the victims and the offenders as illustrated in the case of Diep, an educated woman who came to the United States a few years before the incident.

Diep was living with her fiancé who was a highly educated professional from Taiwan. During an argument occurring a few weeks before their wedding, Diep was kicked several times on her back and her waist by her fiancé who later transported her to the hospital for care. A nurse, after learning about the assault, reported the incident to the police, and Diep's fiancé was arrested at the hospital despite her opposition. As Diep told her story,

I didn't call the police. . . . He slapped and kicked me because I smashed two glasses on the floor to express my anger and he thought I was disrespectful to him. . . . The nurses asked me what had happened. When I told them he had kicked me, they asked if I wanted to press charges against my fiancé. I didn't understand what they were talking about. I thought every family had conflicts, and these had nothing to do with the police . . . but the nurses told me that I was a victim of domestic violence and they were required to report the case to the police. . . . Two police officers arrived to the hospital and talked with my boyfriend and me separately. Then, they said that my fiancé had committed domestic violence and he was under arrest. I strongly opposed their decision, but they handcuffed him and took him to the police car, leaving me alone in the hospital. . . . His arrest was really a trauma for him and for me. The next day, I went to the police jail to post bail for him. When I saw him, I wanted to cry because he looked extremely miserable. . . . He looked like another person, scared, timid, mute. . . . Until now, I still have difficulties thinking of the way they treated him like a criminal. You know, he was an educated and responsible man but they treated him like a murderer, a burglar, a thief. It was fortunate that his parents and his son did not have to see it. Otherwise, they would have felt embarrassed to death. Since that day, I often had nightmares, seeing him handcuffed and taken away by the police. . . . I usually feel guilty for placing him in this disgraceful situation.

New immigrants are particularly fearful of arrest, especially those who came to the United States under the refugee category and still have not yet obtained permanent residency. They have learned from resettlement agencies that having troubles with the law will negatively affect their immigrant status. In addition, new immigrants who receive public assistance do not want resettlement agencies to learn about their domestic violence problems because they are afraid that resettlement caseworkers would see them as "trouble makers" and withdraw public support. To help husbands/partners avoid arrest, women often explicitly ask the police not to make an arrest. They also alter earlier versions of events or statements and deny the abuse when they fear arrest and its consequences. Phuong, who just arrived in the United States several months before the incident, called the police because she wanted to stop the abuse she had suffered since she and her husband were in Vietnam. When she learned that the police were going to arrest her husband, she changed her story because she was afraid that an arrest would cause difficulties for her husband in finding jobs and completing the paperwork with the Immigration and Naturalization Services (INS). Phuong talked about her contact with the police as follows,

After listening to my story through an interpreter, the officers asked my husband to stand facing the wall and handcuffed him immediately. But I didn't want him to be arrested. . . . [Why?] Because I was afraid that he would be in troubles with the refugee agency. . . . I begged the police three times not to arrest my husband, but it didn't work. Finally, I told the police that I had hit my husband, but he hadn't hit me. At that point, the officers gave my husband two options: either leaving the apartment that night, or being arrested. Obviously, my husband agreed to leave home.[2]

While most Vietnamese immigrant women do not want their abusive husbands/partners to be arrested, they do need police intervention to stop the violence. When husbands'/partners' behavior becomes too violent and out of control, abused women are concerned for their safety. They need police help to stop the violence, order their abusers away from the premises temporarily, calm their abusers down, and/or explain to their abusers that they should not use force to solve family conflicts. Because the police represent power, many women ally with the police to empower themselves and tend to think that the presence of the police will stop the assault and deter their husbands/partners from using violence again. Lan, a professional who had been in the United States for more than 20 years, had tremendous confidence in the authority of the police, and she quickly called the police when her husband first used force against her. Lien, an unskilled worker who had been abused for many years, asked her daughter to call the police after she learned from her friends about police intervention in domestic violence. As these women explained,

I thought that the presence of the police would deter him. . . . I wanted the police to write a report on the incident and keep it in file. . . . I thought that when he knew that his name was in the police record, he wouldn't use force against me any more. (Lan)

I just wanted to give him a lesson, warning him that the police would protect me from his violence. . . . I didn't want him to be in jail or to be out of the house. (Lien)

Besides those women who are clear about what they want from police interventions, many other women are confused about their preference for arrest and/or pressing charges. Because the implementation of mandatory arrest policies varies across jurisdictions, women who live in places where these policies are not rigidly followed (e.g., Houston) are often asked whether they prefer arrest. Although many women resent their husbands'/partners' abusive behavior and think that their husbands/partners should receive some sort of punishment, they are worried about the negative consequences of the arrest, including the possibility of their husbands/partners losing jobs and "losing face" with other family members and friends. They are also concerned with the prospect of increasing strain in family relationships that can lead to family breakups. Oanh recalled her first contact with the police almost 10 years ago when mandatory arrest policies were not implemented in California,

At the beginning, I didn't want to report [abuse incidents] to the police because I didn't want him to be involved with the law. According to our [Vietnamese] family traditions, family conflicts should be solved by family members, not outsiders. . . . [Later] I decided to call the police because he continued abusing me and I didn't know whom in the families of both sides I could ask for help. . . . My parents [in Canada] said I was a married woman and I belonged to my husband's family. People in his family considered wife beating as normal . . . nothing was wrong. . . . When the police asked whether I wanted him to be arrested and whether I wanted to press charges, I said no. . . . I just wanted them to stop the violence. . . . [After divorce when] I recalled his abusive behavior, I wished I would have said "yes" because I did want him to be punished for abusing me, but I still don't know why I said no. . . . Probably because I didn't want him to be in trouble with the law.

Under mandatory arrest policies, with some variations in the implementation, those committing domestic assault are likely to be arrested, regardless of the victims' opposition. Police decisions to arrest often move the case to the court and initiate a journey for Vietnamese immigrant women entering the unfamiliar judicial system and participating in the judicial proceedings as witnesses.

The Desire to Drop Charges

Similar to early police practices, traditional judicial responses to domestic violence have been criticized for their indifference to the plight of battered women (R. E. Dobash & R. P. Dobash, 1979). Prosecutors were reluctant to prosecute domestic batterers because they tended to view spouse abuse as a civil and personal matter that did not require either arrests or judicial responses. Some prosecutors even set up obstacles to prosecution in domestic violence cases by charging fees for filing criminal complaints, or by requiring female complainants to return after a period of "cooling off" and sign charges to show their willingness to cooperate with the prosecution (Cahn, 1992; Dunford, Huizinga & Elliot, 1990; Ford, 1983). Prosecutors' unresponsive behavior made abused women feel unsupported in seeking the prosecution of their partners. Moreover, the prosecutors' decision to charge in a domestic violence case tended to be made on the basis of their evaluation of the victim's and the defendant's personal attributes rather than on legal criteria. A victim's negative attributes could reduce the chance of charges being filed if they called into question a woman's status as a victim (Rauma, 1984; Schmidt & Steury, 1989). Many abused women became disinterested in pursuing the case because prosecutors' biases made them feel responsible for their own victimization (Ford, 1983; Lerman, 1986). On the other hand, because the majority of battered women (50% to 80%) wanted to drop charges either by requesting that the courts dismiss their cases, or by failing to appear in court as witnesses, prosecutors often cited high attrition rates caused by victims' lack of cooperation as a principal reason for their unwillingness to prosecute wife assaulters (Ford & Regoli, 1993).

New prosecutorial policies have been created in an attempt to respond more effectively to the domestic violence problem. A prosecutor-filing-charge policy, which requires the prosecutor to file charges in place of the victim in domestic cases in the same manner as in other criminal cases, has been established because it is assumed that the victim's decision to file charges will create an opportunity for the abuser to intimidate her and keep her from pursuing the case (Cahn, 1992). In response to high rates of attrition in domestic violence cases, the no-drop-charge policy, which emphasizes the prosecutor's decision to charge and prosecute, regardless of the victim's desire to drop charges, has been implemented. This new policy aims at regulating prosecutorial discretion in instances where the victim declines to participate (Corsilles, 1994).

Regardless of the intention of new prosecutorial policies to provide more protection for battered women, and despite the expectation from advocates for battered women that new policies would be highly effective in reducing high attrition rates and in facilitating the cooperation of domestic violence victims with the judicial system (Corsilles, 1994), most abused Vietnamese immigrant women whose husbands/partners are arrested for domestic assaults want to drop the charges. The desire of these women to drop the charges reflects the negative attitudes of Vietnamese immigrants toward the legal approach to social conflicts in general, and intimate violence in particular.[3] Because traditional Vietnamese culture emphasizes social harmony, the preferred method for the Vietnamese to solve conflicts has been mediation and conciliation. The avoidance of confrontation and litigation is evidenced in the old saying "*Di hoa vi quy*" (Conciliation is the best policy, translation by Ta, 1999). In addition, experiences of judicial oppression, including French colonial, feudalist, militarist, and communist rule, also caused the Vietnamese to view the legal system with great suspicion. Throughout history, there were very few legal safeguards for those who were involved in the criminal justice system, and coerced confessions often led to a guilty verdict in the court with severe consequences for not only the convicts but also the convicts' families (Ta, 1999). That historical legacy resulted in the fact that most Vietnamese avoid being involved in the judicial process, as reflected in the old saying "*Vo phuc dao tung dinh*" (Woe falls on those who have to go to courts, translation by Ta, 1999).

Although abused Vietnamese immigrant women share a traditional negative view of the legal system, they have different experiences with the prosecution on the basis of their gender and their immigration status. While the ideology of marriage and romantic love often prevents women from leaving their partners, immigrant life serves to reinforce the desire of Vietnamese immigrant women to maintain family relationships. A large proportion of Vietnamese immigrants did not come to the United States with intact families. Women whose relatives were left behind in Vietnam often feel lonely, isolated, and unfamiliar in the new settlement environment of American society. Those whose intimate partners are the

only ones who provide them with emotional and/or financial support have a great
need for maintaining family relationships. In particular, married women who have
children often openly express their concerns that "freedom" in American society
may cause their husbands to leave home and abandon the family. Duc explained
why she continued staying with her husband despite his abusive behavior:

I escaped Vietnam in 1980 and arrived in Thailand where I met him in a refugee camp. Later,
I was allowed to resettle in the United States due to my service in the South Vietnam
military. . . . I first arrived in Florida, but I felt very lonely there and soon moved to Boston
where he was resettled. . . . I decided to marry him because living in an unfamiliar society, I
needed a person who could understand my language and culture, who could give me help
when I face financial and emotional crises. . . . I'm not happy with his violent behavior, but I
have to stay [with him] because I need him. . . . I don't have any relatives, or close friends. I
cannot drive, cannot go anywhere far away, and I often feel lonely.

For women who want to stay with their husbands/partners, prosecution can be a
threat to their relationships because they are required to testify against their intimate partners. To avoid this uncomfortable confrontation, and to help their hus-
bands/partners, abused women often try very hard to convince the prosecutor to
drop the charges. Nga, who experienced severe abuse by her husband, tried to obtain a medical evaluation to backup her request to drop charges against him. As
Nga told her story,

I escaped Vietnam alone to Malaysia before my uncle sponsored me to the United States.
Upon arriving in the United States, I stayed with my uncle who was my only relative
here. . . . He owned a car repair shop, and I was required to work as his housekeeper and the
bookkeeper for the shop without pays to pay back his sponsorship. I was not allowed to learn
English, a vocation, or driving a car. I understood that I was exploited but I did not know
how to get out of the situation. . . . I met him [her husband] at the car shop. He came to the
United States alone like me, leaving his parents and siblings behind. He was also working for
and was exploited by my uncle. Both of us quickly understood each other and fell in
love. . . . Before the wedding, we had a very beautiful relationship. . . . He was always sweet
to me and did what I wanted. When we decided to get married, we had a traditional wedding
ceremony. . . . I still have lots of pictures taken on that day. . . . I will never forget these
beautiful memories. . . . When his abuse first happened, I didn't report because I thought
his violence would be over soon, and also because I loved him and didn't want him to be in
jail. . . . As his violence continued, I had to take the children to women's shelters several
times to escape his violence, but I could not stay there for long. The children and I missed
him, and we came back. . . . I only called the police to stop his violence when his behavior
became too destructive. One time, he attempted to set fire to the apartment. The other time,
he pointed a gun to the children and me, threatening to kill all of us and commit suicide. On
both incidents, he fled before the police arrived. . . . I thought he might suffer some sort of
mental illness as a result of his participation in a special military unit during the war
[Vietnam War]. . . . When he was not violent, he was a nice person. Everybody who knew
him said he was a good person. . . . He was arrested two times. One time because he was
chasing me into a shelter nearby and the security guard stopped him and called the police.

He was put on probation this time. The other time when my friend reported to the women's shelter that he had committed child sexual abuse. . . . The shelter then informed the police. . . . Two days after he was arrested, I bailed him out and went to the court [prosecutor office] to request that charges be dropped. Because the judge [prosecutor] refused my request, I decided to look for a lawyer and asked him to help me obtain an evaluation of my husband's mental illness. I hoped the court would drop the charge if the doctor confirmed that my husband was sick. . . . My husband was required to stay in the hospital for two weeks, and I had to borrow $15,000 to pay for the medical evaluation. . . . I don't understand what the doctor put in the evaluation, but he was tried and sentenced to 12 months on probation and 300 hours of community services.[4]

Besides a desire to maintain the relationship with husbands/partners, being grateful or feeling indebted to husbands who had sponsored and brought them to the United States also pressures abused women to drop charges. Many Vietnamese immigrants escaped Vietnam alone and only re-established their family lives after they have sponsored their spouses and children into the United States. In addition, many Vietnamese immigrant women came to the United States as dependents of their husbands who were allowed to resettle on American soil under the humanitarian program for former Vietnamese political detainees. These women often feel that they owe their husbands for the opportunity to live in the United States, and they do not want to be ungrateful by challenging those who spent effort, commitment, and resources to bring them to this country. As Hanh explained, "I didn't want him to be prosecuted and convicted. He had sponsored me to the United States, and I didn't want to be ungrateful for what he had done to bring me here."

Pressures from the abusers and other family members also caused abused Vietnamese immigrant women to request that charges be dropped. Growing up in a cultural tradition that emphasizes collectivism, many Vietnamese immigrant women often act not only in their own interests, but also in the interests of other family members, including parents, siblings, and children. Abusive men can threaten to harm their wives'/partners' parents or siblings if their wives/partners do not agree to drop charges. As Hien, a young woman in her twenties who had an on-and-off relationship with a Caucasian American man explained, "I requested that charges against him [her boyfriend] be dropped in two different incidents. For the first incident because I loved him and also because I was afraid of him. . . . I didn't want him to hurt anyone in my family. He threatened to blow up my parents' home if I didn't drop the charge. For the second incident . . . because I was afraid that he would kill people in my family." Some parents also want their daughter to drop charges because they are concerned about the consequences of court interventions, including the possibility of their daughter's family breakup, a conviction and prison term for their son-in-law that can cause their grandchildren to become fatherless and bring shame to the whole family. Because of filial piety, children also often ask their mothers to drop charges against their fathers. Fear of loneliness in the new country often forces many women to defer to the desire of their parents, their children, and/or their in-laws in exchange for emotional, and sometimes, financial support. Hanh was sponsored to the United States by her husband and was blamed by her in-laws for her husband's involvement with the law after she reported his violent behavior to the police. As Hanh talked about her experience,

I only wanted him [her husband] to leave me alone, not to yell at me, not to cause family conflicts, not to hit me. . . . After I realized that he couldn't change, I called the police to request a PPO [personal protection order] to be separate from him. In fact, I didn't want him to be prosecuted or to go to court. . . . His family already hated me and alienated me because I had called the police. . . . I didn't want to suffer his abuse, but I didn't want other people to hate me and blame me for his involvement with the law either. . . . When his family asked me to drop the charge against him, I was more than happy to follow their request . . . but the judge didn't approve, and he was sentenced to prison. After his lawyer appealed the conviction and sentence decisions, I went to the second trial to ask the judge to acquit him. . . . I felt relieved when the judge dismissed the case.

Like Hanh, Xuan decided to drop charges to satisfy the demands of her children, and Hue those of her mother.

My children wanted the charges against their father dropped. So, I went to the court [the office of the prosecutor] with my daughter to submit a letter asking the judge [the prosecutor] to drop the charge. But the judge [prosecutor] refused. He said that if he approved all victims' request to drop charge, no abusive men could be prosecuted, convicted, and punished, and they would continue to abuse their wives. (Xuan)

My mother urged me to pay for his bail and take him home. She said: "He's the father of your son, and you cannot leave him in jail." My mother was worried about my husband being convicted and sentenced to prison, and my son would become fatherless. My husband also asked me to go to the court and request that the charge be dropped. I made the request [that charges be dropped] to make my mother feel comfortable. (Hue)[5]

The desire of Vietnamese immigrant women to drop charges is also related to the immigration status of their abuser. Since the late nineteenth century, immigration laws have allowed the deportation of immigrants who commit heinous crimes (Kim, 1996). The new 1996 immigrant reform law, however, includes domestic violence offenses on the list of crimes that can serve as grounds for the deportation of aliens.[6] Although deportation is a fear for all immigrants, it can become a nightmare for those who are former political detainees in Vietnam as well as their relatives. Because resettlement in the United States is the only chance in their lifetime to escape the Vietnamese communist regime, deportation means that they may not be able to reunite with their relatives in the United States. In addition, the conviction of a crime can be a barrier for immigrants in obtaining American citizenship. Consequently, women whose husbands/partners are not American citizens, are often concerned about the possibility that their husbands/partners may be denied American citizenship, as illustrated in the case of Hue:

He [her husband] had received the notice for a citizenship interview two weeks before the incidents. After the arrest, he was afraid that the INS [Immigration and Naturalization Services] would be informed about his problem with the law, and he would be denied American citizenship. . . . He insisted that I ask the prosecutor to drop the charge. . . . I wanted him to go to the court so he could learn a lesson, but I also had the same concerns as he did. . . . He needs to have a citizenship. It will be safer if you have citizenship. . . . Finally, I went to the court and asked that his charge be dropped, but the judge [prosecutor] did not approve my request.[7]

Limited Use of Restraining Orders

In recent years, restraining orders have been used extensively in domestic violence cases because they are considered to play an essential role in protecting abused women from further violence.[8] Although a restraining order is a form of civil protection, a violation of it constitutes the criminal contempt offense that can result in mandatory arrest and punishment by imprisonment (Klein & Orloff, 1999). Depending on jurisdictions, a restraining order can be obtained in a civil court or a criminal court. For example, in Orange County (CA), trial judges can issue a restraining order in a domestic violence case at either pretrial or trial hearings regardless of the victim's request. On the other hand, abused women in Lansing (MI) and Boston (MA) must go to the family court to request a restraining order. In Houston (TX), abused women can obtain an emergency restraining order through police officers who respond to domestic calls and who will contact and ask a judge to issue an emergency order against the abuser.

While the majority of abused women in mainstream society use the restraining order to prevent future violence (Erez & Belknap, 1998a), abused Vietnamese immigrant women do not often use it to protect their personal safety, except for cases where the judge has the discretion to issue a restraining order against the abuser regardless of the victim's desire. The most common reason for not requesting a restraining order among Vietnamese immigrant women is their lack of understanding about its availability and benefits. Although police officers who respond to domestic calls usually distribute printed materials about supportive services available for victims of domestic abuse, including information about the restraining order, language barriers often prevent women from being aware of this type of intervention. In addition, the process of obtaining a restraining order is complex enough to discourage those who attempt to use this service to protect their safety. Those who need a permanent restraining order that can be effective for at least one year, have to go through the formal, though expedited, judicial process, from filing the petition to the execution of the order. Their other option is obtaining an emergency protection order available through police officers, which are only effective for several weeks from the issuing date. Abused women who face no language barriers often need assistance to go through the process, but immigrant women who have difficulties with English also need translation assistance that is not always available. In addition, because it often takes a whole day or two to obtain a protection order, many working women are reluctant to take the time off to complete the paperwork.

The same economic dependency and desire to keep the family intact for the benefit of children that often prevents abused Vietnamese immigrant women from requesting a restraining order also causes them to terminate an existing order. Because a restraining order creates a separation between the victim and her abusive husband/partner, women who do not want, or cannot have, a separation because of economic dependency, are not likely to request one. After Ha reported the abuse incident to the police, she was advised to file a restraining order to prevent future violence, but she refused because she needed her boyfriend's help for child care and transportation. Like Ha, Nguyet did not want to use the restraining order because she depended on her husband's financial support, and she did not want to deprive her children of emotional relationships with their father either. As these women explained,

After he [her boyfriend] was arrested, two victim advocates arrived and explained what would happen for him at the police and the court . . . they also gave me lots of information about where I could go for help. They advised me to request a restraining order . . . because they said it would protect my safety. They told me if I had an order, he would have to stay away from me and he could no longer hurt me . . . but I decided not to have it because I needed him to take care of the baby when I went to work. . . . He worked at night shift and could take care of the baby in daytime. I didn't have money to pay for childcare. . . . It cost about $300 a month. If he were away, who would pay me $300 for childcare? I also need him to take me to work because I couldn't drive. . . . I couldn't pass the driving test because of my [poor] English. (Ha)

I didn't request a PPO [personal protection order]. I needed him to take the children to school because I couldn't drive. . . . The children also liked their father. . . . They even blamed me [for calling the police] . . . they said, "Dad hit Mom because Mom talked back to Dad." He loved the kids, and he often took them out to restaurants or parks on weekends. The kids couldn't have these things if their father was away from home. . . . I don't mean he wasn't allowed to visit his children, but I think he would not be bothered coming home after he was forced to move out. (Nguyet)

Besides the limited use of restraining orders by abused Vietnamese immigrant women, whose women who have restraining orders do not often report the violations by their husbands/partners because they fear their husbands'/partners' retaliation. Hien had an off-and-on relationship with her boyfriend for many years. She reported his abuse to the police and went to shelters twice, but she finally returned to him, partly because she thought he had changed, and partly because she was afraid of his retaliation. As Hien explained, "He didn't care about the order and he continued coming to my father's home to look for me. I didn't want to see him because he was angry and agitated, but I didn't report [his violation] because he threatened to blow up my father's house if I called the police. He told me that the police couldn't keep him in jail forever, and I should not report his violation because when he get out of jail, I would suffer the consequences." In many situations, a woman's decision not to report violations of the restraining order is backed by her desire to reunite with her husband/partner. In fact, many women even violate the restraining order themselves when they let their husbands/partners return home, or when they continue contact with their husbands/partners through telephone and the mail but do not officially terminate the order. These women attempt to use the restraining order to protect their personal safety while maintaining the relationship because they believe that their husbands/partners will be deterred from using force by more severe sanctions for their violations of the order. As Xuan and Ly explained,

I allowed him to return home because he had no place to live. He had no relatives. . . he stayed with his friend for some time and had a very difficult time. He was depressed, got sick, and couldn't work. When the children learned that he was sick, they asked me to let their father come back home, so they could take care of him. I felt pity for him and agreed to let him back. However, I didn't ask the judge to remove the PPO. I wanted to use it to warn him not to hit me again. I told him that if he hit me, I would call the police and he would be charged with a more severe offense. (Xuan)[9]

I didn't request a restraining order. The judge granted it as a part of the no-contact bond for his release pending trial, and he moved in to his sister. A few weeks later, I called him back, but I didn't request to remove the order. . . . I planned to keep the order for one year, and if he felt remorse and learned the lesson, I would ask the judge to remove it. (Ly)

BARRIERS TO PARTICIPATION IN THE CRIMINAL JUSTICE PROCESS

Communication Issues

For immigrants with limited English proficiency, the language poses a great hardship in contacts with government officials and constrains their willingness to participate in the criminal justice process (Berk-Seligson, 1990; Shusta et al., 1995). The lack of language skills often makes it difficult, or even impossible, for victims of crime to communicate effectively and provide the necessary information to help law enforcement officials understand the situation. The trauma caused by victimization also impedes the victim's ability to verbally use their limited English (Shusta et al., 1995). Some law enforcement officers modify their speech so that they can be better understood, but most officers often feel frustrated by language barriers and fail to speak slowly or listen carefully.

As with other immigrants, Vietnamese immigrant women who contact the criminal justice system as victims of domestic violence face difficulties in communicating with police officers who respond to their calls. Two-thirds of women whom I interviewed reported such difficulties. Translation assistance can be beneficial, but only a small number of women receive this service, either in person or via telephone, by law enforcement agencies. A lack of resources is often the reason cited for the unavailability of interpretation assistance. In areas with large concentrations of Vietnamese

immigrants, such as Orange County (CA) and Houston (TX), where many Vietnamese serve in law enforcement agencies, interpretation assistance is more likely to
be available than in areas that have smaller Vietnamese-American populations. In
Lansing (MI), for example, where the Vietnamese population is less than 4,000,
translation assistance for abused Vietnamese immigrant women who contact the
criminal justice system is infrequent because it depends on the limited free time of
Vietnamese staff at refugee resettlement agencies. Women who do not receive translation or interpretation assistance have to rely on the help of neighbors or relatives,
or they have to manage the problem by themselves.

Language barriers cause poor communication and affect police performance. Victims often misperceive police work, and may not rely on law enforcement services
for future abuse incidents. When women with limited English proficiency are unable
to explain clearly to the authorities the complicated situations of their families as well
as their expectations of the police, responding officers are unlikely to provide services
that meet their needs. The disjunction between expectations and services can cause
Vietnamese immigrant women to think negatively about police work. As members
of a minority group, Vietnamese immigrants have heard about, and/or have experienced, racial discrimination in American society. They tend to attribute any police
failure to support their requests to racial discrimination. Nguyet had reported the
abuse by her husband several times, but she stopped calling the police after she realized that responding officers failed to do what she expected. In fact, there were misunderstandings on the part of Nguyet about police responsibilities, and on the part
of the police about the victim's expectations of them. As Nguyet told her story:

I'd called the police several times, but they didn't do anything to help me, so I've decided not
to call them anymore. . . . He [her husband] even made fun me when I tried to call the police
because the police didn't do anything against him. . . . One time, I called 911 when my
husband hit me, and he tried unsuccessfully to flee before the police arrived because I kept
his car key. When the police arrived, he told the police that we had arguments because I was
jealous and kept his car key to prevent him from going with his friend. When the police
learned that he was the car owner, they ordered me to return him the key. I tried but
couldn't make the police understand that he had hit me and wanted to escape. . . . They even
told me that they would arrest me if I refused to give the key back to my husband. . . . The
last time I had contacts with the police was two months ago. On that day, his friend called
and asked him to go gambling. . . . This guy usually called my husband to go gambling and I
hated him. The next day, I called this guy and swore at him on the phone. . . . This guy
retaliated and caused me troubles by calling the police and lying that my husband needed to
go to the emergency room. When the police arrived, they were angry and accused me of
lying to the police. I tried to explain the situation, but I was so nervous that I couldn't know
what to say. . . . I wanted the police to advise my husband not to gamble, but they didn't do
it. . . . It seemed to me that the police didn't want to protect me. I felt like people who
couldn't speak English did not deserve police protection.

Language barriers and a lack of understanding about judicial proceedings are
some of the difficulties that immigrants face in court. Because legal terms are more

difficult to comprehend than conversational language, immigrants who want to understand the proceeding would need the same familiarity with English legal terms as a native English speaker (Moore & Mamiya, 1999). In addition, cultural differences in concepts of justice also cause difficulties for immigrants even when they are translated into the immigrants' native language (Davis, Erez & Avitabile, 1998). In order to help immigrants participate in court proceedings, the Court Interpreters Act of 1978 provided interpreters to non-English-speaking defendants, litigants, and witnesses in federal courts (Berk-Seligson, 1990; Moore & Mamiya, 1999). Despite the importance of court interpreters, not all court participants who need interpretation can get assistance. For example, among twelve abused Vietnamese immigrant women I interviewed who went to pretrial hearings as witnesses, ten had limited English proficiency, but only one received translation assistance from the court. Among five women who attended trials, only two received court interpretation assistance.

In addition to a lack of resources, organizational views of how domestic violence cases should proceed also affect the probability that an abused immigrant woman will get interpretation assistance. More often, the court is not active in providing interpreters for non-English-speaking witnesses. Instead, victim advocates often have to ask the court for translation assistance on behalf of abused immigrant women. Due to limited resources, not all requests for interpretation assistance are honored because translation services are often reserved for victims who cooperate with the system and help it achieve the organizational goal of successful prosecutions. Victim advocates have often refused to help women who seek to drop charges against their abusive husbands/partners because they are not considered useful witnesses for the case. Xuan, who requested but did not receive translation assistance, explained her situation:

Before I went to the pretrial hearing, I learned that there would be no translator at the court. Therefore, my 20-year-old daughter went with me to help me in the court with translation. . . . I had asked a victim's advocate for help [with translation] but she said that she couldn't help me because I had requested that charges be dropped. She told me that she could only help me if I agreed to testify against him, or to file divorce and child custody.

Women who do not have translation assistance often feel lost and confused because they do not understand the proceedings and what the prosecutors, judges, and other court officials say. Even when they have questions, they do not know how to communicate with the prosecutors and other court officials. Hue did not know much English, but she decided to attend the pretrial hearing upon the advice of a victim advocate. She had been told that her presence at the court would strengthen her position in the relationship because her husband would learn that her "voice" could affect the court outcome. Although the victim advocate had promised it, she could not provide translation assistance for Hue at the court. Therefore, Hue did not have a chance to explain her situation to the prosecutor as she had planned, and she did not even understand the outcome of the hearing.

Although translation assistance can reduce communication difficulties, it can create other kinds of problems. When an abused woman relies on an interpreter to communicate, there is no guarantee that what she says in her native language will be accurately translated into English without losing its original meanings. In addition, the interpreter can consciously change the story according to his or her perception of the situation and people involved. Relatives, neighbors, or friends who provide translation assistance often alter the stories to help abusive husbands/partners avoid involvement with the law because they are on the side of the abusers, or because they fear the retaliation by the abusers. As Nguyet and Xuan, who had negative experiences with translation assistance told their stories:

I had called [the police] several times. . . . Because I couldn't speak English well, I dialed 911 and said, "Help! Help!" When the police came, his children [with his former wife] did the translation. They told the police that I was crazy and nothing had happened. After listening to the children, the police left. Through this experience, I learned that because I couldn't speak English, I couldn't do anything [about his abuse]. (Nguyet)

He beat me many times before, but I just reported recently. . . . I asked my children to call the police. Because I was very confused and nervous, I asked my neighbors to come and help me. . . . I also wanted them to witness the situation because both were leaders in the local Vietnamese community. After the police talked with the children, my husband, and me, they decided to arrest him. When the police took my husband out of the house, he angrily looked at me and said that when he was released, he would kill me. One police officer asked my neighbor to translate what my husband just said to me. She [her neighbor] later told me that she was concerned with the possibility that my husband would be in deeper trouble with the law should she report exactly his statement. So, she told the officer that my husband said he hated me. (Xuan)

Translation assistance can cause unintended consequences for abused women when the translator reports abuse incidents that the victims want to hide because they do not want their husbands/partners to be involved with the law. Nga had a strong emotional relationship with her husband and did not want him to be in trouble with the law, but her friend, who provided interpretation assistance, reported to the authorities his sexual abuse of children that led to his arrest. As Nga told her story,

My English wasn't good, so I asked my friend to go with me [to a women's center] and help me with translation. My friend was a social worker and she said more things than what I wanted her to tell staff at the women's center. On the basis of her report, the staff found out that my husband had sexually abused the children, and later threatened to kill them when he was drunk. The center staff filed a report with the police, and my husband was arrested for child abuse. . . . Since that time, I didn't see my friend again.

Problems also arise in the courtroom with certified interpreters. Inaccurate interpretation of testimony and distortions of court materials have been the most frequent phenomena in bilingual courtrooms (Moore & Mamiya, 1999). Because no one in the courtroom, other than the court interpreter, is able to speak both languages, the court interpreter is put in a position where he or she can choose between upholding the standards of ethics or undermining them. Conflicts of interest can pose another problem, and the court hears not what the party is saying, but what the interpreters think the facts should be when friends and relatives are interpreters. In domestic violence cases, the gender of the interpreter can influence his/her task. A male interpreter may take the side of the male abuser and become biased against the female victim. Van had a court-assigned male interpreter who insisted that she should contact her abuser to notify him of the restraining order hearing. As she explained,

After I filed a request for a restraining order, an [male] interpreter asked me to contact my ex-husband and tell him to appear at the restraining order hearing. Although I explained that I didn't want to contact him because I was afraid of his harassment and stalking, the interpreter repeated several times that I had to contact my ex-husband, or there would be no hearing for restraining order. I finally had to ask a friend to call him and let him know about the hearing. Later, I learned from other people at the court that because my ex-husband had a history of harassment and abuse, I should not have been asked to contact my ex-husband.

Lack of Understanding about the American Judicial System

Because both procedural and substantive laws are anchored in American social reality and culture, they may not be easily understood by Vietnamese Americans who come from a different culture. Even when women do understand English, court objectives, procedures, and proceedings may differ radically from the workings of the criminal justice system in their country of origin. The lack of knowledge of the law often has negative consequences in child custody and child support cases following intimate abuse incidents. Because abusive men often threaten to take away women's right to custody or refuse to pay child support as part of their control tactics, fear of losing custody and child support often cause abused women to defer to the demands of the abusive party. Because of the abuser's manipulation, women who do not understand the law can lose custody and have to pay child support, as illustrated in the case of Van. As she explained:

He had an extra affair in Vietnam and had two children with his girlfriend. He tried to add these two children in the immigration application but the fraud was discovered, and all my children, three of them, were left behind . . . because U.S. officials after discovering the fraud viewed all documents he provided as suspicious and they needed time to investigate. . . . Because he continued to abuse me after we arrived in the United States, I decided to leave the relationship. After I left, he filed for divorce. . . . Before I received the court notification about the divorce case, I was asked by the court to take a blood test, but I didn't understand why. . . . No one explained it for me. At the divorce hearing, a Vietnamese man who appeared to me as a court official asked if I agreed to sign the divorce paper or not. I asked him whether, after the divorce, I could see my 10-year-old son should he arrive in the United States, but he didn't respond to my question. Instead, he told me firmly that I had to say "yes" or "no." I was confused and felt intimidated. So, I said "yes." Later, I learned that this man was my husband's lawyer. I also learned that my 10-year-old son had come to the United States and stayed with my husband, but he didn't let me know. I also learned that the blood test was for establishing the proof of maternity that my husband used to ask me to pay for child support. . . . I was not informed about the child custody case, so I did not attend the hearing. As a result, I lost the custody and didn't have child visitation. I also had to pay for child support. Because the amount of child support was too high, I went to a refugee service agency and asked for legal help. They referred me to a public law center. The lawyer who helped me in the child support case was a young Vietnamese but she didn't speak Vietnamese well [as she grew up in the United States]. Because of communication problems, I gave her wrong information, which in turn didn't help reduce much of the amount of money I had to pay. . . .I felt totally helpless. All bad things happened to me just because I didn't understand English and the law.

Prosecutors' and judges' demeanors, shaped by organizational goals, also cause abused women to feel excluded from the system. Literature has long documented prosecutors' indifference and unresponsiveness to women's complaints of domestic violence (Cahn, 1992; Ford, 1983; Ford & Regoli, 1993; Lerman, 1986). To address the problem of prosecutors' disinterest in domestic violence cases, the no-drop-charge policy has been established to regulate prosecution discretion in cases where abused women want to drop charges and decline to participate. Because the goal of the no-drop-charge policy is to bring more domestic violence offenders into the court system and make them responsible for their abusive behavior through success-ful prosecutions, many prosecutors have become indifferent and insensitive to the needs of intimate violence victims who ask that charges against their assailants be dropped. Abused Vietnamese immigrant women who actively contact prosecutors and other court officials to help their husbands/partners avoid prosecution often feel alienated and unwelcome in the court. Diep is a highly educated woman whose fiancé was arrested when he took her to the hospital after a violent incident. Diep wanted to contact the prosecutor to help her fiancé avoid a criminal record. As she explained,

I didn't have problem with the language, but I didn't understand much of the court procedure because I didn't understand the law. . . . A victim advocate told me that the prosecutor would be willing to talk with the victim, but when the prosecutor learned that I wanted to drop the charge, he didn't want to talk with me. I went to his office three times and tried to explain my situation. . . . I wanted to tell him that this was an accident, and my fiancé was a good, responsible person. . . . He [the prosecutor] was not available for the first two times when I went to the DA office. On the third time, he told me that it didn't matter whether I provided him information or went to the court to testify because he would prosecute, and the court would try, on the basis of the police report.

Abused women whose husbands are prosecuted often do not attend court hear-ings. Contrary to the popular notion of noncooperative victims, many abused Vietnamese immigrant women do not attend trials because the court does not ask them to appear. Most domestic violence cases are misdemeanors that prosecutors try to handle through pleabargaining, and many victims of domestic violence are not asked to attend sentencing hearings after their abusive husbands/partners have pleaded guilty for a domestic assault offense. However, abused Vietnamese immigrant women who receive summons notices from the court often comply with the request to appear because they think that they are obliged to attend, or because they want to have a chance to ask the judges for leniency on behalf of their husbands/partners. Only a small number of abused women fail to attend court hearings because they do not want to testify against their husbands/partners at the trial.

Court delays often create another barrier to the participation of domestic violence victims in the judicial process. Court hearings are only held on business time, and abused women who attend trials have to take time off from work, and/or arrange for childcare. Many abused women have to give up their attempts to attend trials because they are not informed about delays and have to go back and forth to court two or three times without having a hearing. As Nga explained, "I had planned to attend his trial . . . because I wanted to comply to the court order. I took days off from work and went to the court two times, and in both cases, the case was postponed. On the third court schedule, I didn't show up because I had to work."

Abused Vietnamese immigrant women who do attend trials have little interaction with court officials, including judges. Language barriers are part of the reason, but it is also because court officials are not interested in including abused women who are likely to recant their stories at the hearing. Court officials often believe that abused women who want to drop charges cannot serve as useful witnesses; thus, they do not need to be a part of the case and appear at the trial. Even women who have interpretation assistance do not have much communication with court officials. Moreover, many women do not understand the progress of the case or sentencing decisions. As Huong explained, "I didn't know that he got probation. . . . He told me that everything was okay, and he only needed to attend counseling and study law [batterers' program] that I had to pay for him. About four or five months later, a woman contacted me and said that she was the probationer officer who supervised my husband. . . . She was going to prepare a report on my husband, and she wanted to know whether my husband had abused me again. I didn't understand what was probation until I had her explanations."

COOPERATION WITH THE JUDICIAL SYSTEM: THE ROLE OF SUPPORT SERVICES

Domestic violence is a social problem that requires intervention from both victim service and criminal justice agencies, each of which had individualized responsibilities. The diverse needs of victims require cooperative efforts from different agencies to coordinate their activities (Johnson, Sigler & Crowley, 1994). Besides police responses that often lead to judicial interventions, abused women also need services that provide support for their participation in the criminal justice process and their escape from abuse. These include legal counsel, victim advocacy, and public assistance.

Police Referrals

The police can serve as a critical link between the victim and other social services deemed necessary for battered women to escape abuse. Police officers who respond to domestic calls can help abused women contact women's shelters and/or give them information about available services. Thus, referrals have become an important element of the police response to domestic violence (Ferraro, 1989; Belknap & McCall, 1994). Almost half of all abused women who use women's shelters learn about this service from police officers who gave them information about the shelters' services or who provided them transportation to the shelters (Coulter et al., 1999). According to two victim's service programs that serve abused Asian Americans in Boston (MA) and Houston (TX), about 20% to 30% of their clients were referred by the police (Personal communications, November 1999; March, 2000).

Abused Vietnamese immigrant women who have reported intimate violence incidents to the police often receive referrals, but not all of them find these services helpful. When officers distribute information packets as part of their routine but do not consider the special needs of abused immigrant women, including language barriers and culture differences, the referral service is of little help. For example, even when bilingual materials are available in many areas, such as in Boston (MA), Orange County (CA), and Houston (TX), responding officers still give the English versions that many abused immigrant women cannot understand. In many situations, responding officers also refer non-English-speaking victims to service agencies that have no Vietnamese-speaking staff, despite the availability of bilingual-service agencies in the local area. Some police officers also carelessly transport victims of domestic violence to homeless shelters where the environment often gives abused women little comfort. As Nga talked about her experience,

> When the police came, my husband had already fled the scene. I asked the police to take the children and me to a women's shelter because I couldn't drive, but they took us to a homeless shelter instead. . . . The children felt very scared of the condition there and wanted to go home. . . . I felt humiliated. . . . You know, we were not homeless people. . . . Because we didn't feel comfortable staying there, we left [the homeless shelter] the next day. . . . I asked a person working there, and she helped me contact a women's shelter nearby where my children and I stayed for almost a month.

Victim Advocacy Services

The treatment of abused women by court officials, victim advocates, or service providers is pivotal for successful prosecutions because positive responses and encouragement from court officials can facilitate abused women's participation in the criminal justice process (Erez & Belknap, 1998a; Cahn, 1992; Ford & Regoli,

1993). As victims of domestic violence often refuse to appear in court as witnesses, many offices of the district attorneys have created victim advocacy programs to provide support for victims, encourage victim cooperation with the prosecution, and enhance case survival rates (Cahn, 1992). Victim advocates can help prosecutors get additional information on the history of abuse and the nature of the violence. They also provide support and counseling and explain the criminal justice system to the victim.

Although criminal courts in most jurisdictions have victim advocacy programs, few Vietnamese immigrant women who are involved in the criminal justice process as witnesses can benefit from their services. In many cases, there is no contact between victim advocates and abused Vietnamese women because of language barriers and the absence of bilingual staff or translators. However, victim advocacy agencies outside the court, especially when they have bilingual staff, often provide better services for abused Vietnamese immigrant women. By coordinating their services with the police, the judicial system, legal services, women's shelters, and social welfare agencies, victim advocacy programs try to provide abused women with the support that they need to avoid further victimization. This often includes both emotional and material support to help overcome confusions, adjust to changes after violent episodes, especially when their husbands/partners have been arrested, and take steps to prevent violence in the future. Bilingual victim advocates also provide translation assistance for abused women during legal counseling sessions, accompany them to court hearings, assist them in obtaining a restraining order, or help them apply for public assistance when necessary. Although these programs are rare, abused women who have contact with them often have positive opinions about the services. Nguyet talked about her experience with victim advocates:

In the latest incident, after the police left, two victim advocates came to talk with me in my apartment. Because they spoke English, I only understood part of what they told me. The next day, another victim advocate who spoke Vietnamese called me to make sure that I was aware of available services. . . . She later helped me obtain a PPO [personal protection order] and assisted me with translation when I went to the legal aid to get counseling for child custody and child support. . . . I could speak a little bit of English, but because I didn't know how to say the right thing, I usually felt scared and nervous when I had contacts with the authorities. . . . I didn't know if I said something wrong, what the consequence would be. . . . I felt comfortable with her presence. Before I met her, my ex-husband had threatened to take away my custody should I get remarried to another man. . . . I don't worry anymore because she already explained the law and helped me understand my right to custody and safety.

Domestic violence units have also been created in many health care services to identify victims and provide necessary counseling and referrals because domestic violence is seen not only as a social problem but also a public health issue. Van had overheard discussions about women's shelters, but she did not know how to contact these services until she was hospitalized for surgery and talked about her experience of abuse with the doctor [through an interpreter] who then referred her to a women's shelter. As Van explained:

I had suffered his abuse for a long time . . . before we came to the United States, and his abuse continued in the United States. . . . He even tried to kill me, but I didn't know where I could get help. . . . I heard people talking about women's shelters, but I didn't know the location. . . . When I was in the hospital for a surgery, I told the doctor, with the help of an interpreter, about the abuse, and he helped me contact a women's center [shelter]. When I was released from the hospital, staff from the center came to the hospital and took me to the center where I stayed for a month.

Abused Vietnamese immigrant women also often follow the advice of victim advocates to appear in court. Contrary to the common wisdom that only abused women who want to testify against their husbands/partners attend trials, many Vietnamese immigrant women appear in court to help their husbands/partners. With the assistance of victim advocates, they see their helping acts as a way to empower themselves by building an alliance with the judicial system. Both Diep and Hue did not want their husbands/partners to be in trouble with the law, but they decided to follow the advice of their victim advocates and attend the trial to help their husbands. As they explained:

I attended the pretrial and the final trial to help him by saying good things about him. . . . A victim advocate advised me to attend his trial to have my say in the case, and I wanted him to understand that my say would affect his life. (Diep)

A victim advocate encouraged me to go to the court and tell the judge what I wanted. She said that my opinions can have effects on the court decision. . . . I talked with my husband and made clear to him that if he changed his behavior, I would say good things about him at the court to help him out. I also told him that the court usually protected me, and I had a lawyer [victim advocate] who could help me whenever I needed. At first, he didn't believe me. . . . He used to think I couldn't do anything because I couldn't speak and understand English. . . . I did appear at the pretrial, but I didn't have a chance to talk with the judge. However, when my husband was aware of the fact that I had a victim advocate who helped me, he became apprehensive [smiled]. . . . He said Vietnamese women in the US had lots of support that men didn't. (Hue)

Victim advocacy services also have an influence on the use of restraining orders to prevent future violence among Vietnamese immigrant women. Because of cultural isolation, Vietnamese immigrant women are not often aware of the availability of restraining orders, and those who request one had often learned about the service and its benefits from the police, legal counsel, or victim advocates. Women who have learned about the restraining order often want to use it to protect their safety and the safety of their families, especially when they plan to leave the relationship or empower themselves by making an alliance with the court to transform the relationship. The influence of victim advocates, however, is particularly important because they can provide assistance for abused women during the process of obtaining the order. Without the help of victim advocates, many abused women may not be able to go through the process. As Duc and Huong talked about their experiences,

When he hit me and caused me bruises all over my chest, I didn't call the police because I didn't want him to be in jail. I told my co-workers and they took me to see health care staff at the agency [where she worked]. . . . The heath care staff helped me obtain a restraining order. . . . I wanted to teach him a lesson by using the restraining order, and I hoped that he would be afraid of the judge [who issued the order] and stop hitting me. (Duc)

A victim advocate explained the PPO and helped me obtain one. . . . I requested an order because I decided not to live with him any more, and I didn't want him to come to my home and my work to harass me. . . . I wanted to protect my mother and my siblings from his threats. . . . She [the victim advocate] went with me to the PPO office and helped me fill out the form. . . . She accompanied me to several offices at the court to complete the paperwork. . . . It took a whole day before I could receive the order. (Huong)

Legal Services and Public Assistance

Public legal services also have an important impact on the participation of abused Vietnamese immigrant women in the criminal justice process. The inability to understand the law and the criminal justice process often makes abused immigrant women feel confused, intimidated, and lost in the system. Those who depend on their husbands'/partners' financial support also fear negative economic consequences from troubles with the law. Abused women who are confused about the consequences of their participation in criminal proceedings are often reluctant to cooperate with the criminal court. However, those who learn from victim advocates and legal counsel about the benefits of attending trials are often willing to participate in the criminal justice process. Twice, Huong called the police to report abuse by her husband, but she did not appear in court to testify the first time partly because she feared her husband would retaliate, and partly because she needed him to work to support the family and did not want him to be in trouble with the law. However, Huong decided to go to the court after the second incident because a victim advocate assisted her in obtaining free legal counsel who helped her understand the protections allowed by law. As Huong explained,

A victim advocate helped me go through the whole process. . . . She was a Vietnamese and she contacted legal counsel services and interpreted for me. . . . Without her help, I could not have understood anything . . . because the legal service did not have translators. . . . My lawyer advised me to appear in court. He said because I had filed for the custody [of three children] and child support, my testimony of my husband's violent behavior would strengthen the custody and the child support case. My husband also harassed me after he left home to go with his girlfriend, and his girlfriend also threatened to harm my mother, my siblings, and myself. . . . My lawyer advised me to appear in court to give the judge all information he needed to decide on the case and protect my family and myself. (Huong)

In addition to legal counsel, public assistance can influence the cooperation of a domestic violence victim with the criminal justice process. Welfare assistance has been seen as an opportunity for women to exercise power by relying on the state to break their dependency on men (Piven, 1990). Many abused women are fed up with violence but are reluctant to leave the abusive relationship and avoid criminal justice interventions because they depend on their abusers' financial support and fear negative economic consequences from the arrest and imprisonment of their providers. However, when these women can rely on public assistance to adjust their lives to new situations after assault incidents, their need to depend on their abusers for support diminishes. They become comfortable with criminal justice interventions because they are no longer afraid to leave their abusive husbands/partners. Phuong could not work because she had to devote all of her time to take care of her eight-year old daughter who became paralyzed shortly after her birth in a refugee camp. When her husband became too violent, Phuong moved out and had a de facto separation because she needed his financial support for the child and did not want him to be in trouble with the law. After a victim service agency helped Phuong get public assistance for her daughter and apply for housing assistance, Phuong no longer thought about returning to the abusive relationship. Instead, she decided to file for divorce. Similar to Phuong, Huong felt comfortable with public assistance, which enabled her to live free of abuse and fear. As these women explained,

When his violence became unbearable, I had to move out with my daughter . . . and my financial situation became worse very soon. I had a lot of difficulties finding money for daily necessities, and I was constantly worried about how to have money to survive, but enduring his abuse was even more difficult. . . . After a victim service agency helped me get SSI [Supplementary Social Security Income] for my daughter, I also received financial assistance from other agencies. . . . Currently, I'm not worried very much. . . . I filed a divorce a few months ago, and I just completed an application for housing recently. I believe things would be better soon. (Phuong)

When I moved out, I had lots of [financial] difficulties. I had to pay rent and bills, and I had to work. He even threatened to take away my children if I got remarried with another person. . . . Now, I don't have to worry so much about money because the combination of welfare benefits, child support, and earnings from my part-time job is enough to support my three children and myself. The court also ordered child support money to be taken directly from his paycheck, so I don't have to worry about his failure to pay. I feel that I have more freedom and no longer live in fear . . . (Huong)[10]

Public housing assistance is particularly important for Vietnamese immigrant women who want to leave the abusive relationship. Because a majority of Vietnamese immigrant women either hold low-paying jobs due to their low levels of education and English proficiency, or stay home to do child care and housework, many do not have the financial resources to rent their own apartment or house. Many abused Vietnamese women express a desire to receive housing assistance to make a new life, but only a few victim advocacy programs actively help them apply for public housing and assist them throughout the process. Chau was among a small number of women who could receive housing assistance to live independently and free of abuse. As Chau told her story,

I was forced to marry him in a refugee camp in Hong Kong. He was a tough man who could hit anyone he wanted, and he constantly abused me since. After arriving in the United States, I still had to live with him because I had no relative here. . . . When I learned that the police could intervene, I called the police. They referred me to the Asian Task Force [a women's shelter]. . . . A Vietnamese woman caseworker helped me get a PPO [personal protection order] and apply for housing because I had no place to live. . . . When my husband and I just arrived in the United States, we shared an apartment with his relatives because we didn't have money to rent our own, but his relatives did not want us to stay because he was causing troubles all the time. . . . I stayed in the shelter for two months while waiting for housing assistance. . . . After I got housing, I felt very much relieved. . . . Housing assistance saved me lots of money . . . because the rent cost only one third of my income. I felt like I was born again. . . . I don't feel lonely as I did before because I can contact the caseworker at the Asian Task Force whenever I need help.

∾

Abused Vietnamese immigrant women still face many difficulties with their decision to reach out to the criminal justice system for help, and their experiences are shaped by both their personal situations and the practices of criminal agencies. The traditional negative perception of a legal approach to solve family conflicts, fear of economic hardship, concerns with losing relationships with the abusers and the extended families, and immigration status often make abused Vietnamese immigrants disinterested in the arrest and prosecution of their abusive husbands/partners. The failure of criminal justice agencies to understand the need to preserve family relationships that these women have and the lack of bilingual services for those with limited English proficiency create further barriers to Vietnamese immigrant women's participation in the criminal justice process. Bilingual victim advocacy programs, public assistance, and legal counsel services can respond to the needs of abused Vietnamese immigrant woman and help them cope with the aftermath of abuse incidents, but these services are still very limited compared to the demand for them.

NOTES

1. See Appendix B for details of the survey of Vietnamese Americans' attitudes toward criminal justice approaches to intimate violence.

2. This quote is from my article "Help-seeking behavior among abused immigrant women: A case of Vietnamese American women," *Violence Against Women, 9,* (2), p. 220. Copyright © 2003 by Sage Publications. Reprinted by permission of Sage Publications, Inc.

3. See note 1.

4. Many Vietnamese immigrant women cannot distinguish prosecutors from judges.

5. This quote is from my article "Help-seeking behavior among abused immigrant women: A case of Vietnamese American women," *Violence Against Women*, 9, (2), p. 233. Copyright © 2003 by Sage Publications. Reprinted by permission of Sage Publications, Inc.

6. The Illegal Immigration Reform and Responsibility Act of 1996, Section 350, provides that domestic violence is grounds for deportation of aliens.

7. See note 6.

8. Depending on the jurisdiction, the restraining order may be called a personal protection order or PPO.

9. This quote is from my article "Help-seeking behavior among abused immigrant women: A case of Vietnamese American women," *Violence Against Women*, 9, (2), p. 221. Copyright © 2003 by Sage Publications. Reprinted by permission of Sage Publications, Inc.

10. This quote is from my article "Help-seeking behavior among abused immigrant women: A case of Vietnamese American women," *Violence Against Women*, 9, (2), p. 229. Copyright © 2003 by Sage Publications. Reprinted by permission of Sage Publications, Inc.

4
WHEN VICTIMS BECOME OFFENDERS

Two hours after the arrest, my husband went to the police station and admitted that
he had lied to the police, that I had not attempted to stab him with a knife. He asked
the police to release me but the police did not agree to release me without bail. When
the judge decided the bail amount, my husband refused to pay on my behalf. . . . My
lawyer worked with the court, and he advised me to plead guilty to a misdemeanor to
receive a less severe sentence. I was told if I didn't plead guilty, I would be taken back
to jail. Because I didn't want going back to jail and having more troubles, I pleaded
guilty to an offense that I did not commit . . . to let things over so I could go back to
my business and take care of my daughter. The judge sentenced me to 3 years on supervision [probation], 30 days of community service, and 52 weeks on counseling.
                                                                (Interview with Mai)

After the implementation of mandatory arrest policies in many areas, scholars acknowledged the problem of women being arrested in domestic violence cases (E.
Buzawa & C. Buzawa, 1993; Walsh, 1995; Wanless, 1996). Under mandatory arrest
policies, police officers are required to make arrests when there is evidence suggest-
ing that violence has taken place, regardless of the victim's preference for or opposition to arrest. As presumptive and mandatory arrests become popular policies, a
concomitant increase in women arrested for domestic violence offenses has resulted, either as part of dual arrest in which the victim is arrested along with her
abuser or as a sole suspect (Miller, 2001). Although many criminal justice professionals and victim service providers do not believe that violence by women has increased, the number of women arrested for domestic offenses has risen following
changes in arrest policies (Miller, 2001). Under these policies, many Vietnamese
immigrant women have been arrested and charged with domestic assault. Their in-

volvement in the criminal justice system often occurs within the complex context of male control and domination, and their experiences with the system are conditioned by their gender, their immigration status, and the practices of criminal justice agencies.

THE POLITICAL CONTEXT OF ABUSE AND ARRESTS

Similar to battered women who are victims of male domination, Vietnamese immigrant women charged with domestic assaults are often victims of their husbands/partners who rely on domestic law to exert their control. Unlike most Vietnamese women who call the police in an attempt to stop violence but do not want their husbands/partners to be arrested, many Vietnamese men call the police in an attempt to have their wives/partners arrested. In order to do so, they may exaggerate the problem, distort the nature of the incident, or fabricate evidence to blame their wives/partners. The male's malicious intent is often supported by police practices that consider the party who has visible injuries as the victim, regardless of his/her contribution to the incident, and information provided by the complainant as a sole basis for arrest and charge decisions. Within the social and political context of immigration and resettlement, police practices in domestic violence cases make Vietnamese immigrant women more vulnerable to their partners' control and manipulation.

For many Vietnamese, the end of the Vietnam War was also the beginning of the exodus of people who escaped the country to avoid communism and search for a better life in other countries. More specifically, a number of people involved with the South Vietnamese government feared the retaliation of the new communist regime and wanted to leave Vietnam. Gradually, discriminatory policies of the new government against southerners and ethnic Chinese, as well as the widespread poverty that resulted from socialist-oriented economic reforms created a desire among members of all social classes to search for a better life in other countries, especially in the United States. While clandestine escapes were costly and dangerous, permission to leave the country officially was only granted to a limited number of people, such as those sponsored by immediate relatives (e.g., parents, siblings, spouses), Amerasians, and former political detainees.[1] However, the family-oriented nature of American immigration policies also allowed spouses and children of aliens who qualified for admission under the provisions of the law to enter the United States, or allowed American residents and citizens to sponsor their spouses and/or children as legal immigrants (Houston, Kramer & Barrett, 1984). As a result, many Vietnamese women have depended on their husbands for their immigration to the United States. This is partly because Vietnamese men tended to dominate the early waves of immigration to the United States, and thus sponsor their spouses, and partly because Vietnamese men were more likely than women to obtain permission to resettle in the United States due to their participation in the South Vietnam government. Women who had already arrived in the United States but did not meet the requirements for obtaining permanent legal status needed to marry American citizens or permanent residents and rely on their sponsorship in order to stay in the country.

Vietnamese women who have depended on men to enter the United States or to obtain legal status are often vulnerable to their husbands' control. If they respond to their husbands' abuse, they can be subject to retaliation. Many of these women experienced abuse in Vietnam, and they often suffered in silence to complete immigration paperwork. After they arrive in the United States, fears of negative economic and emotional consequences from their husbands' arrests, prosecutions, and convictions often prevent them from reporting violent incidents to the police. They do not want to risk angering their husbands/partners, ending the relationship, or causing them to lose a chance to obtain a legal status. A number of Vietnamese immigrant women, however, do respond to abuse by fighting back verbally or physically because they are fed up with the abuse and cannot take it anymore. They also warn their husbands about the prohibition of domestic violence in the United States. Coming from a country where corporal punishment of children and wives was permissible, a majority of Vietnamese immigrants need to be made aware of the prohibition of domestic violence in the United States (Bui, 2002; also see Appendix B). Ironically, while women rely on the law to protect them from men's violence, men can use the law as a power tool to control their female partners.

Cam was charged with domestic assaults based on a false report by her husband. He made up the source of his injuries in an attempt to retaliate when Cam did not give him the money he wanted. As Cam told her story,

I married K [her husband] because I wanted to go to the United States. I had tried to escape many times but no success. In my last attempt in 1988, I arrived in Thailand but I was sent back to Vietnam. When I learned that former military officers who had been detained in communist re-education camps for at least three years were allowed to resettle in the United States with their spouses and children, I planned to find a man who qualified to the program to marry. . . . K had been detained for almost 9 years. We married in 1990 and applied for resettlement in the United States shortly after the wedding. Two years before we went to the United States, K told me that he had a son in another relationship and he wanted to divorce me so that he could take his son and his girlfriend with him to the United States. I didn't agree. Then, he asked me for 10 "pieces" of gold to give his girlfriend and his son, and I didn't agree either.[2] Since that time, he caused me troubles all the time. We weren't happy with each other . . . we often had arguments, and he also beat me several times before we left Vietnam. . . . [Did he hit you in the U.S.?] No, but he usually initiated arguments on money. He didn't try to find a job . . . he only hanged around with his friends, drinking and gambling, but he wanted me to work hard and give him money he needed for his son and his girlfriend in Vietnam. . . . He also had another woman here, in the United States, and he threatened to divorce me many times, but I didn't care. . . . It's OK for me now to live without him. One time, I told him that I agreed to divorce and I was ready to sign the paperwork. Since then, he didn't threaten to divorce me anymore. . . . The incident happened three months after I gave birth to my first child. He left home after we had an argument, using bad words against each other. . . . We argued because he forced me to work and make money while I just had a surgery. Four days later, I received a letter from the police asking me to show up at the police station for an assault case. At the police station, I was stunned to learn that he had made up a story telling the police that I had attacked him and caused him several scratches and bleeding on his face. . . . [Why?] I think he had an incident while he was drunk, but he wanted to blame me, to retaliate. . . . He usually made me feel like I owed him for my ticket to the United States, and I had to pay him. He constantly asked me for money, but I didn't give him the money he wanted.

Vietnamese women who came to the United States as dependents of their husbands also have experienced emotional abuse in the form of neglect and/or threats of abandonment by their husbands. When families broke apart during the Vietnamese exodus, many Vietnamese men sought intimate relationships for the sole purpose of reducing their loneliness after all other members of their families (e.g., parents and siblings) had left the country. In fact, Vietnamese men who spent several years in labor camps often found upon release that they were the only member of their family left in the country. Immigration to the United States, however, changed things. Reunification with other family members can weaken the relationships of these men with their wives, especially when they realize that they and their wives are not compatible in terms of education and/or social class. Collectivism in Vietnamese family traditions can cause these men to abandon their wives under the pressure of their parents and/or siblings. Although the neglect and abandonment of wives was not uncommon in Vietnam and often caused a great deal of economic and emotional hardship for these women, Vietnamese women who are neglected and abandoned by their husbands during the early periods of their resettlement in the United States may experience even greater difficulties because they still have to adjust economically and culturally to the new environment. In addition, they often lack the support from the family network that is usually available for women in Vietnam.[3]

Dung's story illustrates how the cruelty of an abusive man combines with the conspiracy of his family, domestic violence law, police practices, and his wife's immigration status to make his victim become an offender. Growing up in a rural area near Saigon and finishing only an elementary education, Dung met P. after he was repatriated from a refugee camp in Thailand. Because his parents and siblings already left the country, P. had no place to live and had to rely on housing and financial support from friends and relatives. After he met Dung, he moved in with her and they got married. One year later, Dung's husband applied for resettlement in the United States under the ROVR program;[4] Dung and their newborn son were allowed to accompany him to the United States as his dependents. Upon arriving in the United States, Dung totally depended on her husband emotionally and financially because she had no other relatives in the United States and had to stay home to take care of their son. While Dung had no opportunities to learn the language and vocational skills to work and make money, her husband studied English, received training in auto mechanics, and went to work when their public assistance programs ended. Dung's husband also received financial help from his parents and siblings who did not welcome Dung into their family because of her rural background. They attempted to separate the couple. As Dung told her story,

After we arrived in the U.S., we often had conflicts and we argued a lot. It seemed to me that he didn't care about the baby and me but only his parents and siblings. He had a close relationship with them, and they also helped him a lot, financially, when we just came here. I had more difficulties because I didn't have any relative in the U.S. . . . His parents, sisters, and brothers often called him to their houses to play games, party, and drink, but they didn't like me. I knew full well that they tried to separate him from me, and I also tried to keep him with me because I was afraid that he would abandon the baby and me. His sister sometimes jokingly told him that if he agreed she would match him with her friend who was more intelligent and beautiful than me. . . . This caused a lot of problems to our family . . . because we often argued about his drinking, playing games, and spending time with his family. . . . He hit me one time during an argument . . . but I didn't report. . . . On the day of the incident, we invited his parents to our apartment for lunch. When it was close to the lunch time, his sister called him to her house to play games. I asked him to stay home but he didn't care. I was so disappointed and frustrated that I just wanted to die. . . . I held a kitchen knife I was using to prepare lunch, pointed to my stomach and told him that if he didn't stay home, I would kill myself in front of him. His parents intervened, took away the knife, and left. He also went with his parents. . . . Two hours later, the police knock the door, and said something I really didn't understand. Then, one officer took away my son I hold in my arms, while the other officer handcuffed me and transported me to jail. I was so surprised by what just happened that I couldn't say a word. . . . Once in jail, they explained to me that I was arrested and charged with "threatening a family member with a knife" because my mother-in-law had called the police and reported that I attempted to stab my husband. When I said I only attempted to kill myself and showed them a small scratch in my belly caused by the knife, the police transferred me to the suicide watch area, leaving me there waiting for trial.

Cuc did not rely on her husband to enter the United States, as she was already in the country when she met him, but she still needed his sponsorship to get a permanent resident status. Leaving Vietnam when she was two years old, Cuc, her father and her sister were resettled in the Netherlands as refugees. Her father died when she was 13 years old, and because she had no adult relatives in the Netherlands, Cuc was allowed to move to the United States under the sponsorship of her uncle. Three years later, when her sister finished high school, Cuc and her sister left their uncle because they could not establish close bonds with him. After Cuc and her sister left, her uncle also terminated his sponsorship, and as a result, Cuc had no legal status in the United States. As a teenager who did not finish high school, had no working skills, and no legal status in the United States, Cuc had to rely on her sister for emotional and financial support. Cuc met a man who later became her husband after her sister got married, which had left her alone in a desperate situation. Cuc's emotional, financial, and legal dependency on her husband reinforced his power control and abusive behavior. Despite the physical abuse that began early in their relationship and continued almost weekly, causing multiple injuries all over her body, Cuc did not think about leaving the relationship or reporting the abuse.

On the other hand, when she fought back her husband's attacks, he used the law and domestic violence policies to control her behavior. As Cuc reported the incident leading to her arrest,

On that day, we had an argument because he went out, drank, and came home, causing troubles. . . . He swore and yelled at me as he used to when he was drunk. I was so angry that I threw a TV remote control at him, but it failed. . . . He then grasped me in an attempt to hit me and pushed me to the wall. I resisted by grasping his shoulder to push him back, and my fingernails accidentally caused several scratches on his neck. He became enraged and said that he would call the police to arrest me and put me in jail to teach me a lesson. . . . Because I didn't have immigration paper, I felt scared when thinking that I would be deported. I asked him to let me flee before the police came, but he didn't agree. He said he wanted me to be arrested and die in jail. . . . He locked all the doors to prevent me from fleeing until the police came. . . . One officer, after listening to my explanation of the incident, assured me that what I had done wasn't serious, and I didn't have to worry. However, the other officer who talked with my husband, after discussing with the one who talked with me, told me that I was under arrest for a felony domestic offense because I had attacked my husband with a weapon. Surprised, I asked him what kind of weapon. They took me to the living room where I saw two more officers talking with my husband who reported that I had attempted to stab him with a pocketknife.

Under police practices that consider visible injuries as evidence of assaults and give more weight to information provided by those who report the incidents than those who get injured, the exaggeration or distortions of responses to abuse can lead to the arrests of women for domestic offenses. Somini Sengupta (2001) has indicated that because police officers who respond to domestic violence calls are often ill-trained and unable to discern who is to blame in a messy domestic dispute, a minor bruise can lead to the arrest of a victim who has struck back in self-defense. Immigrant women are particularly vulnerable to men's manipulation of the law and the system when they cannot present their side of the story because of language barriers, and/or when they become confused or emotionally exhausted by the attacks. Quyen was frequently abused by her common-law husband, and before mandatory arrest policies were implemented, Quyen responded to abuse by calling the police to warn her partner and stop his violence, but she did not request an arrest or press charges. However, after the implementation of mandatory arrest policies, Quyen did not call the police because she financially depended on him and did not want him to be arrested. Instead, she fought back or sometimes left home to avoid abuse because she realized that her partner was much stronger than herself, making her counterattacks ineffective. Her responses to abuse, however, made her become a victim of retaliation by her partner who took advantage of her inability to communicate with the police to distort the story. Quyen told her story as follows,

I had a brother in Grand Rapids who wanted to move to California to live near me. I wanted to help my brother and asked my husband to let my brother move in. My husband agreed, but after my brother moved in with us, my husband became difficult with me and caused me troubles. He accused me of giving my brother too much care and neglecting him. . . . He said the presence of my brother in our home invaded his privacy. Then, he swore at me and used bad words all the time. One day, he asked me to moved out after we argued against each other. . . . I had moved out several times and stayed with my friends as he often asked me to moved out when we had conflicts. So, this time, I planned to do the same thing. We had two cars, but he didn't give me the [car] key because he didn't allow me to use any of them. He held the key in his hand and said I had to walk out of his house. I felt very angry. When I reached out, attempting to take the key in his hand, he pushed me back so hard that I fell on the floor and against the door. . . . I struggled to take the key, and when I was able to take the key, I accidentally hit his right eye with the key. His eye was swollen and bleeding a little bit, but he became enraged by my reaction. He screamed, "Dare you hit me. . . . I will call the police to arrest you and make you stop." When the police came, he told the police that I hit him because he didn't give me the key. The police officer asked if I hit him first. . . . I was confused. I saw his eye bleeding and I said yes. I didn't think that he hit me when he pushed me back and made me fall on the floor. . . . Before they handcuffed me and took me to jail, they took pictures of his injuries. Only when I was in jail, I realized that that my arm was swollen and bruised because of his push.

Similarly, Mai's husband also exaggerated the problems and distorted the nature of her behavior by reporting that she attempted to stab him with a kitchen knife when she tapped the door with the knife several times to express her anger. As Mai explained,

This happened because of his involvement in day-trading. . . . That day, while I was preparing dinner, he started blaming me for causing him to lose [money]. Tired of his blaming, as it already happened so many times, I tapped the kitchen knife I was using to prepare dinner on the door several times to express my anger and told him to shut up. He saw my behavior as provocative, and he threatened to call the police to put me in jail. I dared him to call, and he did. When the police came, he reported that I attempted to attack him with a knife. . . . I was arrested and charged with a felony [domestic assault with a weapon].

Unlike Quyen's husband who distorted the nature of her behavior and details of the incident, Thao's husband fabricated his injury to have Thao arrested when she responded to his emotional abuse. She talked about her experience as follows,

My husband was a womanizer . . . he had relationships with several women. He took me out to dancing clubs but he talked and danced with other women as if I had not been there. When returning home, we often had arguments and verbal fights. . . . He never used force against me, never hit me, but his behavior was very insulting and it hurt me a lot. . . . Several months before the incident, I knew something wrong in the relationship between him and his own daughter [with his former wife]. . . . I thought he had committed incest. After I warned him, he became very angry with me. . . . One day, I discovered that someone had entered my bedroom and stolen my jewelry. I thought of his daughter, and I told him my suspicion about his relationship with his daughter. He admitted the relationship by telling me that he treated her as a woman, not as his daughter. Speechless, I grasped a bread loaf (French baguette) on the dinner table nearby and threw at him, but it failed. . . . I then took a flat shoe and threw it at him again. This time, the shoe hit his shoulder. . . . He didn't say anything, but opened the door and went out. I also left and went up stair and go to sleep. Two hours later, the police knocked the door and asked me to come down stair. I was stunned to learn that my husband had called the police and reported that I had hit him, causing him scratches and bleeding on his arms. I looked around the dinning room and realized that all furniture was disturbed as if there had been a big fight happening there. I told the police that I had no idea about how my husband got injuries because I only threw a loaf of bread and a flat shoe at him. The officer examined the shoe and said that there was nothing important. He gave my husband information materials and told him to contact the city court if he wanted to file a complaint. Because my husband wasn't satisfied with the police's decision not to arrest me, two other officers were called. After these officers talked with my husband and discussed with their colleagues, they decided to arrest me for domestic assault. They didn't allow me to explain, didn't allow me to take my personal items or change my nightgown but took me to the police car and transported me to the city jail. . . . The next day, my friend came to my house to take some clothes I needed in jail, she saw my husband's daughter sleeping in my bed.

The above stories indicate that many Vietnamese immigrant women arrested for domestic violence offenses had experienced abuse, physically or emotionally, before the incidents leading to their arrests. They also suggest that police practices that rely primarily on visible injuries and information provided by those who report abuse incidents to make arrests without thorough investigations can create opportunities for abusive men to distort, exaggerate, and even blatantly lie about the incidents to control and/or retaliate against wives/partners who have fought against emotional and/or physical abuse.

GENDER AND THE LABELING PROCESS

When Vietnamese immigrant women enter the criminal justice system as domestic violence offenders, their fates are largely determined not by their behavior (their violation of the law), but by the power relationship between them and other actors in the labeling process, including their husbands/partners acting as witnesses, their defense lawyers, court interpreters, prosecutors, and judges. Throughout the criminal justice process, from pretrial release to plea-bargaining and trial, Vietnamese immigrant women are often in disadvantaged situations because of their position in the hierarchy of class, gender, and immigration status.

Men's Control of Women's Bail Status

The original intent of bail was to ensure that a person accused of a crime would appear for trial, and it was traditional for a friend or neighbor to act as a surety and assume the responsibility for the defendant's appearance in court (Sorin, 1985). Cash bail, however, has replaced personal surety and become the dominant approach since the late nineteenth century. With massive urbanization, the number of individuals who were not well known in the community increased, and there was no other means deemed forceful enough to ensure the appearance of the accused at trial (Mann, 1993). Under the cash bail system, a defendant is obliged to put up money that is subject to forfeiture if he or she fails to appear in court in exchange for his/her pretrial release (Sorin, 1985).

Vietnamese immigrant women arrested for domestic assault are more likely than their male counterparts to remain in jail waiting trial. Their experiences run contrary to the assumption that women offenders who committed offenses other than prostitution often receive chivalrous treatments by the court (Bernat, 1985; Kruttschnitt, 1984). Chivalry theory assumes that women are a vulnerable class requiring protection from the evils of world, including prisons and jails, while prostitutes who have violated the purity and delicacy of womanhood and motherhood need to be punished (Feinman, 1992). While there is no indication that the court considers women domestic violence offenders as deserving harsher treatment, it is clear that women's subordinate status and men's control contribute to the probability that a woman arrested and charged with domestic offense will stay in jail or be released, pending trial. Normally, people arrested and sent to jail have to ask their relatives, generally spouses if married, to bring money to post bail for them. Vietnamese women who report abuse usually post bail for their abusive husbands/partners and take them home, partly because they emotionally and/or financially depend on their husbands/partners, and partly because they want to keep the family intact for the benefit of their children. On the other hand, Vietnamese men often report abuse incidents in an attempt to control their wives/partners and therefore are unlikely to post bail for them. Women who cannot depend on the help of their husbands/partners have to remain in jail, waiting trial. Mai was arrested and charged with a felony based on her husband's false report. After the arrest, her husband admitted to the police that he had lied about the nature of the incident, but his claim did not count. When the judge set the bail amount for the pretrial release, Mai's husband refused to post bail on her behalf. As a result, Mai was detained for three days until she agreed to plead guilty to a misdemeanor in order to get out of jail. Without the help from their husbands/partners, many Vietnamese immigrant women, such as Quyen and Thao, had to rely on the assistance of friends and relatives. These women talked about their experiences as follows,

When I was in jail, I called and asked him [her husband] to post bail for me, but he refused to talk with me. . . . My brother had to find money to help me. I was detained three days and charged with a misdemeanor domestic offense. (Quyen)

I called him from jail to ask him to pay for my bail, but he didn't respond to my call. I had to ask my friend to help me. (Thao)

Staying in jail is also the fate of poor people and those who do not have a support network to help. In some jurisdictions, such as in Orange County (CA), bail for domestic offenses ranges from $15,000 to $50,000. These expenses are beyond the reach of immigrants who have not yet economically adjusted to the new society because of language barriers and the lack of vocational skills. Dung was arrested less than a year after she left her parents and siblings behind in Vietnam and came to the United States with her husband. Since she arrived in the United States, Dung had not worked but stayed home to take care of her young child. Her husband only started working about three months before the incident leading to her arrest, and he still occasionally needed financial support from his parents. Because her husband did not post bail for her, Dung had to stay in jail for three weeks until she agreed to plead guilty to the offense she did not commit. As Dung explained, "My husband didn't pay for my bail . . . about $5,000 probably because he didn't have money, and his parents didn't want to help. They didn't like me and they wanted him to divorce me."[5]

Women's Powerlessness in Plea Bargaining

Men's control, women's subordination, and the lack of legal counsel keep Vietnamese immigrant women at a great disadvantage in the American court system. Unlike abused women who often want to drop charges against their husbands/partners, men who report domestic violence do not often ask the court to drop the case against their wives/partners. In addition, women who want to drop charges to help their abusive husbands/partners often mitigate the seriousness of the incidents or recant in court what they said during police investigations at the scene. This is in sharp contrast to the situation in which men lie about the incident or exaggerate the seriousness of the problem in an attempt to involve their wives/partners in the criminal justice system. Although mandatory prosecution and no-drop policies have been implemented, their application is not absolute across jurisdictions. In fact, prosecution decisions are often made on the basis of a prosecutor's calculation of how strong the witness's testimony will be, and a case can be dismissed when the victim wants to drop charges and refuses to appear in court (Davis & Smith, 1995). Men's unwillingness to request that charges against their wives/partners be dropped combined with prosecutorial practices that rely heavily on police reports reflecting men's versions of the story make women's prosecutions very likely.

Following prosecution decisions is the process of plea bargaining, which has become an essential part of the criminal process in the United States.[6] Although the United States Supreme Court considered plea bargaining "an essential part of the criminal process which can benefit all concerned" (cited in Stitt & Chaires, 1993, p. 70), Josefina Figueria-McDonough (1985) has indicated that women are less able to bargain and more willing to plead guilty because of limited access to attorneys, education, and experience. Theoretically, plea bargaining requires the defendant to be represented by counsel to maintain its present quasi legitimacy (Stitt & Chaires, 1993). This legal protection, however, is not often experienced by Vietnamese immigrant women charged with domestic offenses. Although the right to legal counsel is one of the constitutional protections for a fair trial, many women do not have legal counsel when they need it. Because of their lack of understanding about the American legal system, many Vietnamese immigrant women are not aware of their constitutional right to legal counsel. Quyen did not have a lawyer for the whole criminal proceeding because, as she said, "I didn't know that I had the right to have a free lawyer to defend me. No one told me about this." For women who are aware of their right and ask for it, legal counseling services often come too late to help. Dung, who was charged with a domestic violence felony (threatening a family member with a weapon) on the basis of her mother-in-law's false report, did not have legal counsel at two pretrial hearings in which she pleaded not guilty. She was provided with counsel at the third hearing when she gave up efforts to defend her innocence because of emotional exhaustion caused by imprisonment and lack of legal counsel. Dung explained her situation as follows,

I had to appear in court [pretrial hearing] three times. At the first appearance, I asked for a defense lawyer, but they did not provided one for me. . . . Then, the judge [prosecutor] told me that if I pled guilty, I would be sentenced to one month in prison, three years on probation, 300 hours of community services, and one year on counseling. Otherwise, I would receive a harsher sentence at trial. Because I didn't attempt to stab my husband, I pled not guilty and I was taken back to jail. One week later, they took me to the court at the second time [pretrial hearing], and I still didn't have a lawyer. . . . I continued to plead not guilty. At the third court appearance [pretrial hearing], I felt very depressed and emotionally exhausted because I had been in jail for 16 days. So, I pled guilty to get out of jail. This time, they gave me a lawyer but he could not help because he only met with me 15 minutes before the hearing. At that time, I already decided to plead guilty to avoid unpleasant conditions in jail and go home with my baby.

Women are also disadvantaged because of the collusion between defense lawyers and prosecutors during the plea-bargaining process. In principle, the responsibility of defense counsel, according to the ABA Model Code of Professional Responsibility, is to represent a client zealously within the boundary of the law (Stitt & Chaires, 1993). However, defense counsel often assumes that the client is guilty and tries to bargain with the prosecutor for a lesser offense and sentence, without challenging evidence used by the court. Theoretically, the practice of plea bargaining is considered fair because both sides, the prosecutor and the defendant, feel that they can benefit (Stitt & Chaires, 1993). In the case of the prosecutor, the benefit is a sure conviction that saves the costs of trial and subsequent appeals. On the part of the defendant, the benefit is a plea to a lesser class of crime and a reduction in sentence. In practice, however, the prosecutor and the defendant, with the defense counsel operating as a mediator, are forming a contract by which the prosecutor can engage in false promises, misrepresentation of the condition, or threats to put pressure on the defendant and make him or her accept guilt (Gershman, 1990).

Combined with a lack of appropriate legal counsel, women's traditional responsibilities, the need to go back to work and make money, and threats by court officials can create strong pressures on Vietnamese immigrant women. Court officials often threaten that if the women do not accept pleas offered by prosecutors, they will be sent back to jail to wait for trial, and they will receive more severe sentences at the trial. The sentencing package accompanying a guilty plea in domestic violence cases is often probation for first-time misdemeanor offenders, or a short prison term for first-time felony offenders, in combination with counseling treatments and community service. Because Vietnamese immigrant women do not understand the consequences of pleading guilty, many agree to give up their right to trial and accept the conviction in order to get out of filthy jails and go home to work and take care of their children. Mai was charged with a domestic violence felony on the basis of her husband's false report concerning the nature of the incident. Although Mai maintained that she did not commit the offense, she agreed to plead guilty to a misdemeanor based on the advice of her defense lawyer. On the basis of her husband's report, Quyen was charged with domestic assault for causing injuries to her husband. Although the incident involved mutual combat provoked by her husband, only Quyen was arrested, charged, prosecuted, and detained in jail for three days. At the pretrial hearing after she was released on bail posted by a brother on her behalf, Quyen pleaded guilty without counsel and under a threat by court officials that she would be returned to jail if she refused to accept the guilty plea. Quyen explained her situation as follows,

They [court officials] told me that if I didn't plead guilty, I would be sent back to jail waiting for trial and would receive a more severe sentence. I didn't want to remain in jail any longer. . . . I missed my baby so much, and I wanted to go home with my baby. I was also afraid that I would be sentenced to a jail term at the trial. So, I agreed to plead guilty because I wanted thing to be over, and I would be placed only under supervision [probation].

For many Vietnamese immigrant women, problems in translation create misunderstandings of the meanings and consequences of court decisions and also contribute to their decision to accept guilty pleas. The mistranslation of the term "probation" into the Vietnamese term "*quan che*" (supervision) has created a misperception about the meaning of probation in the American legal system.[7] Many women understand probation as a form of "administrative supervision" that has become popular in Vietnam since 1975 when it applied to those released from re-education camps. Because administrative supervision in Vietnam only required periodic reports to local authorities, many Vietnamese immigrant women simply perceive probation as "a little bit inconvenience in life," without understanding the full consequences of probation in terms of a criminal record and possible probation violations. Consequently, many women who still maintain their innocence but fear jail detention see pleading guilty as an acceptable alternative to incarceration.

Court's Culture and Biases

What surprises and frustrates many Vietnamese immigrant women charged with domestic offenses is the quick way that cases are processed at the court as well as the prosecutors' and judges' acceptance of the police reports without further investigation; the cronyism between defense lawyers, prosecutors, and judges; or the court delays. At pretrial and trial hearings, prosecutors and judges alike make decisions mainly on the basis of police reports that may not reflect accurate accounts of the incidents, while women offenders do not often have opportunities to present their versions of the story. The lack of a careful examination of evidence may indicate the devaluation of domestic violence cases in the judicial system. Jeffrey Fagan (1996) has indicated that despite mandatory prosecution and no-drop policies aimed at enforcing domestic violence laws, domestic violence cases are still assigned a lower priority for prosecution and punishment compared with other violence cases involving strangers. As a result, prosecutors and judges are reluctant to stretch their limited resources to domestic offense cases.

When prosecutors and judges unquestioningly accept police investigations, it reflects the court's biases and lack of understanding of the differences in life experiences between men and women. For one thing, men often resort to violence to control and dominate their wives/partners, while women who are arrested and charged with domestic violence have often resorted to violence to fight back against abuses (Miller, 2001; Hooper, 1996). In addition, while women report violence to seek protection, men often report domestic incidents to control their female partners. Therefore, men may lie, distort the story, and fabricate injuries. Because of the inherent imbalance in relationships, abused women are often reluctant to provide the information necessary for the successful prosecution and conviction of their husbands/partners. As a result, many jurisdictions have developed strategies to try domestic violence cases solely on the basis of police reports under an assumption that police reports can provide enough information and more accurate accounts of the incidents than those of women victims who often minimize the problems to help their husbands/partners. By relying heavily on police reports, the court has unfairly applied policies, which were originally developed to handle men who use violence to control and dominate, to women who use violence to fight back against abuse. Mai, who tapped a kitchen knife on the door to express her anger during an argument with her husband, was charged with a felony on the basis of her husband's exaggeration that she attempted to stab him with a kitchen knife. Although her husband did come to the police later to admit that he had lied about the incident, the prosecutor did not take into account this detail. As Mai explained: "The pretrial was very short and brief. The judge [prosecutor] didn't spend enough time to listen to all details about the case. He only looked at the police report on that day [the date when the incident occurred]. They didn't take into account my husband's confession that he had lied about the incidents and all of his emotional abuse I suffered in the last three or four years." Thao was charged with a domestic misdemeanor on the basis of her husband's false complaints and the injuries that he had fabricated. Unlike Mai, Thao refused to plead guilty but went to trial. Thao told her story as follows: "My lawyer only discussed the case with me two days before the trial. . . I didn't have any opportunity to tell my story at the court. . . . I was convicted of a misdemeanor domestic offense and sentenced to six months on probation for the offense that I did not commit. . . . The judge also issued a restraining order against me to protect my husband."

Court bias and a lack of understanding of the women's subordinate status among court officials are also apparent in the requirement that any claim of past abuse must be supported by police record. While most women who are charged with domestic violence are acting in response to their husbands'/partners' violence (Hooper, 1996; Miller, 2001), not many of them can meet this requirement because they do not often report violence by their husbands/partners to the police. Cuc regularly experienced severe abuse by her husband but did not report it because she did not want her husband to be arrested. She was charged with domestic assault on the basis of her husband's complaints and his injuries accidentally caused when she countered his attack. Cuc tried to explain to the judge that her fighting back was in response to his abuse, but her defense was not accepted. As Cuc explained: "My lawyer advised me to plead guilty. . . . I told the judge that I had been abused for many years, that I had been put up with his abuse, and I had to defend myself. . . . However, the judge said because I didn't call the police before, there was no record about his abuse that I could use for my defense."

Court delays are another problem for women charged with domestic offenses as they can affect the trial outcomes. Besides legitimate motions that both sides, defendants and prosecutors (or plaintiffs), can request to gather additional information and evidence, delays can be a tactic that one side uses to suppress the damaging testimony of the other. In domestic violence cases, not only male batterers but also men who falsely claim victimization can benefit from court delays. Because the testimony of the victim is crucial for a conviction, defense lawyers can request delays in an attempt to discourage women victims' testimony. Difficulties with child care, women's household responsibilities, and the lack of financial resources and transportation have prevented many women victims from appearing in court. As a result, court delays can cause them to give up their attempts to attend pretrial or trial hearings (Hart, 1993). When women are charged with domestic assault, they need to rely on witnesses who are willing to testify on their behalf. However, court delays can discourage witnesses from continuing their efforts to attend court hearings. Cam was charged with an assault that injured her husband. Cam maintained that she was innocent, and she had two witnesses, her supervisor at the garment factory where she worked and her child's baby-sitter, who could provide support for her alibi. Both of Cam's witnesses, however, could not appear in court on the date of trial to testify on her behalf due to court delays. As Cam explained,

My boss at the factory and the baby-sitter for my son agreed to testify that I was at work at the time my husband claimed that I assaulted him and caused him injuries, but none of them appeared at the trial. . . . In fact, both of them were very good to me, and they agreed to testify on my behalf. They said it would be injustice when I didn't do anything wrong but was punished. They both appeared on the first and second dates planned for the trail, but the case was postponed. On the third date set for the trial, they did not showed up because they became tired of going back and forth to the court and gave up their attempt to testify for me. Because I didn't have witnesses who could support my alibi, I was convicted of domestic assault, sentenced to one month in prison, three years on supervision [probation], and 52 weeks on counseling.

Problems with Defense Counsel

Normally, people who are involved in the legal system tend to rely on their legal counsel for advice and protection, but many also find the performance of defense lawyers problematic. Discussing the work of legal counsel in domestic violence cases, Miller (2001) indicated that despite the adversary system, defense lawyers were not interested in challenging evidence provided by the court, but they and other court officials often acted as a friendly courtroom work group. Besides the cronyism between defense lawyers and court officials, Vietnamese immigrant women charged with domestic offenses also have problems with lawyers who violate their professional ethics. Defense lawyers, both private and public, often spend little time preparing to defend their clients, or helping their clients, especially those who are unfamiliar with the American legal system, understand case processing. The absence of defense counsels' efforts to challenge damaging evidence and to defend the innocence of their clients can be attributed to the legal context where plea bargaining is emphasized and domestic violence cases are assigned lower priorities relative to other criminal cases. It can also reflect defense counsel's assumption of a client's guilt. Under the threat by court officials of being held in jails and the lack of appropriate legal assistance, women offenders often feel frustrated and betrayed. Helpless and uncertain about the outcomes of the cases, many plead guilty to offenses they do not commit. More damaging is the violation of professional ethics committed by lawyers who do not take their defense task seriously and fail to show up at the court to assist their clients. Thao hired a lawyer of Vietnamese background with a hope that he would help her clear the charge at the pretrial stage. She thought that a private lawyer would take care of her case better than public defenders who often have heavy caseloads but receive low wages. Her lawyer, however, was late to the pretrial hearing and only arrived in court after the case was called. Disappointed, Thao hired another lawyer to defend her at the trial, but her second lawyer was no better than the first one. As Thao told her story,

I hired a Vietnamese lawyer to defend me at the pretrial, hoping that the charge would be dismissed. In fact, I didn't assault my husband nor did I cause him injuries. On the day of the pretrial hearing, he [the lawyer] didn't show up on time. . . . He was late and couldn't help me. I hired another lawyer for the trial, this time, an American lawyer. Because I didn't know much about lawyers, I followed the recommendation of my friends. He was no better than the first one. He only examined the case two days before the trial and spent very little time talking with me about the incident. I don't know how he could understand all details about the case that the police didn't put into the report. . . . I thought I would have a jury trial, but it was not a jury trial. . . . There was no jury at all, and I didn't understand why. After the trial, I asked but he didn't explain to me why this happened. . . . The judge convicted me for the assault charge, a misdemeanor, and sentenced me to probation. I think that if I had pled guilty to the charge at the pretrial, I wouldn't need to spend money for the second lawyer who didn't help me anything.

Similar to Thao, Cam also had problems with her defense counsel who did not show up at the hearing. Cam was convicted of a misdemeanor domestic assault and sentenced to a combination of jail time, probation, mandatory counseling, and community service. Because Cam did not assault her husband, she appealed the conviction and sentence. Her lawyer did not show up for the first two preliminary appeal hearings. When I interviewed Cam, she was attending a counseling program for batterers, and she was not sure whether her lawyer would appear at the third hearing, or if she would have to start serving her jail term. As Cam explained:

At the pretrial hearing, the prosecutor suggested that if I pled guilty to a misdemeanor I would receive probation and no jail time. Because I didn't assault my husband, I refused to plead guilty. At the trial, I was convicted and sentenced to one month in prison and three years on probation. I thought that the conviction and sentence were unfair because I did not commit the offense, so I decided to appeal. I hired an American lawyer. . . . He filed the appeal but did not appear at the first two preliminary hearings. I didn't know why, but he just kept telling me he would appear the next time. I'm very worried because the next court appearance will be five days from today, and if he doesn't appear, I will have to serve my term in jail. . . . I don't know what kind of defense he used when he advised me to attend the counseling program for batterers while I am waiting for appeal decision. I'm not a batterer. . . . I never hit my husband. I don't know why I have to do that.

The lack of English proficiency also creates problems in preparing a defense. With language barriers, Vietnamese immigrant women tend to choose lawyers from the same ethnic background to avoid problems in communication. They also hope their lawyers, who share their culture and family traditions, can understand their situations better than lawyers from different cultures. However, relying on Vietnamese lawyers can be problematic. For one thing, only a very small number of lawyers are of Vietnamese background, and they tend not to be specialized in domestic violence. As a result, those who need a Vietnamese lawyer do not have many choices. Second, some of these male lawyers still hold traditional gender norms and are biased against women charged with domestic assaults.[8] When they happen to have prior social relationships with their clients' husbands/partners, their biases increase, making them identify with and feel sympathetic to men who claim to be assaulted by their wives/partners. Because a majority of Vietnamese immigrants are unfamiliar with the American legal system and laws, these lawyers can take advantage of their clients' ignorance and violate their own professional ethics, which works against their clients as illustrated in the case of Cam. Charged with a domestic assault, Cam hired a Vietnamese lawyer to defend her. After several meetings with the lawyer, Cam learned that her lawyer and her husband knew each other through their social hours at a community organization. Cam talked about her experience as follows:

My first lawyer was Vietnamese. . . . I didn't know much about lawyers or about him. Some of my friends saw his advertisement in a Vietnamese newspaper and told me that he was a good lawyer. I was so confused and worried by the charged that I didn't know what to do, so I followed the suggestion of my friends. . . . I wasn't aware that he and my husband knew each other until he told me. That day, he looked at the file, saw my husband's name, and told me that it was familiar to him. After asking me a few questions about my husband, he said that he knew my husband and they often met each other at a community mutual assistance association. Since then, he was not interested in learning about the incident from me but instead from my husband, and he understood the problem through my husband's version of the story. . . . He said my husband's injuries were the evidence that I had hit him, and he insisted that I should plead guilty to avoid trial and more severe sentences. . . . It seemed to me that he believed my husband, took sides with my husband, and did not want to help me. . . . Later, I learned from a friend, who knew both my husband and my lawyer, that he [her lawyer] told my husband many details from the conversation between him [her lawyer] and me.

CONSEQUENCES OF CONVICTIONS AND SENTENCES

The enforcement of mandatory arrests, prosecutions, and enhanced penalties for domestic violence offenses has eliminated the diversion alternative to conviction with punitive consequences (Hooper, 1996). Those who are charged with and convicted of domestic offenses for the first time are often sentenced to probation, if the offense is a misdemeanor, or jail terms, in combination with mandatory counseling and community service, if the offense is a felony. Depending on jurisdictions, probation terms for first time offenders can range from six months to three years, and treatment programs can last from four months to one year. In addition, most domestic violence offenders are also subject to restraining orders. In some jurisdictions, restraining orders are included in the "sentencing package," regardless of the victim's request. For women charged with domestic offenses, the consequences of a conviction can go beyond their basic punitive intent and affect the women's safety and child custody rights.

A majority of women who are involved in the criminal justice system as domestic violence offenders have been physically abused before the incidents leading to their convictions. Many continue to be abused or harassed by their husbands/partners after court proceedings, but they cannot receive assistance from victim services because of their convictions. Under the practices of victim services and criminal justice agencies, the victim is an entity separate from the offender. Consequently, a person can be defined as either the victim or the offender, but she cannot be both the victim and the offender of intimate violence. Even when service caseworkers are well aware that a woman convicted of domestic offenses has been and continues to be abused by her partner, they cannot provide help because the woman does not fit the definition of "the victim" required by the state.

The unilateral definition of the victim does not reflect the power dynamics in intimate relationships and, as a result, has an important implication for women's safety. In the culture of male domination, many men perceive the ability to control their female partners as part of their masculinity (Messerschmidt, 1993). Although men often use force to keep their female partners under control, other means, including psychological pressures, financial resources, and harassment, can also help men achieve the same goal. Women convicted of domestic offenses are often subject to a restraining order that creates a de facto separation and can prevent, to some extent, their husbands'/partners' abuse. However, many women still experience harassment by their husbands/partners who are trying to keep them under control. Thao's husband violated the restraining order by trying to contact her through the mail and the phone, asking her to come back to him. When Thao refused to communicate with her husband, he took advantage of her loss of credibility due to her conviction to spread negative stories about her around the small community where everybody knew each other. Quyen's husband verbally abused her at her workplace after she refused to come back to him. Because of their convictions, these women were ineligible for assistance from victim service agencies, and could not request a restraining order against their husbands/partners to avoid harassment. As Thao and Quyen talked about their experiences,

After the trial, I moved out because of the restraining order [against her], but he continued following me and causing me troubles at the restaurant [where she worked]. . . . He came to the restaurant several times a week and asked to talk with me while I was working. . . . He tried to ask me to come back to him. I refused to talk with him because I didn't want to violate the order. Then, he would yell in front of all customers, calling me a "whore" who abandoned the family, husband, and children to go with other men. I had to change my job a number of times, but he still discovered the place where I worked. . . . I went to a women's center and ask for help, but they said that I was not qualified for the service because I was convicted of a domestic offense. . . . I was not a victim. (Quyen)[9]

I left home since I was arrested. . . . After the court case was over, he started calling me at home, sending me letters, asking to talk with me. He said he wanted me to come back home and start the relationship again . . . but I didn't believe him. I thought he was trying to trick me, making me violate the [restraining] order and causing me to be back in jail. Because I didn't want to violate the [restraining] order, I ignored his requests. This made him angry. . . . He talked bad about me in the church and in other social events in our community. . . . He accused me of abandoning him . . . that I had a boyfriend. He even wrote letters to my son who was in college at that time, telling my son that I was the one who broke up the family because I refused to come back home while he was ready to forgive me for having assaulted him. When his harassment became unbearable, I talked with my counselor at the batterers' program that I was required to attend. My counselor said I was a victim of domestic abuse and she advised me to seek help from a women's center. . . . The caseworker at the women's center was very sympathetic to my situation, but she said I was not qualified for the service because I had been convicted of a domestic offense. I returned to my lawyer and asked him to request a restraining order against my husband, but my lawyer also said it would be very difficult because I already had one against me. It appeared to me that he was not interested in helping me obtain a restraining order. (Thao)

Losing custody of one's children is another detrimental effect of a conviction on Vietnamese immigrant women. Generally, to protect the physical, emotional, and economic safety of children, custody is often given to caring parents and/or parents who have the economic resources necessary to raise their children. A conviction can cause a female offender to lose a custody case. A conviction of domestic assault can influence the court to see a woman as an unsuitable parent due to the violent nature of the offense, even though most women use force for self-defense. Arrests and jail terms can cause working women to lose their jobs. Finding a place to live and the separation required by restraining orders makes their lives more difficult as the household is reduced to only one income. For Vietnamese immigrant women, besides the "violent and abusive parent" label, the lack of economic resources and unfamiliarity with the American legal system can negatively impact their custody status. Vietnamese immigrant women tend to have low education levels and limited English proficiency as well as few vocational skills. They often work in low-paying jobs or stay home, depending on the financial support of their husbands/partners. In addition, because of immigration, many women do not have the support network of the extended family from which they can seek help when needed. Separations following convictions and sentences can cause women to leave the home of their husbands/partners with nothing, and consequently lose custody of their children. As Quyen explained,

I lost the custody of my son because I didn't have income. . . . I didn't work when I lived with him [her husband]. After I moved out because of the restraining order, he asked and was given the custody of my son. The court said my son would be better off under the care of his father because he had stable income and housing while I had no job, no money, and no permanent place to live. . . . I only had visitation. Currently, I'm working but the court still considers me as unemployed because I don't report my income. [Why?] I cannot report my income because I don't have immigration papers, and I have to work for cash.

Dung had to stay in jail for three weeks before she pleaded guilty because she did not have money or relatives who could post bail for her. After she was sentenced to probation, Dung could not return home to see her three-year-old son because of the restraining order. Almost a year later, Dung learned that the court had given custody to her husband. As Dung talked about her experience,

I haven't seen my son since I was arrested. I was in jail for three weeks and after I was released, I could not return home because of the restraining order. . . . People told me to ask the court for visitation but I didn't know how to contact the court. Almost a year later, my husband's lawyer came to the shop [the garment factory where she worked] and gave me divorce and custody papers. . . . I didn't know anything about my husband's decision to divorce because I had no contact with him since the trial. When I asked the lawyer why my husband and the court did not let me know about the divorce and custody case, he said that I had no right to notification because I was a convict. I didn't know what he said was true or not. I asked other people and they said my husband and his lawyer cheated on me. I don't know how to deal with them because I lost both custody and visitation. . . . I want to ask a lawyer to help me but I don't have money. I may have to wait for three years until I have completed my probation terms to ask the court for visitation or custody.

~

Trends in mandatory arrest, mandatory prosecution, and penalty enhance-
ments have drawn many Vietnamese immigrant women into the criminal justice
system as offenders of domestic assaults. Although these policies seem to be gen-
der-neutral, as they are applied equally for men and women, they are, in fact, biased against women in many aspects. Because the nature of violent behavior is not
often considered, women who use force as self-defense are unfairly treated under
the same law applied to men who use violence to control and dominate their female partners. Throughout the criminal justice process, Vietnamese immigrant
women are often in disadvantaged situations not only because of their gender and
the practices of criminal justice officials, but also because of their immigration status. The lack of economic resources and the absence of extended family support
networks often causes these women to stay in jail waiting for trial. Unfamiliarity
with the American criminal justice system, ineffective defense counsel, and the demands of traditional women's responsibilities often cause these women to plead
guilty, even to an offense they did not commit, without full understanding of the
potential consequences of having a criminal record. The practices of criminal justice officials who rely solely on information provided by the complainants not only
cause innocent women to be arrested, convicted, and sentenced but also provide
support for men who know how to use domestic violence laws to control their female partners (see Miller, 2001). For many women, the consequence of their
convictions, in addition to punitive sentences, can include the loss of child custody
and other victim services when they are subject to abuse again.

NOTES

1. A program initiated in 1989 allowed survivors of communist labor camps to resettle in
the United States as refugees (H. Nguyen & Haines, 1996).
2. In Vietnam, people used the term "a piece of gold" to indicate an amount of gold equal
to 1.2 ounces. Ten pieces of gold were worth about US$4,000, a significant sum at that time.
3. According to Abraham (2000), the network of the extended family can provide important emotional and financial support for abused women.
4. ROVR (Resettlement Opportunities of Vietnamese Returnees) was a resettlement program for those who volunteered to repatriate after they escaped Vietnam and stayed temporarily in a Southeast Asian country.
5. An offender can pay 10% of the bail amount to a bail company that insures his/her appearance in court. The money paid for bail is nonrefundable even after the court appearance.
6. In *Santabello v. New York* (1971) and *Blackedge v. Allison* (1977), the U.S. Supreme
Court called plea bargaining "an essential part of the criminal process which can benefit all
concerned (cited in Stitt & Chaires, 1993, p. 70).
7. The Vietnamese version of court materials and materials in counseling programs for
Vietnamese batterers in Orange County (CA) used the term "quan che" (supervision) to refer to probation.
8. My conversation with a male lawyer of Vietnamese background in California indicated
his biases and lack of understanding of the power dynamics in intimate relationships. Dis-

cussing the reason why many women victims who had reported violent incidents but refused to testify against their husbands/partners, the lawyer explained that these women had lied to the police about the incidents and did not want to continue lying. He also contended that Vietnamese women had learned from their American counterparts to become more aggressive, while Vietnamese men lost a great deal of power in the family.

9. This quote is from my article "Help-seeking behavior among abused immigrant women: A case of Vietnamese American women," *Violence Against Women*, *9*, (2), p. 231. Copyright © 2003 by Sage Publications. Reprinted by permission of Sage Publications, Inc.

5

WOMEN'S SAFETY AND FAMILY LIFE

Shortly after I obtained the restraining order, he was very angry because he was forced to move out. Then, he would use phone to yell at me and curse me, using very bad words several times a week. . . . Because of the children, I removed the restraining order. Once he went back home, he didn't change because he refrained from beating me after the arrest, but he verbally abused me more often. . . . While he didn't use force to attack me, he used words, and his language caused me a lot of pain. He criticized me for everything almost everyday to the point that I became emotionally exhausted and drained. I thought that it might be better for me to die in peace than to live with his mental torture. I finally had to file for separation and move to another location to avoid his abuse. . . . When I realized that there was no hope for reconciliation, I decided to file a divorce. . . . I have no longer to worry about his abuse, but I usually feel very sad because the children don't have a family with a father like others.

(Interview with Chau)

The shift from the definition of domestic violence as a private family matter to a view of domestic violence as a crime has led to major changes in criminal justice responses to the problem. There has been general agreement among activists for battered women that this shift in societal reaction to domestic abuse has been beneficial to battered women (Bowman, 1992; Cahn, 1992; Ferraro, 1993; Wanless, 1996). Advocates of criminal justice approaches to domestic violence have considered mandatory arrests, mandatory prosecutions, personal protection orders, and court mandated treatment as effective weapons to fight domestic violence and protect women's safety (Walsh, 1995; Wanless, 1996; Stark, 1993; Corsilles, 1994). These approaches, focusing on the victim and the assailant within the context of criminal laws, are founded on the principle of specific deterrence that invokes the threat of legal sanctions to deter undesired behavior. Despite high expectations for the effectiveness of criminal justice approaches to protecting women's safety, Vietnamese immigrant women have experienced mixed results with criminal justice interventions. While arrests, prosecutions, and personal protection orders cannot guarantee women's safety, criminal justice interventions often interfere with other aspects of family life, including relationships and financial security.

A SENSE OF SAFETY

The protection of women's safety through deterrence is the main concern of those who formulate criminal justice responses to domestic violence, and the absence of re-offending is often a measure of policy effectiveness. The relationships between individuals involved in domestic violence cases complicate the possibility of deterrence with criminal justice approaches, which depend not only on the threat of punitive sanctions but also on the ability of abused women to invoke the power of law.

Immediate Protection and Short-Term Prevention

For most abused Vietnamese immigrant women, seeking help from the criminal justice system is often the last resort when other approaches fail, or when abusive husbands/partners are out of control and cause these women to fear for their own safety. These women's main concern is to seek immediate protection from the police. They also expect that criminal justice interventions can change their husbands'/partners' behavior and prevent violence in the future. Because the police represent power and have the authority to intervene, immediate protection is often achieved with the presence of the police at the scene. In some situations, even a threat to invoke the authority of the police is effective enough to deter abusive men from acting violently. Hong began experiencing abuse by her husband after the couple resettled in the United States. Hong's husband, a former military officer in Vietnam, had difficulties culturally and financially adapting to American society and eventually became an alcoholic. He usually beat Hong when he was drunk, but she did not call the police because she did not want him to be involved with the law. One time, he hit her so hard that she was rendered unconscious, and he fled the scene when a neighbor called 911. After that incident, she did not experience violence as often, and her threat to call the police seemed to stop her husband from hurting her. As Hong said, "I only threatened to call the police by picking up the phone but I didn't actually call. That was enough to make him feel scared and stop hurting me." Because the arrival of the police stops the violence, many women start to feel safe. In most cases, abused women actually receive immediate safety protection from responding police officers who intervene, order violent husbands/partners out of the home, or arrest abusive husbands/partners.

The abused woman's appreciation of police protection can be seen in her satisfaction with police work. The literature on domestic violence suggests that victims' satisfaction with police performance reflects the quality of police work, including enforcing domestic violence laws and serving the needs of victims (Erez & Belknap, 1998a). Victims who are not satisfied with police performance often feel disappointed and frustrated with the system that is supposed to meet their needs, but victims' approval ratings of the police often increase when victims' preferences with regard to arrest have been followed (Buzawa & Austin, 1993). Abused Vietnamese immigrant women expressed satisfaction with police performance not only when the police did what they wanted, but also when they felt protected by police work. As discussed in previous chapters, a majority of abused Vietnamese immigrant women who have reported incidents to the police do not want their husbands/partners to be arrested, but under mandatory arrest policies their husbands/partners are arrested in most of the cases. Women whose preference for arrest is followed feel that their needs are served, but women who oppose arrests are not usually angry or upset because they somehow feel protected by the arrests of their husbands/partners. As these women explained,

I felt very scared when the police arrested him [her husband], but I thought they did protect me. (Le)

The police officer listened when I explained what had happened. They believed me and supported me. They explained the law and what would happen to my husband and gave me information about social services where I could go to get help. . . . I felt sad when they arrested my husband, but I understood that they only did what the law required them to do, and they arrested him to protect me. (Hanh)

The impact of criminal justice interventions on women's safety, however, decreases and almost disappears after the police stop the violence and leave the scene without further actions. When abusive men are not arrested, or when the police do not press charges as requested by abused women, violence tends to continue. Three women, Quyen, Tram, and Phuong, all contacted the police, asking for help with their family problems. Quyen and Phuong called for police help several times when abuse occurred; Tram did not call the police, but she went to the police station to talk with police liaison in the domestic violence unit and asked for advice. In these cases, the police, following the requests of these women, did not make arrests. These women talked about their experiences as follows,

My husband became acting violently after the family business went down causing him unable to make money and support the family. . . . I learned about a domestic violence intervention program of the City Police Department through a radio broadcasting program [a local station], and I went to the police station to ask for help. I told the police liaison that I did not want my husband to be arrested, but I did want him to get help. . . . After the police liaison talked with my husband, the situation in my family became better for awhile, about five or six months, then he continued to make troubles again as usual. (Tram)

I called the police many times before the new law on mandatory arrest. When the police asked if I wanted him to be arrested, I said no, and the police left. . . . The first time when I called the police, he seemed to feel afraid. When he knew that I didn't want him to be arrested, he wasn't afraid any more. He still acted violently, and nothing changed. . . . After the implementation of new domestic violence law [mandatory arrest] in California, I didn't call the police because I depended on his financial support and I didn't want him to be arrested. (Quyen)

He abused me so many times and I had to call the police, but he wasn't arrested because I begged the police not to arrest him. . . . I only wanted the police to stop the violence, stop him from hurting me, but I didn't want him to be involved with the law because I feared his retaliation. Also, we just arrived in the United States, and I was concerned that he couldn't find a job to support the family if he got into troubles with the law. . . . When someone asked him about the incident, he raised his face and said that the police couldn't arrest him because he didn't do anything wrong. Then, he talked bad about me with other people, continued abusing me or threatening to hit me. Because he didn't change, I decided to have a divorce. (Phuong)

Police interventions combined with prosecutions and punishment appear to be more effective than arrests alone in preventing abuse in the future. Abusive husbands/partners who are arrested, prosecuted, and sentenced tend to refrain from violence after criminal justice interventions. Ha and her common-law husband often had conflicts about the use of money, and when Ha's husband could not get the money he needed for his gambling habit, he used force against her to vent his anger. Ha called the police three times to report abuse. The first time, Ha's husband was not arrested based on her request. The second time, he fled the home before the police arrived. A few days later, he came back home, asked her for money again, and assaulted her when she refused to give him money. This time, when Ha called the police, her husband was arrested, prosecuted and sentenced to six months on probation. As Ha talked about the impact of criminal justice interventions, "I'm not happy with my life, but I don't know how to make it better. If he didn't ask me for money [to spend on gambling], everything would be all right. There would be no conflict, no argument, no fight. . . . Currently, he is on probation, and he has to study law [batterers' counseling program]. Since he got sentenced, he didn't bother me to ask for money, and we didn't have problems."

The effectiveness of court interventions in preventing future abuse, however, is often short-lived. For cases that result in probation, the deterrent effect of criminal justice interventions often remains strong during the probation periods when the offenders are under court supervision. Deterred by the possibility of being sent back to jail on a probation violation, abusive men often avoid violating their terms by refraining from using force, but violence often resumes after court supervision is over. Nga called the police several times to seek protection from her husband's violence, which occurred when he was drunk or when she refused to satisfy his demands for sex. Nga had strong emotional ties to her husband and did not want him to be arrested or involved with the law. Therefore, when he was arrested, she refused to provide information to the court or the police during their investigations. Despite her request that the charges be dropped, her husband was prosecuted twice, convicted, and sentenced to probation. However, the prosecutions and punishment of her abusive husband did not provide her long-term protection. As Nga explained, "During his probation, he was all right. After he finished his probation terms, nothing changed. He often scared me, like driving carelessly, or threatening to kill the whole family. He even set fire on my business. I didn't report because I didn't want him to be in deeper troubles with the law, but he was arrested the second time because one of my friends, who was a social worker, reported to the police that he had sexually abuse the children." Hien experienced similar frustrations with criminal justice interventions. Brutally abused by her boyfriend, Hien called the police for help three times, which caused her boyfriend to be arrested, prosecuted, and sentenced. Twice, Hien left her violent boyfriend, but came back to him under his threats. As Hien explained,

It seemed to me that he didn't change even with the intervention of the law. He got one year probation for the first incident and was ordered to attend counseling, but he didn't attend. For the second incident, he was in jail for awhile. After he was released, he continued threatening my family and me. . . . I know that I made a big mistake when I came back with him, but I was so afraid of his retaliation. The law couldn't keep him from going to my parents' home and threatening my parents and siblings.

Along with mandatory arrest and prosecution, the use of restraining orders has become popular in domestic violence cases. In principle, the use of a restraining order can improve a woman's safety because its effects lie mainly in the elimination of the physical proximity between the two parties in the conflict; therefore, it reduces opportunities for one party to assault the other. Abused women who are granted restraining orders against their husbands/partners often feel safe during the time they maintain the order because their husbands/partners are prevented from approaching and attacking them at their residence or elsewhere. Chau called the police for help five times and went to the hospital numerous times to treat injuries caused by her husband during her seven years in the United States. In the past year alone, she went to the hospital three times. Twice, her husband was arrested and prosecuted, but she did not request a restraining order until recently. Chau talked about the effects of a restraining order:

His abuse started in a refugee camp in Hong Kong where I met him and was forced to marry him, and it continued in the United States. I never had a good time with him because he only made me feel scared. . . . I called the police five times; he was arrested and prosecuted but his behavior didn't change. . . . I didn't request a PPO [personal protection order] before because I didn't know about it. This time staff at the Asian Task Force helped me obtain a PPO and arranged for me to move out to my new place. Thanks to the PPO, I don't have to worry about his abuse. . . . He couldn't come to my apartment to hit me, and I don't have to suffer his swearing and yelling at me. . . . This made me feel safe. I had more freedom to move around and I could sleep in peace at night.

Because the main feature of a restraining order is the requirement of physical separation, its impact is often limited to the time abused women maintain the order. When the couple reunites, abuse may continue. Many women terminate restraining orders early because of financial problems that result from their husbands'/partners' absence, because of emotional attachments to abusive men who demand that the restraining order be lifted, or because of the need for the presence of the father at home. In addition, abusive men often violate restraining orders by disregarding the no-contact requirement and return home to threaten or assault their wives/partners. Although in principle, using restraining orders can increase police responsiveness to calls and decrease women's chance of being abused again (Chaudhuri & Daly, 1992), abused Vietnamese immigrant women often do not report restraining order violations to the police. Tam's experience with a restraining order is not unfamiliar to this group of victims. According to the advice of an advocate, Tam requested a restraining order to protect her after police interventions. Shortly after she obtained the restraining order, she went to the court and asked the judge to lift it, so that her husband could return home. As they resumed their family life, her husband continued his abusive behavior, and Tam had to file for a second restraining order. As she explained,

Shortly after the judge issued a PPO [personal protection order, or restraining order] against him, I terminated it because of the request of my husband and his family. I also had financial difficulties, and it was necessary for me to stay with him so he could help me raise the children. However, after we returned to live together, he continued his abuse. When we had conflicts, he would destroy my belongings, yell at me, and assault me. During the time I maintained the PPO, I felt safe because he couldn't come to my apartment to swear at me and assault me. As he continued abusing again, I had to request a PPO for the second time.

Criminal justice interventions also seem to have no effect on men who have been previously involved with the law. Criminal justice approaches to domestic violence assume that punishment that causes pain through shame and a loss of freedom and personal prestige can deter future criminal behavior. However, those who have prior experiences with the criminal justice system may not fear the pain caused by punishment unlike those who have a stake in conformity. Trang did not know that her husband had been in jail in several different states before they were married. Growing up in the United States and aware of the prohibition against domestic violence, Trang warned her husband that she would call the police to report abuse incidents, but her warnings did not stop him from assaulting her. Trang called the police twice, and each time, her husband was arrested, prosecuted, and sentenced to probation. Punishment did not deter her husband, but instead he became more abusive, verbally and physically. As Trang explained, "He got in and out of prisons several times. He probably was not afraid of the law. The law in the United States was not effective."

Women's Empowerment and Deterrence

Arrests, prosecutions, and restraining orders have been considered new resources for abused women to combat domestic abuse; but the effects of these interventions appear to be conditioned by the ability of women to actually invoke the authority of criminal justice agencies to empower themselves, influence their husband's/partner's behavior, and bargain for their safety. Although many abused women have called the police to report abuse, not all of them want to rely on the police to arrest and press charges against their husbands/partners. It is not uncommon to see abused women request that charges against their abusers be dropped. Emotional dependency, fear of reprisal, as well as economic and cultural constraints often prevent women from following through the criminal justice process or using the full force of legal enforcement to empower themselves to fight against domestic abuse. This is illustrated by the experiences of Tram, Phuong, and Quyen discussed in previous sections. On the other hand, when abusive men have a stake in conformity and are aware that their wives/partners have the assertiveness, independence, and access to invoke the authority of the law to combat domestic abuse, criminal justice interventions seem to have a stronger impact on women's safety in the long run. Lien experienced serious abuse by her husband both in Vietnam and in the United States, but the abuse decreased and became less frequent after police interventions. As Lien explained,

My husband was not happy with his life in the United States because he experienced a decline in social status and power. He couldn't deal with stress and easily became angry. . . . My experience of abuse began in Vietnam after he was released from the re-education camp, and his abuse continued in the U.S. Pushing, punching, threatening with gun or knife, choking, slapping, and forcing me to have sex were things he would do to me. . . . One time, he attempted to choke me when I was sleeping. That made me feel fear for my life and I had to report his abuse to the police. . . . He was not arrested because when the police came, my daughter, who interpreted for us, denied everything. I also didn't want him to be arrested, but I wanted to warn him. I told him I would make him arrested if he continued to abuse me, and he knew I would do it. . . . His abuse came less often and less severe after police intervention. . . . Probably he learned from his friends that wife beating was illegal here and he felt deterred by the law.

Similar to police interventions, the deterrent effects of prosecutions and punishment are contingent on the power dynamics of the couple during and after the criminal justice process. Women who emotionally and financially depend on their husbands/partners are often under pressure to request that charges be dropped, and the abuse tends to continue. Regardless of whether prosecutors agree to drop a charge or not, abusive men can take advantage of the dependency of women, who do not want prosecutions and punitive treatments, to take control of the situation. On the other hand, independent women who request that charges be dropped and/or ask for lenient treatment because they want to *help* their abusive husbands/partners may experience long-term reductions of violence. Although most cases are subject to mandatory prosecution and no-drop policies, judges still have discretion in sentencing decisions, and women's requests for lenient treatments may result in lighter sentences for their husbands/partners. It appears that when a

woman who has relative independence decides to help her husband/partner by requesting that charges be dropped, or asks the court for lenient treatments on behalf
of her husband/partner, she sends a message that she has some control over the relationship (see similar findings in Ford & Regoli, 1993). When women take advantage of the power of prosecutors and judges to empower themselves and deal with
abuse, they can change the dynamics of relationships and avoid violence in the future. Because domestic abuse is inherent in male domination and women's lack of
control in family relationships, supportive services for victims of domestic violence
can help improve women's independence and strengthen their ability to use criminal justice interventions to change family dynamics. The stories of two women,
Hue and Huong, who had different experiences with criminal justice interventions, illustrate the importance of women's empowerment in changing the
behavior of abusive husbands/partners.

Hue experienced frequent, severe abuse by her husband but had to struggle to
find a way out. On the one hand, her parents did not support the idea of reporting
abuse incidents to the police because they did not want the problem to be known to
the public, nor did they want her husband to be in jail. On the other hand, Hue also
depended on her husband for financial support and was not aware of services for
victims of domestic violence. When her husband's behavior became a serious
threat to her life, Hue reported the abuse to the police. This happened when her
husband put a knife to her neck. Panicked, Hue called 911 and her husband was arrested. Through her contacts with a victim service agency, Hue learned about the
dynamics of abuse, her legal right to safety, several criminal justice approaches to
family violence, as well as social and legal assistance to domestic violence victims.
When her husband asked her to drop the charges, Hue let him know that she had
the support of a victim advocacy agency, and with the assistance of legal counsel,
she could go to the court and ask the judge to treat him with leniency if he learned
his lesson and took responsibility for his behavior. As Hue talked about her
experience,

When my husband was arrested, I planned to let him stay in jail for awhile, so he could learn
a lesson, but my parents urged me to post bail for him and take him home. . . . After he got
home, he asked me to go to the court and make a request to drop the charge. I followed the
advice of my counselor [a victim advocate] and told him that I could help him if he showed
remorse . . . that means he must take responsibility for his behavior by pleading guilty and I
would ask the judge to give him a light sentence. . . . I wanted my husband to understand
that I could have my say in the case. At first, he did not believe me and felt angry, but after he
found out I did got help from legal and victim services, he seemed to be afraid, and he agreed
with my plan. . . . He pleaded guilty, got probation, and was ordered to attend counseling.
That's what I wanted for him. . . . I began to work to make money after the case was over
because I realized that he wouldn't respect me if I continued to rely on him. . . . He made
good progress. He stopped hitting me; he began treating me with respect; he didn't bring his
friends home to drink despite of me or hang around with his friends outside all night as
often. He agreed to add my name into his bank account after I decided to make money. I told
him that I could work, and I didn't need to depend on him to survive. If he continued to

abuse me, I would leave. Now, I can spend money without asking him every time, and I can also check his spending, especially the money he sent to his family in Vietnam.

Huong began experiencing verbal and physical abuse by her common-law husband when he became addicted to alcohol and gambling, but she only reported her husband's violent behavior after he had abused her several times. Staying home to raise three children, Huong depended on her husband both emotionally and financially. Huong called the police for help three times, but she did not want her husband arrested and prosecuted. Under pressure from her husband, she tried to drop the charges and refused to testify for the prosecutors every time her husband was arrested. Huong told her story as follows,

He hit me five times since we lived together. For the first time, I tolerated his behavior and did not report to the police because I loved him and thought that he wouldn't do it again. . . . In fact, when he was not drunk, he was very nice to me. . . . One year later, on the birthday of my son, he assaulted me again, exactly like the first time. This time, he gave me black eyes, but I still didn't call the police because he promised me that he would never hit me again, and I didn't want him to be in trouble with the law. One month later, when he hit me for the third time, I called the police. He was arrested and prosecuted. He told me that if I loved him, I should denied the charge; I should tell the judge [prosecutor] that he didn't hit me. . . . Because I loved him, and because I didn't want him to lose his job, I denied the assault and asked the judge [prosecutor] to drop the charge, and he was acquitted. . . . He seemed to be afraid for awhile, but after his charge was dropped, he didn't change, and he assaulted me again several months later. This time, I asked the police not to press charge because he was on probation for assaulting his girlfriend and I didn't want him to get a prison sentence. . . . When he assaulted me again recently, he threatened to kill me if I testified at the court. . . . I felt very disappointed because he didn't change.

The preventive effect of a restraining order also rests on the power dynamics in intimate relationships. In principle, restraining orders can have a deterrent effect because the violation of restraining orders is treated as contempt of court, a criminal offense that can result in arrest and even incarceration. However, a woman's economic and emotional dependency often tips the balance of power in a relationship to the man's advantage and puts pressure on the victim, causing her to terminate restraining orders or fail to report violations. On the other hand, women who have some control in the relationship can manage to use restraining orders to improve their safety. Ruth Lewis and colleagues (2000) have indicated that the unique way in which restraining orders operate gives abused women a tool to monitor the behavior of their abusive husbands/partners. In fact, abused women can decide, on the basis of their judgments about their own safety and/or their children's safety, when they need to invoke this form of protection to prevent any contact with their abusive partners. Vietnamese immigrant women have relied on their ability to make these decisions in implementing the restraining orders to bargain for their safety without physical separations. Most are aware that maintaining contact while restraining orders are in effect is illegal, but they accept the return of their husbands/partners without officially terminating restraining orders; the women make it clear to their husbands/partners that they will report the violation if violence occurs, and their husbands/partners will have more trouble with the law for violating restraining orders. When abusive men are aware that their wives/partners are not under emotional and economic pressure but have the ability to invoke the full force of criminal justice interventions, restraining orders can improve women's safety as illustrated in the case of Xuan. A mother of four teenage children and the main provider for the family, Xuan began experiencing assaults by her husband when they were in Vietnam, but the abuse increased in the United States. When Xuan was fed up with the violence, she reported the abuse incidents to the police to teach her husband a lesson. Under the advice of a victim advocate and legal counsel, Xuan requested a restraining order but later allowed her husband to return home. As Xuan talked about her experience,

He was arrested when I called the police to report abuse. . . . He had to move out because I requested a restraining order, and this cause him a lot of difficulties. He couldn't afford to rent his own apartment because he didn't make enough money. You know, he worked only part time at the minimum wage. So, he had to rely on his friends. . . . When the children learned that their father got sick, they asked me to let him return home so they could take care of him. I agreed but didn't ask [the judge] to remove the order. I wanted to use it to prevent him from hitting me again. I told him that if he hit me again, I would call the police and he would be charged with more severe offenses. . . . He seemed to learn the lesson. He knew that I was not afraid of calling the police, and I was ready to file a separation or divorce.

QUALITY OF FAMILY LIFE

The view that domestic violence is a crime has led to reliance on criminal justice approaches as official societal responses to the problem. Because early police responses to domestic violence were criticized for not providing enough protection for women's safety (R. E. Dobash & R. P. Dobash, 1979; Langley & Levy, 1977), current legislation has emphasized the protection of women's physical safety. Consequently, criminal justice approaches to domestic violence, including arrests, prosecutions, and punitive sentences, have been created under the deterrence framework, and the absence of recidivism has become a priority for those formulating system responses to domestic violence (Stephens & Sinden, 2000). Pro-arrest policies have been justified under the assumption that arrest promotes the well-being of the victim because it deters reoffending (Wanless, 1996; Zalman, 1992). In fact, the movement toward pro-arrest and mandatory arrest as preferred policies for domestic violence cases has been facilitated by findings from the Minneapolis Experiment indicating that arrests could deter reoffending (Sherman & Berk, 1984). Similarly, the assumption that prosecutions can protect victims from repeated violence has led to pro-prosecution policies that aim at bringing more domestic violence offenders into the criminal justice system to make them responsible for their behavior (Corsilles, 1994).

Although domestic violence occurs among those who have intimate relationships, official interventions in domestic violence are not very much different from those applied to violence between strangers. Because of intimate relationships between the victim and the offender in domestic violence cases, criminal justice approaches that focus on punishing the offender can have negative impacts on the victim. Vietnamese immigrant women who report abuse incidents to law enforcement agencies are seeking not only immediate safety protections but also long-term prevention and their husbands'/partners' reform, which they expect will ultimately improve their family lives. While arrests, prosecutions, and punitive sentences cannot provide long-term protection in most cases, limited safety protection from criminal justice agencies tends to go hand-in-hand with increased emotional abuse and strained family relationships that can lead to family breakups and economic insecurity.

Increased Emotional Abuse and Family Breakups

For most abused Vietnamese immigrant women, emotional abuse by their husbands/partners tends to increase after criminal justice interventions. Reports of abuse incidents to the authorities by the women can be seen as a challenge to the power of their husbands/partners. Subsequent emotional abuse by the men is a reaction of anger and humiliation resulting from their involvement with the criminal justice system. However, they must restrain themselves from using physical violence. Although men often use both physical and emotional abuse to exert their control, they resort to emotional attacks more often when they cannot use physical violence. Because most criminal justice policies for domestic violence refer only to cases involving physical violence, abusive husbands/partners who feel deterred by the law, especially during the criminal justice process or during their probation terms, can turn to emotional abuse to exert their control and/or to retaliate without violating the law. In addition, abused women who do not experience a decrease in physical abuse after criminal justice interventions can still suffer an increase in emotional abuse as a result of their husbands'/partners' retaliation.

Emotional abuse can be any behavior that causes emotional harm or suffering to the victim, such as economic threats, insults, degradation, debasement, the withdrawal of affection, threats of divorce, and distrust. The goal of emotional attacks is much the same as physical assaults because they are both aimed at causing fear, demeaning the victim, or making the victim feel inferior or worthless. Although emotional abuse is not subject to criminal justice sanctions, many abused women consider emotional attacks the worst aspect of the abuse experience (Heise, Pitanguy & Germain, 1994). Ko-Lin Chin (1994) has indicated that language does not cause physical injuries, but many abused women find it difficult to cope with the foul language their spouses use against them in public or in front of other family members. Abusive men often rely on gender ideology, used to define the appropriate role and behavior of women, as a basis for their emotional attacks against their wives/partners. For example, within the context of immigration resettlement,

Vietnamese immigrant women are expected to do the housework, take care of the children, and at the same time contribute to the family income. Women who lack human capital, including education, English proficiency, and vocational skills, are unlikely to successfully adjust to the new situation and perform the triple role of a new immigrant woman. Criticizing wives/partners for not living up to their new gender-role expectations is a way to attack their self-esteem and self-worth, making them feel guilty for their failure to contribute to the family's economic welfare. The threat of divorce also causes fear among dependent women who feel isolated in the new and unfamiliar society but lack a network of family and friends for emotional and financial support. Linh experienced more of her husband's criticism after she called the police to report an abuse incident. Although Linh's husband spent only one night in jail and was not prosecuted, he considered the arrest to be humiliating because it damaged his authority as the husband and the father in the family. Angry but deterred from using force, Linh's husband resorted to emotional attacks. As Linh explained,

Before [the incident] he did not often criticize me because I used to obey him and did what he wanted. If I did not follow his demands, he would use force against me. . . . He had never believed I could call the police. . . . After I went to jail to bail him out, he did not talk to anyone in the family, including the children, for almost two weeks. . . . He made me feel guilty for his arrest. It was a very tense period, and I felt scared all the time, not knowing when his anger would explode. When we started to talk again, he began to criticize me on almost everything . . . even things he wouldn't mind before. He criticized me for not making money and he compared me with other women. That hurt me a lot. I had tried, but I couldn't make good money because I didn't have English. When I argued against him because of his criticism, he said if I couldn't agree with him, he would want to have a divorce.

Unlike Linh, Nga was not criticized or threatened with divorce by her husband. Instead, her husband threatened to kill himself when his demands were not met. Nga was torn by her husband's threat of suicide and his unreasonable demands. Nga talked about her experience as the following,

After the arrest, he didn't hit me anymore, but he still caused me more pain and fear by his threat of suicide. When I didn't do what he wanted, he would threaten to commit suicide either with a gun or with poisons. One time, he asked me to borrow the money he needed to help his friend. I didn't agree because I knew that once he gave money to someone, it would never come back. This had happened so many times because he let his friends exploited him, and he cared about his friends more than his family. . . . We argued against each other to the point when he took out a gun and told me that if I didn't trust him, he would die in front of me. This was not the first time. . . . When I didn't satisfy his sexual demands he would threaten to castrate himself.

Emotional abuse can become unbearable and cause family break-ups, especially when it happens on a daily basis. In some situations, divorce happens not because of criminal justice interventions but because abused women feel that they cannot stay in an abusive relationship. Increased emotional abuse as a result of criminal justice interventions, however, can also lead to family break-ups. Although emotional attacks do not cause physical injuries, they can cause mental injuries and the subsequent deterioration of physical health. Heise, Pitanguy, and Germain (1994) have indicated that humiliation, criticism, and debasement can be more devastating than physical assaults. Influenced by Vietnamese family traditions that emphasize the ideology of marriage, the subordination of women to men, and the presence of the father in the family, Vietnamese immigrant women often try to stay in the relationship, partly because they are concerned with the future of their children, and partly because they have economic and emotional ties with their husbands/partners. Divorce is often seen as the very last resort when physical and/or emotional abuse reaches a level that threatens the women's safety, causes severe damages to her self-esteem, and strains family relationships to the point that family members cannot carry on their normal lives and feel comfortable with each other. Chau had to file for separation, and then divorce, because of increased emotional abuse by her husband following his arrest and the issuance of a restraining order against him. Refraining from using force, Chau's husband began to criticize her so often that she became emotionally exhausted and drained. Although Chau depended on her husband for financial support and had no relatives in the United States, she was forced to leave the relationship to find peace for herself as well as for her children.

Abusive men can also initiate a divorce because of the humiliation caused by their involvement with the criminal justice system. Men who believe in the supremacy of their gender often see domination and domestic violence as a private family matter totally different from street crime. A woman's solicitation from the criminal justice system can stir distrust in men who consider such interventions inappropriate for solving problems between family members. Combined with the breach of trust that threatens their intimate relationship is the embarrassment and insult experienced by arrested husbands/partners who feel that they are treated like street criminals. Diep felt distrusted and was alienated from her boyfriend who decided to end the relationship because he could not deal with the humiliation and embarrassment caused by his arrest for domestic assault. Devastated by her boyfriend's decision to end the relationship, Diep felt guilty over his arrest even though she did not report the incident to the police but instead tried her very best to help him avoid criminal justice sanctions. Diep talked about her experience as follows,

After the criminal justice process was over and shortly after he participated in a batterers' counseling program, he became very mean, very difficult. He became easily irritated and angry with me. He blamed me for his arrest, and that hurt me a lot. In fact, he should understand that I did not report the incident to the police but instead I had done everything I could to help him. . . . He felt humiliated by the arrest and his participation in a counseling program with other batterers who were alcoholics, drug addicts, and macho men. He said he was not a bad person, and he was highly educated, but they treated him like street criminals. . . . He didn't trust me as he used to. Before the incident, we used to share a bank account, although I didn't work and depended on his support. After the incident, he began to send a large part of his salary to his parents, and he no longer discussed with me about our marriage and wedding. . . . I used to think that he was a good man, but I also realized that he had too much self-love that made him become unreasonable and blame me for every bad thing he experienced. . . . I still wanted to stay in the relationship, especially because of my son. I wanted my son to have a family and a father, but I felt very disappointed when he told me he could not continue the relationship without thinking about the incident and the problem.

Besides divorce, loss of child custody was what Lam suffered for her reliance on a legal response to her husband's abuse. As Lam explained,

I knew that he didn't love me; he only wanted to marry me to go to the United States. . . . That would be fine if he was not so violent. Because he had beaten me so many times, I had to called the police for help. . . . After he was arrested and placed on probation, our relationship became very strained. . . . He tried to find my mistakes to criticize me, to make me feel guilty and hurt my self-esteem. He caused me troubles because he wanted to retaliate for his involvement with the law. He accused me for disloyalty and threatened to file a divorce. I felt insulted when he said I fooled around because I had mixed blood and acted like my mother. I found it very difficult to tolerate someone who said bad things about my background and my mother. . . . We finally had a divorce, and I moved on with my new life. However, he was not happy when he learned that I had a boyfriend shortly after the divorce. He felt jealous and planned to retaliate by taking away my custody. He was aware that I received welfare but worked for cash and did not report [income], and he learned that one time I went out late with my boyfriend, leaving the children at home alone. So, he told the court that I didn't have financial resources to provide good care for my children. He also told the court that I neglected the children, and he asked the court to give him custody. . . . I lost the custody because I didn't understand the law to defend myself.

Family breakups are also an unintended consequence of using restraining orders to prevent future physical abuse. Separations required by restraining orders that protect women's physical safety can create opportunities for men to abandon the family or cut off relationships with their wives/partners. Double standards seem to allow men more freedom to engage in sexual relationships, and often men engage in extramarital affairs when, for whatever reasons, they live away from their families. Forced to leave home because of a restraining order, many men feel the need for emotional companionship to heal their damaged egos and self-esteem. A combination of sexual and emotional needs can make men engage in new intimate relationships that, in many situations, lead to family breakups. For women who wish to maintain family relationships, the separations created by restraining orders can become a threat to their family lives. Ly explained her situation as follows,

After he was released from jail, he came to stay with his sister because of the PPO [personal protection order]. . . . He did ask me to remove the order but I didn't agree because I planned to keep the order in force for one year. I thought he had a pattern of violence against me and the children, and I wanted to use the PPO to force him to think about his behavior. A few months after he was forced to move out, I learned that he had a relationship with a co-worker and had moved in with her. I felt hurt and sad. . . . While I didn't know what to do, my children urged me to remove the PPO to let him return home and prevent family breakup. I did what they wanted, but it was too late. He came back and talked with me about divorce. He said he couldn't continue the relationship when I treated him like a stranger. Under his view, only strangers would use the law to solve family problems. . . . He wanted to blame me for the problem because I had called the police and caused him to be arrested and get probation, but I think the real problem was the PPO. Because he could not go home, he had an opportunity to form relationship with another woman, and you know, when men have extramarital affairs, it's hard to break their new relationships.

Problems with Other Family Members

Criminal justice interventions can negatively affect not only the couple's relationship but also those between couples and other family members as well. Because the concept of the family in Vietnamese traditions includes both the nuclear family and members of the extended family, the confrontational nature of criminal justice approaches to domestic violence, which are not consistent with the cultural emphasis on conciliation and family cohesion, can create problematic relationships between abused women and members of their abusers' extended families, including grandparents, parents, and siblings. The collectivist nature of Vietnamese family traditions means that what happens to a person also affects other members in his or her family. A person can rely on the support of his/her family, but when a person does something that causes him/her to "lose face," his/her family also shares the disgrace. Consequently, a woman's report of abuse to the police that causes her husband/partner to be arrested can jeopardize her relationship with her in-laws. On the one hand, her in-laws can resent and blame her for causing their son (or brother) to be arrested. On the other hand, they often pressure her to drop charges and refuse to testify against their son (or brother) in court. Women who disregard these demands can experience hostility or become alienated from the family. Hanh, whose experience with the criminal justice process has been discussed in previous sections, felt alienated and hated by her husband's family. Because she wanted to maintain as good a relationship with her in-laws as possible, especially in the context of immigration where the support network of the extended family was not always available for her and her children, Hanh, like other women in the same situation, asked the court to drop the charges to satisfy the demands of these family members. Nga also deferred to the wishes of her children and dropped the charges against her husband and allowed him to return home while the restraining order was still in effect. As Nga said, "The children didn't agree with their father's violent behavior, but they didn't want their father to be arrested and involved with the law. They wanted their father to go home."

Besides the extended family, abused women who rely on legal approaches for solving domestic violence problems can also experience conflict in relationships with their children as well as their husbands' distant relatives and friends who hold traditional views of women and do not support the intervention of the criminal justice system. Although children may not agree with their fathers' use of force against their mothers, they do not want their fathers arrested and jailed. Because of filial piety traditions in Vietnamese culture, children often want their mothers to help their fathers avoid criminal justice sanctions. When children have good relationships with their fathers but do not understand the dynamics of abuse, they may take the side of their fathers and blame their mothers for the problems. Nguyet had three children under 18 years old who did not want her to call the police to report the violence she experienced. When violence occurred, they tended to blame her for the problem. As Nguyet explained,

The kids loved their father, and they criticized me for yelling all the time. . . . They liked him because he took them to school and to parks, restaurants, or movies on weekends. I couldn't do these things for my kids because I couldn't drive and I didn't have money. Because he didn't give me any money, all I could do for my kids was to feed them and take care of the housework. . . . I had to use food stamps to buy foods for the whole family, but my kids didn't understand my situation. They didn't understand that I was yelling because he treated me badly and made me angry. When he beaten me, the kids went away to hide themselves. When I called the police, they said I was crazy.

Similar to Nguyet, Lan had a strained relationship with her daughter who took the side of her father and blamed Lan for worsening family problems by reporting abuse incidents to the police. Lan was also alienated by her husband's relatives and friends who did not support the use of criminal justice approaches to family problems. Lan talked about her experience this way:

My family life became more strained and more difficult after I reported his violence to the police. . . . Even though my husband spent only one night in jail and was not prosecuted, my daughter didn't agree with my action and thought that I treated my husband too harsh. She was on the side of my husband because he gave her a lot of favor, such as allowing her to use his credit cards, or promising to buy her a new car when she graduated from high school, while I wanted more disciplines for her. . . . His family obviously was on his side. They didn't welcome me to family gathering. His friends also criticized me; some didn't want their wives to socialize with me because they thought I was too Americanized.

While women may experience more difficult relationships with other family members as a result of criminal justice interventions, they are also concerned with the effects of these interventions on the relationships between parents and children. Under Vietnamese family traditions, women often rely on men to raise and discipline children. Because men have the ultimate power in the family as the father, important decisions about the future and the discipline of children are often men's responsibilities. Arrests can undermine the authority of the father in the family and make the task of raising children more difficult. As Linh explained, "I want my children to well behave, to study well, and to have a good future. That's the reason why we left our country to America. . . . After the arrest, the kids' respect for their father declined; they didn't listen to him as often as before. . . . I'm worried because children who don't listen to their parents can go to the wrong way and will have no future."

Financial Costs

Criminal justice interventions in intimate violence also create financial burdens for abused women due to forced family separations as well as the arrests of abusive men. Because most women do not want their husbands/partners in jail, they feel compelled to post bail for their release after the arrest. Bail amounts for misdemeanor domestic violence cases vary widely across jurisdictions, ranging from $100 to $15,000, and can drastically deplete family savings.[1] When bail amounts are beyond the family budget, abused women can accrue debt because they have to borrow the money they need to post bail on behalf of their husbands/partners. Besides money for bail, abused women often have to pay court fees and expenses for their abusive husbands/partners to attend batterers' counseling programs. In principle, court fees and payments for batterers' counseling are the responsibilities of the offender, but the relationship between the victim and the offender in domestic violence means that the costs come from the collective budget. In fact, many abused women want their husbands/partners to get counseled and rehabilitated, and they are willing to pay these fees, hoping that their husbands/partners will change, and their relationships will improve. However, many are disappointed because their husbands/partners fail to attend the counseling programs for which they have paid. When expert testimony is needed for the defense of abusive men, abused women also have to pay the fees to help their husbands/partners avoid involvement with the law as in the case of Nga. Believing that her husband had a mental health problem that caused him to behave violently, Nga spent $15,000 on a mental health evaluation for him, because she hoped a medical certification of his mental illness would help him avoid prosecution.

Abused women can also experience a loss of family income resulting from criminal justice interventions. During arrest and prosecution, a man's work can be disrupted while he is in police custody, in jail, and attending pretrial/trial hearings. Arrest and prosecution also interfere with a woman's job when the victim has to spend time to bail her husband/partner out and participate in the criminal justice process as a witness. Both Ha and her common-law husband worked for minimum wage in a garment factory. The arrest of her husband for domestic assault resulted in a loss of income for both of them. As Ha explained,

I reported his abuse to the police three times, but he was arrested only twice. The first time I called the police, he fled before the police arrived . . . but I had to pay $300 for his first bail, and $500 for the second time. The court returned the money when he appeared in court, but I had to pay $350 court fees for each time. . . . For the most recent arrest, he lost his income for one week. That was because I didn't have money to post bail for him right away, and I needed time to borrow the money. I also lost my income for one week because I had to stay

home to take care of the baby while he was in jail. . . . That was because we took turn to take
care of our baby. We did not have enough money to send the baby to baby-sitter because it
would cost me $300 [a month], and that was a half of my paycheck. . . . He used to make me
so angry that I lost my mind, and I was so stupid to call the police that time. . . . I will never
do it again.

Diep's daily activities were totally disrupted after her boyfriend was arrested as a result of a report by emergency medical staff. She was so worried about her boyfriend's arrest and its influence on their relationship that she devoted all her time
and energy to trying to help him avoid involvement with the law. Diep told her
story as follows,

I couldn't sleep the night he was arrested. I was told that he could be released on bail, so I
called the police and ask them the location of the city jail. . . . The next day, I went to the jail
in the morning and waited for the judge to sign his release at about noontime. I paid $300 for
his bond, but he couldn't return home because it was a no-contact bond. Because he had no
relatives in the area, he had to stay in his office. I felt terrified by the possibility that his
colleagues and his boss would find out about the problem. . . . After I talked with my legal
counsel and learned about the court process, I went to the court and asked for the removal of
the no-contact condition of his bond. Because the judge was not there, I come back the next
day to get the paper work done. . . . One week later, I received a court notification about his
pretrial. My legal counsel explained to me that he would have a criminal record if found
guilty. In fact, he already admitted with the police that he hit me . . . Because I didn't want
him to be prosecuted and to have a criminal record, I went to the D.A. [District Attorney]
and asked that the charges against him be dropped. I went there three times, but the
prosecutor and his assistant didn't want to talk with me when they learned that I wanted to
drop the charge. . . . I tried to find a lawyer for my boyfriend, but those I talked with said the
only thing they could do for him was bargaining for a guilty plea with a reduced sentence or
a probation. I finally asked my legal counsel to represent both of us. . . . That was unusual,
wasn't it? She explained our situation and proposed a deferred sentence plan. I felt so
relieved when the court agreed with the plan.

Van was in a more complicated situation because she had to deal with child custody in a divorce case following the domestic violence. In order to attend all court
hearings as advised by her legal counsel, Van had to change her work schedule to
the night shift so that she could use her day time to go back and forth to court.

   Forced separations resulting from restraining orders aimed at protecting
women's safety may also have a negative impact on their financial situations. Family incomes are substantially affected when men who are the principal providers of
the family move out. Women who stay home to take care of their children and do
housework are most vulnerable to family separations because the departure of
their husbands also means the departure of the family providers. Abusive men often fail to pay for child support until they are required to by the court. For those
who do pay child support, the amount of support is only a small portion of their income, and women have to struggle to find the resources to fill the holes in family
budgets caused by the men's departures. Public assistance is not available to all

who are in need, especially immigrants who do not have American citizenship, and it is not a stable source of income. It can provide abused women only short-term financial support.[2]

Besides loss of income, separations forced by restraining orders can also cause housing difficulties for abused women, creating barriers to using other household property. When abusive men own the residence, the forced separation required by the restraining order often means that abused women have to move out and find housing elsewhere. Abusive men who are required to leave home can also take with them property they used to share with the family, including cars. Trang did not request a restraining order, but the police ordered her husband out of the house in place of his arrest. Trang talked about her experience with financial difficulties after her husband was required to move out. "He left home because the police ordered him out of the house. A few days later, he returned to take both cars with him . . . because the cars were registered under his name. So, my mother and I didn't have cars to take children to school and move around. He also threatened to cut off health care insurance he had bought for the children and me." Diep experienced similar financial problems when she had to move out because her boyfriend felt humiliated by the arrest and decided to terminate the relationship. Because Diep depended on her fiancé's support while in school, the end of the relationship also meant the end of his housing and financial support.

～

Criminal justice interventions in domestic violence produce limited safety effects for Vietnamese immigrant abused women and have negative effects on their family lives. Because of the relationship between the offender and the victim in domestic violence cases, the consequences of criminal justice policies that emphasize arrest, prosecution, punitive sentences, and restraining orders are conditioned by family dynamics. Police interventions can provide immediate protection for abused women using the state's authority to stop the violence, but the goal of preventing future violent behavior through punishment cannot be achieved when abused women, because of their economic and emotional dependency, are unable to invoke the law to empower themselves and fight against abuse. The relationship between the offender and the victim in domestic violence cases also causes abused women to share the negative effects of punitive treatments given to their abusive husbands/partners. Unlike other victims, abused women have to pay the costs of their husbands'/partners' involvement with the criminal justice system, and they easily become the target of resentment by members of the extended family. They also experience retaliation by abusive husbands/partners who use emotional abuse to express anger and control. Economic insecurity is also the price abused women have to pay for their safety when their husbands/partners leave home because of the requirements of restraining orders or because of family breakups resulting from intensified family conflicts after criminal justice interventions.

NOTES

1. Bail amounts for misdemeanor domestic violence cases range between US$100 and US$500 in Lansing (MI), and between US$15,000 and US$25,000 in Orange County (CA) (Personal communications, April 28, 2000).

2. The Illegal Immigration Reform and Responsibility Act of 1996 provides that legal aliens (who do not have American citizenship) do not qualify for most welfare benefits, except for refugees who could receive public assistance for no more than five years.

6

WOMEN'S DIFFERENCES
AND SOCIAL POLICIES

Two decades after new domestic violence policies were implemented, it is apparent that criminal justice approaches may not be successful in combating the domestic violence problem and improving women's safety. As evident in the experiences of Vietnamese immigrant women, most victims of domestic abuse do not report abuse incidents, nor do they favor the arrest and prosecution of their abusers. The effects of criminal justice interventions tend to be limited to immediate protection and short-term prevention, and women's physical safety often coexists with increased emotional abuse and strained family relationships. In many situations, criminal justice interventions also lead to family breakups to the disappointment of women who have relied on the system to end violence and eventually improve family relationships.

Vietnamese immigrant women are not alone in experiencing unsuccessful criminal justice interventions. Abused women in the general population, following contacts with the police, prosecutors, and the court, also realize that the system has limited capacities and investments in helping them or providing meaningful relief from their abusers (Erez & Belknap, 1998a). Findings from many studies suggest that arrests are not effective in deterring subsequent domestic assaults, have no long-term effects, and can increase hostilities (Hirschel et al., 1992; Berk et al., 1992; Dunford et al., 1990; Sherman et al., 1992; Goolkasian, 1986); prosecution and personal protection orders can reduce violence only for cases involving low levels of prior violence and injury (Chaudhuri & Daly, 1992; Fagan et al., 1984). Consequently, few women embrace criminal justice approaches to domestic violence. Estimates of domestic violence incidents reported by women victims vary from less than 10% to 50% (Rimonte, 1989; Hackler, 1991; Kantor & Straus, 1990; Smith & Klein, 1984; Bureau of Justice Statistics, 1995; Dutton, 1995), and the number of women who desire to drop charges and/or refuse to testify for the courts still remains high, ranging from 50% to 80% (Davis & Smith, 1995; Erez & Belknap, 1998a; Ford & Regoli, 1993; Carlson & Nidey, 1995). A close look at the experiences of abused women with criminal justice interventions and the implementation of domestic violence policies suggests that the failure of criminal justice approaches lie in the narrow vision of the policies, which are inconsistent with the nature of the problems and the needs of women victims. The chapter closes with an argument for more effective interventions that focus on attacking the root cause of the problem and addressing abused women's different life experiences and their diverse needs.

THE NARROW VISION OF DOMESTIC VIOLENCE POLICIES

Focusing on the Individual Offender—Overlooking Family Relationships

Traditionally, criminal justice responses to domestic violence have reflected a pattern of indifference. Until the late 1960s and early 1970s, wife beating was considered a private family matter, not a crime. The notions of the preciousness of the family, the sanctity of the home, and the inferior status of women all contributed to differences in criminal justice treatments of domestic violence and other assaultive cases involving strangers (Binder & Meeker, 1992). The most noticeable aspect of traditional criminal justice interventions was the lack of arrests and rigorous prosecution of domestic violence cases (R. E. Dobash & R. P. Dobash, 1979; Sherman & Berk, 1984). Responding police officers often resolved the disputes, threatened the disputants, or asked one of the parties to leave the premises, and then left themselves. Similarly, prosecutors and judges viewed domestic violence as civil and personal matters requiring no serious judicial responses (R. E. Dobash & R. P. Dobash, 1979). Court officials often refused to file charges, but instead pursued quasi-judicial remedies, including conducting informal hearings and writing out mock divorce papers, in an attempt to deter the offenders while avoiding arrests.

Changes, however, in criminal justice responses to domestic violence have occurred since the 1970s when the issue of domestic violence began to get attention from women's advocates and grassroots feminist organizations who took leadership roles in redefining the problem, initiating legislative changes, and altering police and court procedures (Schechter, 1982). Amid the civil rights movement for social change, advocates for battered women gathered and exposed the public to information about wife abuse. Using court records and agencies' statistics, they attempted to gain recognition of wife assaults as a major social problem (Binder & Meeker, 1992). Criticizing police indifference and asserting that inadequate police protection puts women in the danger of continuing domestic abuse, feminist groups and other advocates for battered women asked for more punitive approaches to the problem. After the movement toward arrest as the preferred policy for domestic violence cases was established, efforts of battered women's advocates to campaign for the enforcement of arrest policies through lawsuits and pressures exerted on legislators resulted in subsequent warrantless and mandatory arrest policies (Wanless, 1996).

The same vigor was used in changing state laws to facilitate the prosecution of domestic violence and increase punishments for repeat domestic violence offenders. Under the assumption that prosecution could protect victims from repeated violence, changes included reorganizing prosecutorial activities to ensure effective responses to the complainants, affirming the state interest in controlling domestic violence, and reducing pressure on victims to appear in court (Corsilles, 1994). Consequently, two prosecutorial innovations, the prosecutor-filing charge and the no-drop charge, have been created in an attempt to provide more effective services for victims of domestic violence. It is assumed that requiring the victim to file charges will create an opportunity for the abuser to intimidate her and keep her from pursuing the case. On the contrary, when prosecutors are responsible for signing charges, a strong message would go to the abuser, making it clear that his action is a crime against both society and the victim (Cahn, 1992). No-drop-charge policies are aimed at regulating prosecutors' discretion and emphasizing prosecutors' decisions to charge and pursue cases, regardless of the victim's desire to drop charges (Corsilles, 1994). Concerned over the failure of the criminal justice system to punish domestic violence offenders, states have enacted laws in an effort to improve court responses. The goals of new approaches are to make domestic violence a specific criminal offense that could result in court-mandated treatment, jail terms, and penalty enhancement for repeated offenders, and to create specialized courts to ensure consistent application of punitive sanctions for offenders and appropriate relief to the victims (Carlson & Nidey, 1995; Fagan, 1996).

The move toward the criminalization of family violence tends to emphasize more sanctions and control of offenders than the protection of victims' safety and family lives. In principle, criminalization serves a symbolic purpose, indicating the moral unacceptability of domestic violence (Stark, 1993). It also has the instrumental purpose of deterrence (specific and general) that enables the state to intervene (Hoyle & Sanders, 2000). Women's advocacy groups that have supported and lobbied for the criminalization of domestic violence expect that it will serve the goal of protecting women victims through the mobilization of legal institutions to take action (Fagan, 1988). Under the assumption of the deterrence framework, arrest, prosecution, and punitive treatment of the offender will prevent future offending. In pursuing victim protection goals, advocates for battered women have also asked criminal justice agencies to refocus their efforts on the protection of victims through the coordination of extralegal and legal services and the development of referral linkages designed to expand the web of social control (Fagan, 1988). This perspective, however, differs from the traditional goals of criminal justice institutions that focus on the assailant, detection, and punishment of crime. Specifically, pro-arrest policies have been created to make police responses to family violence more aggressive, and to address the problem of victims' noncooperation, so that the probability of arrests will increase and the likelihood that sanctions will be forthcoming (Hoyle & Sanders, 2000). Because the effectiveness of interventions is measured mainly in terms of criminal justice sanctions—namely the number of arrests, prosecutions, and convictions—victim assistance programs affiliated with law enforcement agencies are also geared to sustaining victims' commitment to the prosecution efforts but not about protecting them from further violence. Corcoran, Stephenson, Perryman, and Allen (2001) have asserted that the central goal of a police-social work crisis intervention service is to increase the cooperation of victims of domestic violence with the arrest and ultimately the prosecution of the offender; a secondary goal is to increase the efficiency and effectiveness of domestic violence investigations.

Prosecution innovations, including prosecutor-filing-charge and no-drop-charge policies, that emphasize the aggressiveness of prosecution are intended to increase the percentage of cases formally prosecuted and ensure appropriate court treatment of domestic violence cases reported to the police (Fagan, 1988). Other developments in prosecutorial responses to wife assault are aimed at improving the efficiency and effectiveness of the prosecution function in terms of successful convictions. These include victim-witness programs established to provide counsel and referrals to critical social services for victims; legal advocacy to expedite hearings and notification of appearances whenever possible; and special prosecution programs to provide incentives for vigorous prosecutions without competition with other units for scarce investigative or trial resources (Fagan, 1988).

Along with arrest and prosecution, court-mandated treatment of battering is essential to the objective of reducing recidivism (Dutton, 1995). A main element of the punishment package for domestic violence offenders, mandatory battering treatment is considered a form of control that strengthens the traditional probation sanction and a means to protect abused women who choose not to dissolve their relationships, but whose violent partners do not seek treatment voluntarily (Fagan, 1988). Despite the diversity in therapeutic models and approaches, most treatment programs are based on the social control model and reflect personal explanations of domestic violence by stressing offenders' responsibility and behavioral control. Feminist-oriented therapy approaches that call for the resocialization of men, the redirection of men's views of women and gender roles, as well as men's instrumental use of violence to retain power and domination are inconsistent with the social control model of probation supervision and are not often included in the current development of treatment models (Fagan, 1988).

Criminal justice interventions that emphasize punishing the offender have overlooked the reality of women's lives, particularly family relationships and family dynamics. Established within the social organization of the legal system, criminal justice interventions have been modeled on cases involving strangers whose nature is different from that of domestic violence cases involving intimate partners. In fact, battered women are different from most crime victims because of their intimate relationships with the assailants. The adversarial nature of the American legal system creates an inherent paradox for abused women who attempt to use the criminal justice system to solve domestic violence cases because a woman's adversary in the court is also her husband/partner at home (Jones, 1994). Although proponents of criminal justice approaches consider arrests and prosecutions resources for abused women to fight domestic violence, many abused women cannot use these resources to solve the problem because, unlike victims in stranger-assault cases, they are often controlled by their abusers. In addition, arrests and/or prosecutions can become a threat to family relationships when punishing the offender also results in indirect punishment for the victim, financially and emotionally.

Similar to criminal justice interventions, feminist-oriented victim services also overlook family relationships. By focusing their attention on the woman victim and the protection of abused women from further harm, most victim services pay little attention to the family unit as a whole. Although many abused women want to improve family relationships, victim advocacy programs believe that there is a conflict of interest in serving both the victim and a family unit that includes her victimizer (Fagan, 1988). Instead, victim service agencies support criminal justice approaches and at the same time emphasize leaving the abusive relationship as the best way to protect women's safety. Despite the fact that many women do not want their husbands/partners to suffer under the law, victim services providers tend to believe that criminal justice treatments of domestic violence offenders are still too light to send a deterrent message (Erez & Belknap, 1998b). Victim service programs also set up shelters, provide housing assistance and legal counseling for divorce and child custody to encourage women pursuing legal remedies, or help victims avoid violence by getting away and staying away from their abusers (Hoyle & Sanders, 2000; Peled et al., 2000).

Not all abused women, however, consider leaving their husbands/partners or separation as viable options for their situations. Many women resist leaving because it is contrary to the ideology of marriage and the norm of heterosexuality. For these women, relationships and family units are important because marrying and maintaining intimacy are highly valued by the state and religious institutions while divorce and separation are considered failures that should be avoided (Ferraro & Pope, 1993). The need for family relationships is particularly great among immigrants not only because of the traditional values of the immigrant community that emphasize women's subordination and the importance of marriage for women, but also because of social isolation resulting from the process of immigration to the United States. For immigrant women who have left the network of the extended family behind in their county of origin and who feel isolated in the unfamiliar setting and culture of the new society, family relationships are important because the family is their only source of support during financial and emotional crises. Economic isolation also causes immigrant women to depend, totally or partly, on their husbands/partners to meet the financial obligations of everyday life. Because domestic violence interventions do not provide options for women who wish to end the violence while staying with their partners, abused women often have to make a choice between personal safety and family life.

Women's Disempowerment

The criminalization of domestic violence, originally conceived by the battered women's movement as the politics of liberation, has inadvertently become an impediment to women's freedom as criminal justice interventions impose more constraints on women's responses to domestic abuse. Battered women are supposed to be empowered by criminal justice resources to take action and fight domestic violence, but they are, in many cases, totally controlled by the criminal justice process. Mandatory arrest and no-drop prosecution policies have limited the intervention options deemed appropriate to a woman's life circumstances. In fact, not all women equate calling the police with the arrest and/or criminal prosecution of their husbands/partners; many only want the police to stop the violence (Hoyle & Sanders, 2000). This was evident in this current study of Vietnamese immigrant women. However, under mandatory arrest and prosecution laws, women victims have little control over the direction of the cases. No-drop-charge and enhanced penalty policies also undermine women's agency by denying women victims the ability to make choices for themselves. Many women victims turn to the criminal justice system for help in ending domestic abuse but still want to continue the relationship with their abusers. Policies that require the victim to testify against the defendant and a jail sentence for the latter often produce results contrary to the wishes of the victim.

While arrests and prosecutions cannot guarantee women's safety, they can cause abused women to experience further victimization. Besides pain, fear, and confusion resulting from physical attacks, women victims often experience additional anxiety and frustration, or helplessness, when their family lives are subject to unsolicited interventions. They are also blamed for having initiated the whole process by calling the police, and they often become the target of emotional abuse and retaliation by their husbands/partners after criminal justice interventions. Because arrests, prosecutions, and leaving the abusive relationships are the only options offered to women victims, those who wish to avoid these legal consequences have to refrain from reporting violent incidents and continue suffering abuse.

Besides these laws, the organizational goals of criminal justice agencies charged with enforcing domestic violence laws also contribute to the process of disempowering women when they fail to provide women victims with the resources they need to fight and avoid domestic violence. By emphasizing the organizational goal of securing convictions through successful prosecutions, criminal justice agencies have overlooked the victims and become insensitive to their needs. Women victims who have special needs, including those who face language barriers and who experience financial and cultural constraints on their decision to rely on criminal justice approaches, do not receive adequate and appropriate assistance to participate in the criminal justice process. Women victims whose needs are not addressed often feel alienated, abandoned, and/or excluded from the process that is supposed to help them fight domestic abuse.

The arrest of women in domestic violence cases also represents another negative aspect of mandatory arrest laws. Dual arrests in which women who respond to abuse by fighting back are arrested along with their abusers, or sole arrests where police respond to men's reports, serve to diminish women's efforts to combat domestic violence, thereby reinforcing men's domination. In fact, most women use violence for self-defense against physical attacks by their partners, or in response to long-term physical and/or emotional abuse. The neutrality of legal language, however, provides the context for the police to view attacking by men and self-defense by women as mutual combat (Ferraro, 1993). The concept of mutual combat is problematic because it overlooks the power dynamics in intimate relationships, the nature of domestic violence, and women's experience of abuse. The arrest of a battered woman who has defended herself not only fails to deter the abuser and protect the victim but also revictimizes the victim by forcing her to undergo the same arrest procedure as the offender and, at the same time, provides her abuser with a justification for his use of violence (Wanless, 1996). Consequently, battered women subjected to arrest are dissuaded from calling the police when subsequent violence occurs.

Mandatory arrest and prosecution laws appear to be gender-blind as they are applied equally to men and women but they, in fact, inadvertently reinforce women's subordination. Women and men do not experience gender-blind social relationships; instead, gender-biased social practices have placed women in disadvantaged situations relative to men. By focusing only on violent acts and promoting standardized responses to domestic violence, mandatory arrest and prosecution policies prevent criminal justice agencies from differentiating between violence by women and violence by men within the context of intimate relationships. Instead, they apply the same standard that has been created to deal with domestic violence by men to women who are charged with domestic violence (Hooper, 1996). Mandatory arrest laws were created because it is well known that abused women who are under emotional and financial control by their partners are unlikely to report and tend to deny abuse. These laws require arrest when there is evidence, often reported by women victims and/or visible injuries, that violence has occurred. This standard of evidence, however, is not consistent with the experience of many abused women who use violence for self-defense, and women whose husbands/partners have learned how to manipulate the system and make false reports to exert their control (Miller, 2001). On the other hand, women's actual experiences of abuse are rarely taken into judicial consideration because women do not often report abuse incidents, therefore they are unable to use police records to show evidence of past abuse as required by the court. When the same amount of bail is applied regardless of the gender of the accused, women are unlikely to have the same experience of pretrial release as men do because women tend to have fewer financial resources and often depend on their male abusers financially. The application of criminal justice standards based on men's experience to women not only creates loopholes for abusive men to use the law as a tool to dominate, but also undermines abused women's efforts to rely on government interventions to solve the problem of domestic violence.

WOMEN'S EMPOWERMENT, WOMEN'S CHOICE, AND SOCIAL POLICIES

Structural Inequality and Women's Empowerment

Criminal justice approaches to domestic violence that emphasize the sanction of offenders through arrests and prosecutions are more consistent with individual explanations of family violence than with the root cause of the problem that lies in the social structure of gender relations (Fagan, 1988). The traditional division of labor by gender creates the subordination of women to male authority making women economically dependent on men by assigning women the responsibility for domestic work, child care, and emotional support. Laws and rules established by the state as well as religious and political institutions have reinforced women's subordination and institutionalized the control of women by their husbands/partners.

Historically, major institutions have permitted and condoned the use of physical abuse by husbands to control wives. The first law of marriage, proclaimed by Romulus in Rome in the eighth century BC, obliged married women to conform themselves entirely to the temper of their husbands who had the right to rule their wives as inseparable possessions (Martin, 1987). English common law upon which American jurisprudence is based gave a man the right to beat his wife with a whip or rattan no bigger than his thumb to enforce the salutary restraints of domestic discipline (Calvert, 1975). Under the guise of privacy rights and state non-interference in private family spheres, American common law permitted the husband to discipline and beat his wife unless it became excessive (Chaudhuri & Daly, 1992). In 1824, the Mississippi Supreme Court ruled that the husband could administer moderate chastisement and use salutary restraints in every case of misbehavior without being prosecuted (*Bradley v. State*, cited in Calvert, 1975). When wife beating became illegal in most states, the failure to enforce the laws amounted to the recognition of the husband's right to use force to control his wife. For example, in 1874 the North Carolina Supreme Court, arguing for the sanctity of the family, decided that the state would not intervene when there were no severe injuries involved or when a husband's behavior was not malicious, cruel, or dangerous (*State v. Oliver*, 1874). Patterns of indifference in criminal justice responses to domestic violence persisted until the 1970s when policies attempted to give victims of domestic violence the same treatments as victims in stranger-assault cases.

Changes in criminal justice responses to domestic violence have addressed only one aspect of the structure of unequal gender relations, which is the practice of the state condoning men's violence against women. However, social structures that perpetuate men's control of women still exist. The arrest and prosecution of men who batter women cannot change women's economic dependency, or give abused women social resources to enhance their economic status and change the power dynamics in relationships (Ferraro, 1993). In many situations, criminal justice interventions even create economic hardships for women victims. Domestic violence laws cannot do much to change social definitions of masculinity and femininity as well as the ideology of marriage and romantic love that cause women's emotional dependency on men, reinforce women's subordination, and prevent women from breaking the cycle of domestic abuse.

Criminal justice interventions can give domestic violence victims the confidence to do something about the problem, but they have little or no effect unless they are coupled with more direct supportive actions aimed at improving women's status and changing power dynamics within women's family lives. Since the battered women's movement emerged following the growth of the women's movement in the 1960s, advocates for battered women have sought to empower victims of domestic violence by providing shelters, economic assistance, and support groups, and influencing institutional change through the criminalization of domestic violence. Unfortunately, these efforts have a limited impact on changing women's status in the family when these programs are geared to helping women participate in the legal process against their husbands/partners and preparing them to leave the abusive relationship. In addition, while the rhetoric and ideology of empowerment have been served as a guiding principle for interventions, attempts to operationalize the means by which abused women can become empowered are scarce (Peled et al., 2000).

Empowerment theory is based on the assumption that the capacity of people to improve their lives is determined by their ability to control their environment; therefore, powerless individuals or groups become empowered when they gain access to resources (Busch & Valentine, 2000). Empowerment practice facilitates the acquisition of skills, knowledge, emotional as well as material resources aimed at enabling people to master their environment and achieve self-definition (Peled et al., 2000). Abused women are often disadvantaged in the relationship because of their lack of economic resources and a social structure and culture that emphasizes men's power and control. When violence occurs, economic dependency and culturally created women's roles and responsibilities are impediments to their efforts to escape abuse. Thus, empowerment practices must address the structural aspects of the problem in order to be effective. While changing social structures will take time, empowering women victims by providing them with support and resources to reduce the impact of structural inequalities can improve their ability to fight domestic abuse and avoid violence in ways appropriate to their own situations.

Women's Differences and Women's Choices

Women are not a homogeneous group in their circumstances and in their needs. Although all women want to avoid violence, they have different perceptions about solutions to the problem and different needs regarding support for stopping abuse. Women victims may choose to use criminal justice resources to deter future violence, to leave the abusive relationship, or to work with their partners on changes in their relationships, hoping to put an end to the violence and keep the family intact to protect their children. Because abused women bear the burden that this decision making places on them, they have to calculate the costs and benefits in light of their own circumstances. For example, when the cost of interventions outweighs their benefits and leads to more violence, economic hardship, or family breakups, abused women may be less concerned with deterrence than they are with protecting their own safety and the economic security of their children. The empowerment of battered women is achieved not through obedience to the expectations of legal advocates or models, but through acknowledgment of the needs of women victims (Mills, 1996).

There have been gaps, however, between battered women's choices and the solutions commonly offered to them by victim advocates (Mills, 1996; Schechter, 1982). It is commonly assumed that abused women are trapped in violent relationships by external (economic and sociocultural) or internal (psychopathological) factors, and freedom from violence entails leaving the abusers (Peled et al., 2000). This assumption is reflected in increasing numbers of social services and intervention strategies developed to support battered women and their children before, during, and after separation from the perpetrators (Dutton, 1992; Hart, 1991; Kirwood, 1993; Sullivan, 1991). This assumption is also evident in reports describing service providers' goals and standards for success and failure in interventions with battered women and in research designs aimed at understanding why women return to their abusers after a stay in a shelter (Davis, 1988; Gondolf, 1988; McKeel & Sporakowski, 1993; Okun, 1988; Schwartz, 1988; Strube & Barbour, 1983, 1984). Over time, however, women continue to resist the cultural scripts directing them to get away and stay away from their abusers as this study and others have found (Baker, 1997; Mehrotra, 1999).

Facilitating women's freedom of choice as a mechanism for empowerment implies accepting and respecting their choice to stay with their abusers as a viable alternative (Peled et al., 2000). Fed up with abuse, many women left the relationships, but economic hardship caused them to return to their abusive husbands/partners (Okun, 1988; Strube & Barbour, 1983, 1984). This study suggests that women's economic dependency needs to be conceptualized more broadly to include absolute dependency when abused women totally depend on their husbands/partners for financial support, and relative dependency when abused women depend on their husbands'/partners' incomes to maintain their existing lifestyles. In fact, not only unemployed women and women who work in low-paying jobs but also women who earn decent incomes are reluctant to use the criminal justice approach to deal with intimate abuse. While unemployed women and women working in low-paying jobs need their husbands'/partners' incomes to make ends meet, women who earn decent incomes also need their husbands'/partners' incomes to maintain a middle-class lifestyle, or to give their children better care and a better education. For many abused women, staying is the result of a rational decision-making process based on weighing the perceived cost and benefits in the context of a multidimentional relationship. A woman's decision to stay acknowledges not only the constraints that prevent battered women from leaving, but also the positive feelings and perceptions that they may hold regarding their partners and the relationship, namely their love for their partners, their hope that he will change, and their desire that their children maintain a relationship with their father (Schechter, 1982).

Victim advocates also endorse criminal justice approaches and focus on offering support and information expected to encourage victims to pursue legal remedies (Hoyle & Sanders, 2000). For women who are fed up with abuse and want to end the abuse and/or the relationships, criminal justice interventions can be a resource to deal with the situation. In a study conducted by Edna Erez and Joanne Belknap (1998a), the overwhelming majority of participants (98%) cooperated with police requests for information, and the reasons for their cooperation were to protect themselves and to have the offenders arrested or brought to justice. Retribution was a rationale offered by women who wanted their partners to be arrested (Hoyle & Sanders, 2000). Arrest is also sought by women who want to separate, temporarily or permanently, from their abusers (Hoyle & Sanders, 2000). Although criminal justice interventions can give battered women immediate protection and short term prevention, not all women who need safety protection and who contact criminal justice agencies for help to end the violence favor an arrest or prosecution.

Jill Radford and Elizabeth Stanko (1991) have suggested that criminal justice interventions are more appealing to women in mainstream America, but these interventions do not address the needs and concerns of victims who belong to other racial/ethnic groups. Indeed, the intersection of race, class, and gender has created a matrix of domination that shapes the personal, cultural, and social contexts of women's experiences and causes minority women to experience multiple oppressions (Zinn & Dill, 1994). Interventions that seem to be neutral in terms of gender, class, and race in principle are, in fact, insensitive to the plight of women who experience multiple disadvantages not only because of their gender, but also because of their low status in the hierarchies of class and race. Unlike white women, women of color are more aware of racial discrimination in American society. Although they want to stop the violence, many of them do not want their husbands/partners to experience racial discrimination in the criminal justice system. In this study in particular, fear of racial discrimination against their husbands/partners or themselves deterred many women victims from reaching out to criminal justice agencies for help, and personal experiences of racial prejudice stopped women victims from reporting abuse incidents.

The cultural norms of ethnic minority communities impose an additional level of constraint on women's response to abuse. For example, Chinese, South Asian, and Vietnamese women face tremendous pressures when trying to break through the abusive cycle within the cultural milieu of their communities (Lee & Au, 1998; Dasgupta & Warrier, 1996). For women who grew up in the cultural traditions that emphasize collectivism, family privacy, and women's sacrifice, seeking help from outside the family, let alone from inside the criminal justice system, will damage the reputation of their families and result in the "loss of face" for the abusers and other family members. Perceptions of women's appropriate behaviors, women's place, and women's family responsibilities that are shaped by culture also discourage abused women from seeking help from outside the family, or using any approaches that may cause a separation between the husband and wife and between the parents and children. Concerns for their safety cause women victims to call the police, but most of these women do not want an arrest and prosecution. Although they seek government help to stop the violence, they do not want government interventions to jeopardize their relationships and family lives.

Unlike native-born women, immigrant women struggle with legal dependency, fear of deportation, as well as economic and cultural isolation. While deterrence theory assumes that punishing domestic abusers will deter future violence, many abused immigrant women are deterred from reporting abuse incidents by their concern that a prosecution or conviction will result in the deportation of their husbands/partners. Women who entered the United States under the sponsorship of their husbands/partners are reluctant to use the criminal justice approach to deal with abuse because they fear that their abusers may retaliate and may not want to help them complete the paperwork to obtain legal status in the United States as required by the law. Cultural and economic adaptation can improve immigrant women's independence; however, the adaptation process is not the same for all as it is a function of socioeconomic conditions and the division of labor that gives immigrant women opportunities to learn the new language, pursue an education, and initiate contact with mainstream society.

Women have different expectations for domestic violence interventions because they experience different levels of constraints. Depending on their own circumstances and the resources available to them, women victims can invoke different levels of criminal justice interventions to bargain for their safety. For many women, calling the police for help excludes a desire for punishment; instead, it includes a hope for long-term protection through deterrence and improved family relationships through the rehabilitation of their partners. Women victims are not passive recipients of social or legal interventions, but they often make decisions by considering consequences of various legal interventions, including effects on their safety, the couple's finances and relationship, the welfare of the children, and women's connection to the extended family and the community. Women's empowerment entails more than providing resources; it also requires improving women's ability to use social resources under a strategy appropriate for their situations.

Women want the violence to stop but not at all costs. Because the desires of women victims are complex and shaped by their experiences of gender, class, and race relations as well as culture, treating women victims of domestic violence as a common group ignores their many differences. Focusing on the diverse needs of women victims also requires broadening the goals of interventions to include stopping the violence and preserving the family life of those who are in need. The one-size-fits-all solution to domestic violence, namely the criminal justice approach, is unlikely to alleviate the problems but likely to deepen the sense of powerlessness and exacerbate the frustration when the result of intervention is in contrast to the victim's wishes (Erez & Belknap, 1998a). It has been argued that abused women should not bear the burden of making arrest or prosecution decisions because they are under the control of their abusers (Stark, 1993). However, taking away women's choices is by no means equal to giving them freedom. The task of women's empowerment is to reduce the social constraints on women's lives and to make their choices reflect their freedom and self-determination. More importantly, however, effective approaches to domestic violence must focus on correcting gender inequalities and improving women's status to eliminate the root cause of the problem.

Appendix A

About the Study

THE SETTING

My plan to study the experiences of abused immigrant women with criminal justice interventions began after I conducted a pilot study on domestic violence among Vietnamese immigrant families and established contacts with abused Vietnamese immigrant women through my volunteer work with a victim service agency located in a city with a small Vietnamese population. Although no existing official information on characteristics of the Vietnamese immigrant population at the state level was available, I found in the literature on immigration resettlement that socioeconomic conditions and the adaptation of Vietnamese immigrants differed across states, depending on available resettlement programs and funding (Office of Refugee Resettlement, 1993). In addition, criminal justice policies dealing with domestic violence also varied across states and police departments. As these differences would allow an examination of women's diverse experiences within various structural, cultural, and legal contexts, I decided to expand the location of my study to include Vietnamese communities in four different geographical areas in the United States: 1) Orange County, California (the West Coast); 2) Houston, Texas (the South); 3) Boston, Massachusetts (the East Coast); and 4) Lansing, Michigan (the Midwest).

The Vietnamese community in Orange County (CA), with the nickname "Little Saigon," is the largest Vietnamese community in the United States. It was estimated that one out of every four Vietnamese immigrants to California since the 1975 had settled in Orange County (Martell & M. Tran, 2000a). From 1990 to 1996 almost 45,000 legal immigrants from Vietnam arrived in Orange County, adding to the official count of 71,000 in 1990 (Martell & M. Tran, 2000a). With almost 120,000 Vietnamese residents and more than 2,000 small businesses concentrated in four cities, including Westminster, Santa Ana, Garden Grove, and Anaheim, Little Saigon has become the commercial and spiritual capital of Vietnamese immigrants in the United States. Vietnamese residents in Orange County have followed the traditional path to the resettlement and integration of new immigrants to American society and created changes in the profile of the Little Saigon population during the last 25 years. As many of the first-wave Vietnamese immigrants who came mostly from the privileged and military ranks of South Vietnam expanded their residency from the core neighborhood in Westminster to far more affluent regions, including Fountain Valley, Irvine, Fullerton, and Pomona, new arrivals who often came from lower socioeconomic strata moved in and filled the area. During the period between 1986-1996 nearly two-thirds of Vietnamese immigrants in Orange County were students, unemployed, or retirees; laborers and manufacturing workers made up the largest single employment category, accounting for about 10% of Vietnamese immigrants (Martell & M. Tran, 2000a).

Regardless of the traditional path of the community growth and assimilation pattern reflected in the abandonment of the Vietnamese language among children of immigrants, Vietnamese immigrants in Little Saigon, particularly the first-generation immigrants, still retain strong ties to the language and culture of their homeland. A recent media poll showed that most Vietnamese in Little Saigon (93%) viewed themselves as more Vietnamese than American, and two-thirds of them were more comfortable speaking Vietnamese than English (M. Tran, 2000). Because the assimilation to American culture may create changes that strike at the heart of Vietnamese family traditions and generational hierarchy, Vietnamese immigrants in Little Saigon considered assimilation a very serious problem facing the community: only behind crime but above their concerns about discrimination and difficulties in the job market (Martell & M. Tran, 2000b). News and entertainment media in the Vietnamese language are considered the greatest force for conserving Vietnamese culture in Orange County. In a survey of Vietnamese immigrants in Orange County in 2000, 80% of the respondents indicated that they received some or all of their news from Vietnamese newspapers or magazines; more than half of the respondents reported that they listened to Vietnamese radio broadcasting programs every day (Martell & M. Tran, 2000b). The survey also found that three-fourths of young Vietnamese immigrants in Orange County watched Vietnamese videos at least once a week.

Despite a large concentration of Vietnamese residents and numerous social services for the Vietnamese population in four adjacent cities (Westminster, Garden Grove, Anaheim, and Santa Ana), services for Vietnamese victims of domestic violence are scarce. No women's shelter that has Vietnamese staff is located in or near Little Saigon. Orange County has a large counseling program for Vietnamese batters, but no program for Vietnamese victims of domestic violence. Within the criminal justice system, many Vietnamese Americans have worked for the police force in Orange County for many years, but only one city (Garden Grove) has a male police liaison with a Vietnamese background. This officer's responsibility is to provide assistance for all Vietnamese victims of crime, including victims of domestic violence. Interpretation services for those who cannot speak English are provided at different stages in the criminal justice process (the police and the court), but all Vietnamese interpreters, including those who assist female victims of intimate violence, are male. Furthermore, no Vietnamese staff works in victim assistance programs in the Orange County courts.

The second location of my study is the Vietnamese community in Houston (Texas). Located in the southern part of Texas next to the Gulf Coast, Houston has become the home for many Vietnamese immigrants since 1975. The Vietnamese community in Houston experienced a rapid increase in population during the last 10 years with new immigrants from Vietnam and secondary migrants from other states. At the time of the 1990 Census, about 32,500 Vietnamese immigrants had resettled in Houston (United States Census Bureau, cited in H. Nguyen & Haines, 1996). By 1999, the number of Vietnamese Americans in Houston had reached 52,500, making the Vietnamese community in Houston the third largest in the United States (Gold & M. Tran, 2000). Besides an increase in population, the Vietnamese community in Houston also expanded geographically. With an initial concentration around downtown Houston, Vietnamese businesses and residents have moved outward to the southwest region of Houston and created a large Vietnamese business center similar to the business center in Little Saigon in Orange County (CA). As in Little Saigon, Vietnamese media in Houston, including more than a dozen radio stations, newspapers, magazines, and a cable TV network, have become a major part of the Vietnamese community life. However, unlike in the tightly knit Vietnamese enclave in Orange County, Vietnamese residents and businesses in Houston are less concentrated; instead, these residents tend to mingle with other ethnic groups in the local area.

The Vietnamese community in Houston, although smaller than Little Saigon in size, provides more services for Vietnamese victims of intimate violence. A large women's center that has Vietnamese staff is located near the Vietnamese business center in downtown Houston. Many Vietnamese Americans also serve in the Houston Police Department and often provide interpretation services in person or on the phone for those who have contacts with the police but cannot speak English. Particularly, the Domestic Violence Unit of the Houston Police Department has a Vietnamese woman police liaison whose responsibility is to assist Vietnamese victims of domestic violence. Vietnamese staff of the police force and the women's center also contacts Vietnamese staff in other social service agencies, including the court and public welfare offices, to coordinate supportive services for Vietnamese victims of domestic violence.

The third site of my study is a small Vietnamese community in Lansing (MI). Because of cold weather, few Vietnamese immigrants chose Michigan for resettlement. Although official statistics about the Vietnamese population in Lansing are not available, estimates by the community leaders were that about 3,000 to 4,000 Vietnamese immigrants have resettled in Lansing since 1975. Despite a small Vietnamese population, the Vietnamese community in Lansing has enough resources to serve the special cultural needs of its residents. The community has its own

Catholic church and a Buddhist temple where Vietnamese residents can meet and participate in many cultural activities. A few services for Vietnamese victims of domestic violence are also available. Interpretation assistance for those who cannot speak English is coordinated by the court and the local refugee service agencies. In addition, a Vietnamese volunteer for a victim assistance program often assists Vietnamese victims who face language barriers.

The fourth site of my study is the Vietnamese community in Boston (MA). Located on the East Coast, Boston has cold weather similar to that in Lansing. However, the Vietnamese community in Boston has experienced an increase in population during the last 10 years due to a healthy labor market in the local area. By the time of the 1990 Census, almost 10,000 Vietnamese immigrants had chosen Boston and its surrounding areas as their home. By 1999, it was estimated that almost 12,000 Vietnamese had resettled in the greater Boston area, an increase of 20% (Gold & M. Tran, 2000). Most new Vietnamese immigrants live and run their businesses in Dorchester—a small city located in the outskirts of downtown Boston—and form a small ethnic enclave, but many other Vietnamese are integrated into the mainstream population.

Although the Vietnamese community in Boston is much smaller than its counterpart in Orange County, its residents can access many additional services for Vietnamese victims of domestic violence. An Asian women's shelter in Boston is a main service provider for abused Vietnamese immigrant women. Other agencies, including the Boston Police Department as well as many health care and refugee resettlement agencies also have domestic violence units staffed with Vietnamese case workers who provide counseling, interpretation, and referral services for Vietnamese victims of domestic violence. Vietnamese staff in different agencies also coordinates their services to address the diverse needs of abused Vietnamese immigrant women in Boston.

Police departments in these four locations apply mandatory arrest policies that require law enforcement officials to make arrests without warrants when there is evidence that domestic violence has ocurred. However, there are variations in the implementation of mandatory arrest policies in terms of the level of rigidity. For example, police departments in Orange County tend to apply "zero-tolerance" policies while law enforcement officers in Houston take into account, to some extent, the victim's preference for arrest. Case processing as well as punishment for domestic violence offenses also varies across these four locations. Cases are processed more quickly in California and Lansing than in Houston and Boston. Domestic violence offenders in Orange County also receive harsher treatment. A sentence of three years on probation, three months of community service, and 52 weeks of counseling for the least severe domestic violence case (first time misdemeanor) is typical. On the other hand, punishment for a similar offense in Lansing and Houston is a combination of six months on probation and 15 weeks of counseling. With regard to restraining orders, a trial judge in Orange County can issue one order against an intimate violence offender on the basis of his/her judgment regardless of the victim's request. If the victim does not want the restraining order, he/she has to request its removal. On the other hand, domestic violence victims in Houston can obtain an emergency restraining order via police officers who respond to domestic violence calls and who will contact a judge on behalf of these victims. In Lansing and Boston, those who need a restraining order must go to the family court to make the request. Differences between these four locations in terms of their population sizes, levels of ethnic isolation, the salience of Vietnamese culture in the community life, criminal justice policies regarding domestic violence, and supportive services for Vietnamese victims of domestic abuse all have important impacts on the experiences of Vietnamese immigrant women with criminal justice interventions in intimate violence.

SAMPLE SELECTION AND INTERVIEWS

Consistent with the feminist standpoint approach that considers the location and the perspective of study participants as essential for understanding social phenomena, a major source of data for my study was in-depth interviews with a core sample of Vietnamese immigrant women who had experienced abuse by an intimate partner, such as a husband, an ex-husband, boyfriend, or ex-boyfriend. In order to identify factors associated with women's decisions to rely on criminal justice interventions, I selected a purposive sample that included both abused women who had contacts with the criminal justice system and those who did not. The majority of women participants (23) were recruited through referrals from victim service agencies, including a victim assistance program in Lansing; two women's centers in Boston and Houston; a batterers' counseling program in Orange County; and a public law center in Orange County. The rest of the women participants were recruited through two Vietnamese radio talk shows on women's issues in Houston and Orange County (7 women) and referrals from my acquaintances (4 women). These efforts yielded a sample of 34 Vietnamese immigrant women (10 in Orange County; 9 in Houston; 8 in Boston; 7 in Lansing). By the time of the interviews, all women participants had experienced physical and emotional abuse by an intimate partner; of these women, six had been charged with a domestic offense.

Interviews with women in the core sample were conducted in 2000. Depending on the situation, each interview lasted from two to three hours. The majority of interviews (28) were conducted face-to-face; six women were interviewed via telephone upon their requests. The Vietnamese language was used in all interviews, except one in which Vietnamese was mingled with English. In this case, the woman was not fluent in Vietnamese but tried to use it during the interview because she, like many other Vietnamese immigrants, did not consider English an appropriate language for conversations between Vietnamese people.

The second source of data for the study was drawn from interviews with a community sample consisting of Vietnamese Americans who had contacts with abused Vietnamese immigrant women through their jobs. Although feminist scholarship emphasizes the importance of women subjects' direct experiences (Gorelick, 1991;

Harding, 1991; Smith, 1990), the views of those who are knowledgeable of the community life and who have contacts with abused women are also useful because they can provide additional understanding about the social and cultural contexts in which battering and responses to abuse occur. Writing about rape, R. Campbell (1996, p. 39) reasons that people who advocate for rape victims can provide unique information because they stand with "one foot in the world of the . . . victims and one foot in the world of community help systems, and carry the responsibility of mutual translation." The community sample was composed of 11 Vietnamese Americans (seven women and five men), including two hosts of Vietnamese radio talk shows, three counselors for batterers' treatment programs, two coordinators of victim service agencies, two police liaisons, one social worker, and one defense lawyer. Most respondents participated in face-to-face interviews that lasted an hour each. The interview was unstructured but oriented toward the criminal justice process of intimate violence cases, domestic violence policies, legal and social services for victims and offenders of intimate violence in their local areas. More than half of the sample also participated in one or two telephone follow-ups. My volunteer work for a victim service agency also contributed to the study's data.

My experience interviewing the study participants refuted the notion of an objective knowledge detached from subjective experiences. In fact, my ethnic background and my personal experience with immigration actually facilitated the communications during the interview process and improved the quality of data collected. As a first-generation immigrant from Vietnam, my experience and understanding of difficulties faced by most Vietnamese immigrants—such as language barriers, cultural shock, economic hardship, and isolation—and my ability to speak the Vietnamese language—and sometimes a mix of Vietnamese and English as it was commonly used by young Vietnamese immigrants—helped me quickly develop a good rapport with women participants in my study. My knowledge of Vietnamese culture also helped me understand subtle meanings in the words and idioms used by women participants, especially when they were related to issues considered taboo in Vietnamese culture, such as sexuality.

CORE SAMPLE CHARACTERISTICS

The demographic characteristics of women participants in the core sample were marked by economic struggles and cultural isolation. All women were born in Vietnam, but in terms of ethnicity, four were Amerasian and one was Chinese-Vietnamese. Their age ranged from 20 years old to 58 years old with the median of 40 years (see Table A1). The majority of these women came to the United States as adults in their twenties or older; only eight women were less than 20 years old when they arrived in the United States. These women left Vietnam in different situations and by different means. 12 women (35%) escaped Vietnam by boat and arrived in a country in Southeast Asia before being accepted to the United States as refugees; four women (12%) came to United States under the Amerasian Coming Home Program; 11women (32%) came as dependents of their husbands (e.g., accompanying, or sponsored by, their husbands); and six women (18%) as dependents of their parents. Only one woman came to the United States before 1975 as a student. The time these women had lived in the United States ranged from 1 to 28 years. A majority of these women (20) spent fewer than 10 years in the United States; 9 other women spent between 10 to 20 years; only 5 women spent more than 20 years (see Table A2). Of 34 women, 14 already obtained American citizenship, 13 were American permanent residents, and 7 were legal aliens (see Table A3).

A majority of women participants (18) started their intimate relationships in the United States, others in Vietnam or in refugee camps. Most women had same-ethnic husbands/partners; five had husbands/partners who came from different racial/ethnic backgrounds, including Chinese, Chinese-Vietnamese, Laotian, Iraqi, and Caucasian American. The lengths of their relationships ranged from 1 to 35 years. Sixteen women had a relationship shorter than 10 years; nine women had a relationship that lasted between 10 to 20 years; nine other women had a relationship longer than 20 years. At the time of the interviews, about half of the women (16) were legally married or had a live-in boyfriend; 12 women were separate from their partners, either legally or because of a restraining order; 6 women were divorced. Most women participants (30) had children, and the majority of these women had children under 18 years of age.

The levels of educational achievement among women participants in the core sample were lower than those in the general Vietnamese American population. Only 9% of women participants had a college degree earned in the United States compared to 17.5% of the Vietnamese American population at the 1990 Census (reported in Rumbaut, 1996). A majority of women participants had attended language programs (ESL or English as a second language) and vocational training, but most of them still did not understand English very well. Only three women considered their English proficiency as strong; two-thirds of the women (21) reported that their English was weak, but this proportion was similar to the level of English proficiency of the general Vietnamese American population in the 1990 Census (see Rumbaut, 1996). Despite their lack of English proficiency, the majority of women participants worked (24 women, or 71%), and most women participants who were employed worked in manual jobs (18 women); only two women were professionals (see Table A4, Table A5, and Table A6).

Table A1
Core Sample, Showing Years of Age

Years of Age	Number
20–29	8
30–39	8
40–49	11
50 and above	7
Total	34

Table A2
Core Sample, Showing Years in the United States

Years	Number
1–9	20
10–20	9
21 and above	5
Total	34

Table A3
Core Sample, Showing Legal Status

Legal Status	Number
U.S. citizen	14
U.S. permanent resident	13
Legal alien	7
Total	34

Table A4
Core Sample, Showing Educational Achievement in the United States

Educational Achievement	Number
ESL* and vocational	20
High school or less	8
Some college	3
College	3
Total	34

*ESL = English as a second language

Table A5
Core Sample, Showing English Proficiency

English Proficiency	Number
Good	3
Average	10
Weak	21
Total	34

Table A6
Core Sample, Showing Employment/Occupation

Employment/Occupation	Number
Unemployed	10
Manual laborer	18
Technician	2
Professional	2
Self-employed	2
Total	34

ATTITUDES OF VIETNAMESE AMERICANS TOWARD INTIMATE VIOLENCE POLICIES

A survey about the attitudes of Vietnamese Americans toward various criminal justice approaches to intimate violence was conducted in 2000 with a sample of 440 participants randomly selected in four different locations, including Orange County (CA), Houston (TX), Boston (MA), and Lansing (MI). The survey participants were asked about their knowledge of the problem of intimate violence in their communities, their perceptions about the problem's seriousness, their awareness of domestic violence policies, and their attitudes toward criminal justice interventions.

Results of the survey indicated that although Vietnamese immigrants came from a country with different family traditions and legal norms regarding domestic violence, they recognized intimate violence as a social problem and had a positive attitudes toward government interventions in intimate violence. A majority of respondents (72%) considered intimate violence a problem in their communities, although only less than half (38%) perceived it as a serious problem. In terms of their knowledge about domestic violence laws and policies, a large majority of respondents were aware of the prohibition of intimate violence in the United States and arrest policies ((97% and 80%, respectively). However, a smaller proportion of respondents understood that those who committed domestic offenses would be prosecuted (64%) (see Table B1).

Despite differences in their perceptions of the seriousness of the problem and their knowledge of criminal justice policies dealing with domestic violence, respondents to the survey showed strong support for government interventions to stop and eliminate the problem (mean score = 4.5 on a 5-point scale where 5 indicated the highest level of support) and agreed that the police should be called when domestic violence occurred (mean score = 4.4). However, their support for specific criminal justice approaches varied. Court-mandated counseling received the highest support (mean score = 4.4), followed by fines and probation (mean score = 3.8); prosecution and imprisonment received the lowest support (mean scores = 3.5 and 3.3, respectively) (see Table B2).

Table B1
Awareness of Criminal Justice Policies

Awareness of Criminal Justice Policies	Number (%)
Awareness of the prohibition of intimate violence in the U.S. (n = 414)	414 (97%)
Awareness of arrest policy for intimate violence in the U.S. (n = 407)	327 (80%)
Aware of prosecution policy for intimate violence (n = 406)	259 (64%)

Table B2
Attitude Toward Criminal Justice Interventions in Intimate Violence

Attitude	Mean Score*
Agree that intimate violence should be stopped (n = 430)	4.72
Agree that the government should intervene (n = 413)	4.50
Agree that batterers should receive court-mandated counseling (n = 376)	4.43
Agree that police should be called (n = 414)	4.39
Agree that batterers should be arrested (n = 386)	4.03
Agree that batterers should be fined (n = 355)	3.81
Agree that batterers should receive probation (n = 353)	3.81
Agree that batterers should be prosecuted (n = 371)	3.54
Agree that batterers should receive imprisonment (n = 352)	3.30

* On a 5-point scale: 1 = disagree in all situations; 2 = disagree in most situations; 3 = agree in some situations; 4 = agree in most situations; 5 = agree in all situations

BIBLIOGRAPHY

Abraham, M. (1999). Sexual abuse in South Asian immigrant marriages. *Violence Against Women*, 5, 591–618.

Abraham, M. (2000). *Speaking the Unspeakable: Marital Violence among South Asian Immigrants in the United States.* New Brunswick, NJ: Rutgers University Press.

Acker, J. (1989). The problem with patriarchy. *Sociology, 23*, 235–240.

Alexander, M. & Mohanty, C. (1997). Introduction: Genealogies, legacies, movements. In M. Alexander & C. Mohanty (Eds.), *Feminist Genealogies, Colonial Legacies, Democratic Futures* (pp. xiii–xlii). New York: Routledge.

American Bar Association. (1997). *Prosecuting Domestic Violence Cases with Reluctant Victims: Assessing Two Novel Approaches in Milwaukee.* NCJRS #169111.

American Prosecutors Research Institute. (1996). *Prosecution of Domestic Violence Offenses, Final Report.* NCJRS #168057.

American Psychological Association Presidential Task Force on Violence and the Family. (1996). *Violence and the Family.* Washington, D.C.: American Psychological Association.

Baker, P. L. (1997). And I went back: Battered women's negotiation of choice. *Journal of Contemporary Ethnography, 26*, 55–74.

Belknap, J. & McCall, K. (1994). Women battering and police referrals. *Journal of Criminal Justice, 22*, 223–236.

Berg, B. (1998). *Qualitative Research Methods for the Social Sciences.* Needham Heights, MA: Allyn & Bacon.

Berk-Seligson, S. (1990). *The Bilingual Courtroom: Court Interpreters in the Judicial Process.* Chicago: University of Chicago Press.

Berk, R., Berk, S., Newton, P. & Loseke, D. (1984). Cops on call: Summoning the police to the scene of spousal violence. *Law & Society Review, 18*, 479–498.

Berk, R., Campbell, A., Klap, A. & Western, B. (1992). *Bayesian Analysis of the Colorado Springs Spousal Assault Replication Project: Final Report to the National Institute of Justice.* Washington, D.C.: National Institute of Justice.

Bernat, F. (1985). New York State's Prostitution Statute: Case study of the discriminatory application of a gender neutral law. In C. Schweber & C. Feinman (Eds.), *Criminal Justice Politics and Women* (pp. 103–120). New York: Haworth Press.

Binder, A. & Meeker, J. (1988). Experiments as reforms. *Journal of Criminal Justice, 16*, 347–358.

———. (1992). The development of social attitudes toward spousal abuse. In E. Buzawa & C. Buzawa (Eds.), *Domestic Violence: The Changing Criminal Justice Response* (pp. 4–19). Westport, CT: Auburn House.

Black, D. (1978). Production of crime rates. In L. Savitz & N. Johnston (Eds.), *Crime in Society* (pp. 45–60). New York: John Wiley & Sons.

Blumer, H. (1969). *Symbolic Interactionism: Perspective and Method*. Englewood Cliffs, NJ: Prentice- Hall.

Bowker, L. (1982). Police service to battered women: Bad or not so bad? *Criminal Justice and Behavior, 9*, 475–496.

Bowman, C. (1992). The arrest experiments: A feminist critique. *Criminal Law & Criminology, 83*, 201–206.

Brettell, C. & Simon, R. (1986). Immigrant women: An introduction. In R. Simon & C. Brettell (Eds.), *International Migration: The Female Experience* (pp. 3–20). Totowa, NJ: Rowman & Allenheld.

Bright, S. (1994). Counsel for the poor: The death sentence not for the worst crime but for the worst lawyer. *The Yale Law Journal, 103*, 1835–1883.

Brown, S. (1994). Police response to wife beating: Neglect of a crime of violence. *Journal of Criminal Justice, 12*, 277–288.

Bui, H. (2001). Domestic violence victims' behavior in favor of prosecution: Effects of gender relations. *Women & Criminal Justice, 12*, 51–75.

———. (2002). Immigration context of wife abuse: A case of Vietnamese immigrants in the United States. In R. Muraskin (Ed.), *It's a Crime: Women and Justice*. 3rd ed. (pp. 394–410). Prentice-Hall.

———. (2003) Help-seeking behavior among abused immigrant women: A case of Vietnamese American women. *Violence Against Women, 9* (2), 207–239.

Bui, H. & Morash, M. (1999). Domestic violence in the Vietnamese community: An exploratory study. *Violence Against Women, 5*, 769–795.

Bureau of Justice Statistics. (1995). Violence against women: Estimates from the redesigned survey, August 1995. NCJ-154348 (Special Report).

Busch, N. B. & Valentine, D. (2000). Empowerment practices. *Affilia, 15*, 82–95.

Buzawa, E. & Austin, T. (1993). Determining police response to domestic violence victims. *American Behavioral Scientist, 36*, 610–623.

Buzawa, E. & Buzawa, C. (1985). Legislative trends in the criminal justice response to domestic violence. In A. Lincoln & M. Straus (Eds.), *Crime in the Family* (pp. 134–147). Springfield, IL: Charles C. Thomas.

———. (1990). *Domestic Violence: The Criminal Justice Response*. Newbury Park, CA: Sage.

———. (1993). The Scientific evidence is not conclusive: Arrest is no panacea. In R. Gelles & D. R. Loseke (Eds.), *Current Controversies on Family Violence* (pp. 337–356). Newbury Park, CA: Sage.

Cahn, N. R. (1992). Innovative approaches to the prosecution of domestic violence crimes: An overview. In E. S. Buzawa & C. G. Buzawa (Eds.), *Domestic Violence: The Changing Criminal Justice Response* (pp. 161–180). Westport, CT: Auburn House.

Calvert, R. (1975). Criminal and civil liability in husband-wife assaults. In S. Steinmetz & M. Straus (Eds.), *Violence in the Family* (pp. 88–90). New York: Dodd, Mead.

Campbell, J. C. (1992). Wife-battering: Cultural context versus Western social sciences. In D. A. Counts, K. Brown & J. C. Campbell (Eds.), *Sanctioned and Sanctuary: Cultural Perspectives on the Beating of Wives* (pp. 229–249). Boulder, CO: Westview Press.

Campbell, R. (1996). The community response to rape: An ecological conception of victims' experiences (Doctoral dissertation, Michigan State University, 1996). *Dissertation Abstracts International, 57,* 3403.

Capellaro, C. (1999). Help for battered immigrant women. *The Progressive, 61,* 15.

Caputo, R. (1988). Police response to domestic violence. *Social Casework, 69,* 81–87.

Carlson, C. & Nidey, F. (1995). Mandatory penalties, victim cooperation, and the judicial processing of domestic abuse assault cases. *Crime and Delinquency, 41,* 132–149.

Casper, J. D. & Brereton, D. (1984). Evaluating criminal justice reforms. *Law & Society Review, 18,* 122–144.

Chalk, R. & King, P. (1998). *Violence in Families: Assessing Prevention and Treatment Programs.* Washington, D. C.: National Academy Press.

Chaudhuri, M. & Daly, K. (1992). Do restraining orders help? Battered women's experience with male violence and legal process. In E. S. Buzawa & C. G. Buzawa (Eds.), *Domestic Violence: The Changing Criminal Justice Response* (pp. 227–252). Westport, CT: Auburn House.

Chin, K. (1994). Out-of-town brides: International marriage and wife abuse among Chinese immigrants. *Journal of Comparative Family Studies, 25,* 53–70.

Chow, E. N. (1987). The development of feminist consciousness among Asian American women. *Gender & Society, 1,* 284–299.

Cohn, E. (1987). Changing the domestic violence policies of urban police departments: Impact of the Minneapolis Experiment. *Response, 10,* 22–25.

Collins, P. H. (1991). *Black Feminist Thought: Knowledge, Consciousness, and the Politics of Empowerment.* New York: Routledge.

Connell, R. (1987). *Gender & Power.* Stanford, CA: Stanford University Press.

———. (1996). New directions in gender theory, masculinity research, and gender politics. *Ethnos, 6,* 157–176.

Corcoran, J., Stephenson, M., Perryman, D. & Allen, S. (2001). Perceptions and utilization of a police-social work crisis intervention approach to domestic violence. *Families in Society, 82,* 393–398.

Corsilles, A. (1994). No-drop policies in the prosecution of domestic violence cases: Guarantee to action or dangerous solution? *Fordham Law Review, 63,* 853–881.

Coulter, M., Kuehnle, K., Byers, R. & Alfonso, M. (1999). Police-reporting behavior and victim-police interactions as described by women in a domestic shelter. *Journal of Interpersonal Violence, 14,* 1290–1298.

Crowell, N. A. & Burgess, A. W. (1996). *Understanding Violence Against Women.* Washington, D.C.: National Academy Press.

Dasgupta, S. D. & Warrier, S. (1996). In the footsteps of "Arundhati": Asian Indian women's experience of domestic violence in the United States. *Violence Against Women, 2,* 238–259.

Davis, L. (1988). Shelters for battered women: Social policy responses to interpersonal violence. *Social Science Journal, 29,* 243–250.

Davis, R., Erez, E. & Avitabile, N. (1998). Immigrants and the criminal justice system: An exploratory study. *Violence & Victims, 13,* 21–30.

Davis, R. & Smith, B. (1995). Domestic violence reforms: Empty promises or fulfilled expectations? *Crime & Delinquency, 41*, 541–552.

Davis, R. & Taylor, B. (1999). Does batterer treatment reduce violence? A synthesis of the literature. *Women & Criminal Justice, 10*, 69–93.

Davis, W. (1985). Language and the justice system: Problems and issues. *Justice System Journal, 10*, 353–364.

Dill, B. (1988). Other mothers' grief: Racial and ethnic women and the maintenance of families. *Journal of Family History, 13*, 415–431.

Do, H. (1999). *The Vietnamese Americans*. Westport, CT: Greenwood Press.

Dobash, R. E. & Dobash, R. P. (1979). *Violence Against Wives: A Case Against Patriarchy*. New York: Free Press.

Dunford, F., Huizinga, D. & Elliot, D. (1990). The role of arrest in domestic assault: The Omaha Police Experiment. *Criminology, 28*, 183–206.

Dutton, D. (1995). *The Domestic Assault of Women*. Boston: Allyn & Bacon.

Dutton, D., Hart, S., Kennedy, L. & Williams, K. (1992). Arrest and the reduction of repeat wife assault. In E. S. Buzawa & C. G. Buzawa (Eds.), *Domestic Violence: The Changing Criminal Justice Response* (pp. 111–127). Westport, CT: Auburn House.

Dutton, M. A. (1992). *Empowerment and Healing the Battered Women: A Model for Assessment and Intervention*. New York: Springer.

Ellis, D. (1993). Family courts, marital conflict mediation, and wife assault. In N. Z. Hilton (Ed.), *Legal Response to Wife Assault: Current Trends and Evaluations* (pp.165–187). Newbury Park, CA: Sage.

Erez, E. & Belknap, J. (1998a). In their own words: Battered women's assessment of the criminal processing system's responses. *Violence & Victims, 13*, 251–268.

———. (1998b). Battered women and the criminal justice system: The service providers' perspective. *European Journal on Criminal Policy and Research, 6*, 37–57.

Fagan, J. (1988). Contributions of family violence research to criminal justice policy on wife assault: Paradigms of science and social control. *Violence and Victims, 3*, 159–186.

———. (1996). *The Criminalization of Domestic Violence: Promises and Limits*. Research Report. Washington, D.C.: National Institute of Justice.

Fagan, J., Friedman, E., Wexler, S. & Lewis V. (1984). *Family Violence and Public Policy: The Final Evaluation Report of the LEEA Family Violence Program*. Washington, D.C.: U.S. Department of Justice.

Feder, L. (1999). Police handling of domestic violence calls: An overview and further investigation. *Women & Criminal Justice, 10*, 49–68.

Feinman, C. (1992). Criminal code, criminal justice and female offenders: New Jersey as a case study. In I. Moyer (Ed.), *The Changing Roles of Women in the Criminal Justice System* (pp. 57–68). Prospect Heights, IL: Waveland Press.

Fernandez, M., Iwamoto, K. & Muscat, B. (1997). Dependency and severity of abuse: Impact on women's persistence in utilizing the court system as protection against domestic violence. *Women & Criminal Justice, 9*, 39–63.

Ferraro, K. J. (1989). Policing women battering. *Social Problems, 36*, 61–71.

———. (1993). Cops, courts, and woman beating. In P. B. Bart & E. G. Moran (Eds.), *Violence Against Women: The Bloody Footprints* (pp. 165–176). Newbury Park, CA: Sage.

Ferraro, K. J. & Pope, L. (1993). Irreconcilable differences: Battered women, police, and the law. In N. Z. Hilton (Ed.), *Legal Response to Wife Assault: Current Trends and Evaluation* (pp. 96–123). Newbury Park, CA: Sage.

Figueira-McDonough, J. (1985). Gender differences in formal processing: A look at charge bargaining and sentence reduction in Washington, D.C. *Journal of Research in Crime and Delinquency, 22,* 101–133.

Finnen, C. & Cooperstein, R. (1983). *South East Asian Refugee Resettlement at the Local Level.* Menlo Park, CA: SRI International.

Fischer, K. & Rose, M. (1995). When 'enough is enough': Battered women's decision making around court orders of protection. *Crime & Delinquency, 41,* 414–429.

Fix, M. & Passel, J. (1994). *Immigration and Immigrants.* Washington, D.C. : The Urban Institute.

Ford, D. A. (1983). Wife battery and criminal justice: A study of victim decision-making. *Family Relations, 32,* 463–475.

Ford, D. A. & Regoli, M. J. (1993). The criminal prosecution of wife assaulters. In N. Z. Hilton (Ed.), *Legal Response to Wife Assault: Current Trends and Evaluation* (pp. 127–164). Newbury Park, CA: Sage.

Friedman, L. & Shulman, M. (1990). Domestic Violence: The Criminal Justice Response. In A. Lurigio, W. Skogan & R. Davis (Eds.), *Victim of Crime: Problems, Policies, and Programs* (pp. 87–103). Newbury Park, CA: Sage.

Gabaccia, D. (1994). *From the Other Side: Women, Gender, and Immigrant life in the U.S. 1820–1990.* Bloomington, IN: Bloomington University Press.

Gelles, R. (1976). Abused wives: Why do they stay? *Journal of Marriage and the Family, 33,* 659–668.

Gershman, B. L. (1990). *Prosecutorial Misconduct.* New York: Clark Boardman.

Glenn, E. (1986). *Issei, Nisei, War Brides: Three Generations of Japanese American Women at Domestic Services.* Philadelphia: Temple University Press.

Glenn, G. (1994) *Michigan Criminal Law and Procedure.* Rochester, NY: Lawyers Cooperative Publishing.

Gold, Scott & Tran, M. (2000). Vietnamese refugees finally find home. *The Los Angeles Times,* April 24.

Gold, Steven. (1992). *Refugee Communities.* Newbury Park, CA: Sage.

Gondolf, E. W. (1988). *Battered Women as Survivors: An Alternative to Treating Learned Helplessness.* Lexington, MA: Lexington Books.

Goolkasian, G. (1986). *Confronting Domestic Violence: A Guide for Criminal Justice Agencies.* Washington, D.C.: National Institute of Justice.

Gordon, M. (1964). *Assimilation in American Life: The Role of Race, Religion, and National Origins.* New York: Oxford University Press.

Gorelick, S. (1991). Contradictions of feminist methodology. *Gender & Society, 5,* 459–477.

Grau, J., Fagan, J. & Wexler, S. (1984). Restraining orders for battered women: Issues in access and efficacy. *Women & Politics, 4,* 13–28.

Hackler, J. (1991). The reduction of violent crime through economic equality for women. *Journal of Family Violence, 6,* 199–216.

Hagan, F. (1993). *Research Methods in Criminal Justice and Criminology.* New York: Macmillan.

Haines, D. (1986). Vietnamese refugee women in the U.S. labor force: Continuity or change? In R. J. Simon & C. B. Brettell (Eds.), *International Migration: The Female Experience* (pp. 62–75). Totowa, NJ: Rowman & Allenheld.

Harding, S. (1986). *The Science Question of Feminism: From Feminist Empiricism to Feminist Standpoint Epistemologies.* Ithaca, NY: Cornell University Press.

———. (1987). *Feminism and Methodology.* Bloomington, IN: Indiana University Press.

————. (1991). *Whose Science? Whose Knowledge? Thinking from Women's Lives.* Ithaca, NY: Cornell University Press.

Harrell, A. & Smith, B. (1996). Effects of restraining orders on domestic violence victims. In E. Buzawa & C. Buzawa (Eds.), *Do Arrests and Restraining Orders Work?* (pp. 214–242). Thousand Oaks, CA: Sage.

Hart, B. (1991). *The Legal Road to Freedom.* Harrisburg, PA: Pennsylvania Coalition Against Domestic Violence.

————. (1993). Battered women and the criminal justice system. *American Behavioral Scientist, 36,* 624–638.

Hartsock, N. (1983). The feminist standpoint: Developing the ground for a specifically feminist historical materialism. In S. Harding & M. Hintikka (Eds.), *Discovering Reality* (pp. 283–310). New York: D. Reidel Publishing.

Heise, L., Pitanguy, J. & Germain, A. (1994). *Violence Against Women: The Hidden Health Burden.* Washington, D.C.: The World Bank.

Hilton, N. (1989). One in ten: The struggle and disempowerment of the battered women's movement. *Canadian Journal of Family Law, 7,* 315–335.

————. (1993). Police intervention and public opinion. In N. Hilton (Ed.), *Legal Response to Wife Assault: Current Trends and Evaluations* (pp. 37–61). Newbury Park, CA: Sage.

Hirschel, J., Hutchinson, I. & Dean, C. (1992). The failure of arrest to deter spouse abuse. *Journal of Research in Crime and Delinquency, 29,* 7–33.

hooks, b. (1984). *Feminist Theory: From Margin to Center.* Boston: South End Press.

Hooper, M. (1996). When domestic violence diversion is no longer an option: What to do with the female offender. *Berkeley Women's Law Journal, 6,* 168–181.

Houston, M., Kramer, R. & Barrett, J. (1984). Female predominance in immigration to the US since 1930: A first look. *International Migration Review, 18,* 908–957.

Hoyle, C. & Sanders, A. (2000). Police response to domestic violence: From victim choice to victim empowerment? *British Journal of Criminology, 40,* 14–36.

Huisman, K. (1996). Wife battering in Asian American communities: Identifying the service needs of an overlooked segment of the U.S. population. *Violence Against Women, 2,* 260–283.

Hutchison, I. & Hirschel, D. (1998). Abused Women. *Violence Against Women, 4,* 436–456.

Jaffe, P. G., Hastings, E., Reitzel, D. & Austin, G. W. (1993). The impact of police laying charges. In N. Z. Hilton (Ed.), *Legal Response to Wife Assault: Current Trends and Evaluation* (pp. 62–95). Newbury Park, CA: Sage.

Jamieson, N. (1993). *Understanding Vietnam.* Berkeley, CA: University of California Press.

Jang, D., Lee, D. & Morello-Frosch, R. (1990). Domestic violence in the immigrant and refugee community: Responding to the needs of immigrant women. *Response, 13,* 2–7.

Johnson, I. (1990). A loglinear analysis of abused wives' decisions to call the police in domestic violence disputes. *Journal of Criminal Justice, 18,* 147–159.

Johnson, I., Sigler, R. & Crowley, J. (1994). Domestic violence: A Comparative study of perceptions and attitudes toward domestic abuse cases among social service and criminal justice professionals. *Journal of Criminal Justice, 22,* 237–248.

Jones, A. (1994). *Next Time, She'll Be Dead: Battering and How to Stop It.* Boston: Beacon Press.

Kaci, J. (1992). A study of protective orders issued under California's Domestic Violence Prevention Act. *Criminal Justice Review, 17,* 61–76.

Kandiyoti, D. (1991). Bargaining with patriarchy. In J. Lorber and S. Farrell (Eds.), *The Social Construction of Gender* (pp. 104–118). Newbury, CA: Sage.

Kantor, K. & Straus, M. (1990). Response of victims and the police to assaults on wives. In M. Straus & R. Gelles (Eds.), *Physical Violence in American Families: Risk Factor and Adaptation to Violence in 8,145 Families* (pp. 473–486). New Brunswick, NJ: Transaction.

Kanuha, V. (1996). Domestic violence, racism, and the battered women's movement in the Unites States. In J. L. Edleson & Z. C. Eisikovits (Eds.), *Future Interventions with Battered Women and Their Families* (pp. 34–50). Thousand Oaks, CA: Sage.

Kennedy, D. & Homant R. (1983). Attitudes of abused women toward male and female police officers. *Criminal Justice & Behavior, 10*, 391–405.

Keyes, C. (1977). *The Golden Peninsula.* New York: Macmillan.

Kibria, N. (1993). *Family Tightrope: The Changing Lives of Vietnamese Americans.* Princeton, NJ: Princeton University Press.

Kim, H. (1996). American naturalization and immigration policy: Asian-American perspective. In H. Kim (Ed.), *Asian Americans and Congress.* Westport, CT: Greenwood Press.

Kirwood, C. (1993). *Leaving Abusive Partners.* London: Sage.

Klein, C. & Orloff, L. (1999). Protecting battered women: Latest trends in civil legal relief. *Women & Criminal Justice, 10*, 29–47.

Koss, M. , Goodman, L., Browne, A., Fitzgerald, L. & Russo, N. (1994). *No Safe Haven: Male Violence Against Women at Home, at Work, and in the Community.* Washington, D.C.: American Psychological Association.

Kruttschnitt, C. (1984). Sex and criminal justice court dispositions: The unresolved controversy. *Research in Crime and Delinquency, 21*, 213–231.

Lamphere, L., Zavella, P. & Gonzales, F. (1993). *Sunbelt Working Mothers: Reconciling Family and Factory.* Ithaca, NY: Cornell University Press.

Langley, R. & Levy, R. (1977). *Wife Beating: The Silent Crisis.* New York: E. P. Dutton.

Lee, M. & Au, P. (1998). Chinese battered women in North America: Their experiences and treatment. In A. Roberts (Ed.), *Battered Women and Their Families: Intervention and Treatment Programs* (pp. 448–482). New York: Springer.

Lempert, R. 1989. Humility is a Virtue: On the publicization of policy relevant research. *Law & Society Review, 23*, 145–161.

Lerman, L. G. (1986). Prosecution of wife beaters: Institutional obstacles and innovations. In M. Lystad (Ed.), *Violence in the Home: Interdisciplinary Perspectives* (pp. 250–295). New York: Brunner-Mazel.

Lewis, R., Dobash, R. P., Dobash, R. E. & Cavanagh, K. (2000). Protection, prevention, rehabilitation or justice? Women's use of the law to challenge domestic violence. *International Review of Victimology, 7* (Special Issue), 179–205.

Lin, K., Tazuma, L. & Masuda, M. (1979). Adaptation problems of Vietnamese refugees. *Archives of General Psychiatry, 36*, 955–961.

Lincoln, Y. & Guba, E. (1985). Postpositivism and the naturalist paradigm. In Y. Lincoln & E. Guba (Eds.), *Naturalistic Inquiry* (pp. 14–46). Newbury Park, CA: Sage.

Maguire, P. (1987). Doing participatory research: Feminist approach. *Perspectives, 5*, 33–37.

Mahoney, M. (1994). Victimization of oppression? Women's lives, violence, and agency. In M. A. Fineman & R. Mykitiuk (Eds.), *The Public Nature of Private Violence* (pp. 59–92). New York: Routledge.

Mann, C. R. (1993). *Unequal Justice: A Question of Color.* Bloomington, IN: Indiana University Press.

Manning, P. (1993). The preventive conceit: The black box in market context. *American Behavioral Scientist, 36,* 639–650.

Martell, S. & Tran, M. (2000a). 25 years after the fall of Saigon, a Vietnamese enclave thrives. *The Los Angeles Times,* April 28. Available: http://www. latimes.com/cgi-bin/print.cgi.

———. (2000b). A generation removed: War refugees find a haven in Orange County and change it forever. *The Los Angles Times,* April 28. Available: http://www.latimes. com/cgi-bin/print.cgi.

Martin, D. (1978). Battered women: Society's problem. In J. Chapman & M. Gates (Eds.). *The Victimization of Women* (pp. 111–141). Beverly Hills, CA: Sage.

———. (1987). The historical root of domestic violence. In D. J. Sonkin (Ed.), *Domestic Violence on Trial* (pp. 3–21). New York: Springer.

Maxfield, M. & Babbie, E. (1998). *Research Methods for Criminal Justice and Criminology.* Belmont, CA: West/Wadsworth.

McCall, M. & Becker, H. (1990). Introduction. In H. Becker & M. McCall (Eds.), *Symbolic Interaction and Cultural Studies* (pp. 1–15). Chicago, IL: University of Chicago Press.

McCall, M. & Wittner, J. (1990). The good news about life history. In H. Becker & M. McCall (Eds.), *Symbolic Interaction and Cultural Studies* (pp. 46–89). Chicago, IL: University of Chicago Press.

McKeel, A. J. & Sporakowski, M. J. (1993). How shelter counselors' views about responsibility of wife abuse relate to services they provide to battered wives. *Journal of Family Violence, 8,* 101, 107.

McKinnon, C. (1987). Feminism, marxism, method, and the state: Toward feminist jurisprudence. In S. Harding (Ed.), *Feminism and Methodology* (pp. 135–155). Bloomington, IN: Indiana University Press.

McLeod, M. (1983). Victim non-cooperation in the prosecution of domestic assault. *Criminology, 21,* 395–408.

Mehrotra, M. (1999). The social construction of wife abuse: Experiences of Asian Indian women in the U.S. *Violence Against Women, 5,* 619–640.

Merriam, S. (1998). *Qualitative Research and Case Study Applications in Education.* San Francisco, CA: Jossey-Bass.

Messerschmidt, J. (1993). *Masculinities and Crime.* Boston: Rowman & Littlefield.

Miller, S. (2001). The paradox of women arrested for domestic violence. *Violence Against Women, 7,* 1339–1376.

Mills, L. (1996). Empowering battered women transnationally: The case for postmodern interventions. *Social Work, 41,* 261–268.

Mills, W. (1959). *Sociological Imagination.* New York: Oxford University Press.

Mohanty, C. (1991). Under Western eyes. In C. Mohanty, A. Russo & L. Torres (Eds.), *Third World Women and the Politics of Feminism* (pp. 51–80). Bloomington: Indiana University Press.

Moore, J. & Mamiya, R. (1999). Interpreters in court proceedings. In J. Moore (Ed.), *Immigrants in Courts* (pp. 29–45). Seattle, WA: University of Washington Press.

Morash, M., Bui, H. & Santiago, A. (2000). Cultural-specific gender ideology and wife abuse in Mexican-descent families. *International Review of Victimology, 7* (Special Issue), 67–91.

Nguyen, H. & Haines, D. (1996). Vietnamese. In D. Haines (Ed.), *Refugees in America in the 1990s* (pp. 305–327). Westport, CT: Greenwood Press.

Nguyen, L. (1987). Cross cultural adjustment of Vietnamese in the U.S. In L. Truong (Ed.), *Borrowing and Adaptation in Vietnamese Culture* (pp. 1–21). Hawaii: University of Hawaii at Manoa.

Okun, L. (1988). Termination or resumption of co-habitation in women battering relationships: A statistical study. In G. T. Hotaling, D. Finkerhor, J. T. Kirkpatrick & M. A. Straus (Eds.), *Coping with Family Violence: Research and Policy Perspectives* (pp. 107–121). Newbury Park, CA: Sage.

Office of Refugee Resettlement. (1993). *Report to the Congress: Refugee Resettlement Program (FY 1993)*. U.S. Department of Health and Human Services.

Oppenlander, N. (1988). Coping or copping out. *Criminology, 20*, 449–465.

Orloff, L., Jang, D. & Klein, C. (1995). With no place to turn: Improving advocacy for battered immigrant women. *Family Law Quarterly, 29*, 312–329.

Parnas, R. (1967). The police response to the domestic disturbance. *Wisconsin Law Review*, Fall: 914–960.

Pate, A. & Hamilton, E. (1992). Formal and informal deterrent to domestic violence: The Dale County Spouse Assault Experiment. *American Sociological Review, 57*, 691–697.

Pearson, J., Thoennes, N. & Griswold, E. (1999). Child support and domestic violence: The victims speak out. *Violence Against Women, 5*, 427–448.

Peled, E., Eisikivits, Z., Enosh, G. & Winstok, Z. (2000). Choice and empowerment for battered women who stay: Toward a constructivist model. *Social Work, 45*, 9–25.

Piven, F. (1990). Ideology and the state: Women, power, and the welfare state. In L. Gordon (Ed.), *Women, the State, and Welfare* (pp. 250–264). Madison, WI: University of Wisconsin Press.

Pleck, E. (1987). *Domestic Tyranny: The Making of Social Policy Against Family Violence from Colonial Times to the Present*. New York: Oxford University Press.

Portes, A. & Rumbaut, R. (1996). *Immigrant America: A Portrait*. Berkeley, CA: University of California Press.

Preisser, A. (1999). Domestic violence in South Asian communities in America: Advocacy and intervention. *Violence Against Women, 5*, 684–699.

Radford, J. & Stanko, E. (1991). Violence against women and children: The contradictions of crime control under patriarchy. In K. Stenson & D. Cowell (Eds.), *The Politics of Crime Control* (pp. 188–202). London: Sage.

Raj, A., Silverman, J., Wingood, G. & DiClemente, R. (1999). Prevalence and correlates of relationship abuse among a community-based sample of low-income African American women. *Violence Against Women, 5*, 273–291.

Rasche, C. (1988). Minority women and domestic violence: The unique dilemma of battered women of color. *Journal of Contemporary Criminal Justice, 4*, 151–171.

Rauma, D. (1984). Going for the gold: Prosecutorial decision making in cases of wife assault. *Social Science Research, 13*, 321–351.

Reinharz, S. (1992). *Feminist Methods in Social Research*. New York: Oxford University Press.

Rimonte, N. (1989). Domestic violence among Pacific Asians: In Asian Women United of California (Ed.), *Making Waves: An Anthology of Writings by and about Asian American Women* (pp. 327–337). Boston: Beacon Press.

Roberts, A. & Starr, P. (1989). Differential reference group assimilation among Vietnamese refugees. In D. Haines (Ed.), *Refugees as Immigrants: Cambodians, Laotians, and Vietnamese in America* (pp. 40–54). Totowa, NJ: Rowman & Littlefield.

Roy, M. (1977). *Battered Women*. New York: Van Nostrand Reinhold.

Rumbaut, R. (1996). Origins and destinies: Immigration, race, and ethnicity in contempo-
   rary America. In S. Pedraza & R. Rumbaut (Eds.), *Origins and Destinies: Immigration,
   Race, and Ethnicity in America* (pp. 21–42). Belmont, CA: Wadsworth.
Schechter, S. (1982). *Women and Male Violence: The Visions and Struggles of the Battered
   Women's Movement.* London: Pluto Press.
Schmidt, J. & Steury, E. (1989). Prosecutorial discretion in filing charges in domestic vio-
   lence cases. *Criminology, 27,* 487–502.
Schwartz. M. D. (1988). Marital status and women abuse theory. *Journal of Family Violence,
   3,* 239–248.
Scott, J. (1986). Gender: A useful category of historical analysis. *American Historical Review,
   91,* 1053–1075.
Sengupta, S. (2001). Domestic violence law set to be renewed. *The New York Time,* June 11,
   p. B.6.
Sherman, L. (1988). *Domestic Violence.* Washington, D.C.: U.S. Department of Justice, Na-
   tional Institute of Justice.
———. (1992). The influence of criminology on criminal law: Evaluating arrests for mis-
   demeanor domestic violence. *Journal of Criminal Law & Criminology, 83,* 1–45.
Sherman, L. & Berk, R. (1984). The specific deterrent effects of arrests for domestic assault.
   American Sociological Review, 27, 487–519.
Sherman, L. & Cohn, E. (1989). The impact of research on legal policy: The Minneapolis
   Domestic Violence Experiment. *Law & Society Review, 23,* (1), 117–144.
Sherman. L., Schmidt, J., Rogan, D., Smith, D., Gartin, P., Cohn, E., Collins, D. & Bacich, A.
   (1992). The variable effects of arrest on criminal careers: The Milwaukee Domestic Vi-
   olence Experiment. *Journal of Criminal Law and Criminology, 83,* 137–169.
Shusta, R., Levine, D., Harris, P. & Wong, H. (1995). *Multicultural Law Enforcement.* Saddle
   River, NJ: Prentice-Hall.
Singer, S. (1988). The fear of reprisal and the failure of victims to report a personal crime.
   Journal of Quantitative Criminology, 4, 289–302.
Singh, R. & Uinnithan, P. (1999). Wife burning: Cultural cues for lethal violence against
   women among Asian Indians in the U.S. *Violence Against Women, 5,* 641–653.
Smith, D. (1987). *The Everyday Work as Problematic: A Feminist Sociology.* Boston: North-
   eastern University Press.
———. (1990). Women's experience as radical critique of sociology. In D. Smith (Ed.),
   The Conceptual Practices of Power (pp. 11–28). Boston: Northeastern University Press.
Smith, D. & Klein, J. (1984). Police control of interpersonal disputes. *Social Problems, 31,*
   468–481.
Sorin, M. D. (1985). *Out on Bail.* Washington, D.C.: U.S. Department of Justice.
Spangenberg, R. (1989). We are still not defending the poor properly. *Criminal Justice, 4,*
   11–13, 44–46.
Spelman, E. (1988). *Inessential Woman: The Problems of Exclusion in Feminist Thoughts.*
   Boston: Beacon Press.
Stalans, L. & Lurigio, A. (1995). Public preferences for the court's handling of domestic vio-
   lence situations. *Crime and Delinquency, 41,* 399–413.
Stark, E. (1993). Mandatory arrest of batterers: A reply to its critics. *American Behavioral Sci-
   entist, 35,* 651–680.
Stark, E. & Flitscraft, A. H. (1992). Spouse abuse. In J. M. Last & R. B. Wallace (Eds.), *Public
   Health and Preventive Medicine* (pp. 1040–1043). Norwalk, CT: Appleton & Lange.

Stephens, B.J. & Sinden, P. G. (2000). Victims' voices. *Journal of Interpersonal Violence, 15,* 534–547.

Stith, S. (1990). Police response to domestic violence: The influence of individual and familial factors. *Violence and Victims, 5,* 37–49.

Stitt, G. & Chaires, R. (1993). Plea bargaining: Ethical issues and emerging perspectives. *The Justice Professional, 7,* 69–91.

Straus, M. A., Gelles, R. J. & Steinmetz, S. K. (1980). *Behind Closed Doors: Violence in American Families.* Garden City, NY: Anchor Press/Doubleday.

Straus, M. & Gelles, R. (1986). Societal change and change in family violence from 1975–1985 as revealed by two national surveys. *Journal of Marriage and the Family, 48,* 465–480.

Strauss, A. (1987). *Qualitative Analysis for Social Scientists.* New York: Cambridge University Press.

Strube, M. J. & Barbour, L. S. (1983). The decision to leave an abusive relationship: Economic dependence and psychological commitment. *Journal of Marriage and the Family, 45,* 785–793.

———. (1984). Factors related to the decision to leave an abusive relationship. *Journal of Marriage and the Family, 46,* 837–844.

Sullivan, C. (1991). The provision of advocacy services to women leaving abusive partners. *Journal of Interpersonal Violence, 5,* 41–54.

Ta, T. (1981). The Status of women in traditional Vietnam: A comparison of the Code of the Le Dynasty (1428–1788) with the Chinese Codes. *Journal of Asian History, 15,* 97–145.

———. (1999). Vietnamese immigrants in American courts. In J. Moore (Ed.), *Immigrants in Courts* (pp.140–157). Seattle, WA: University of Washington Press.

Thompson, G. (1999). Deportation risk grows for abused illegal residents. *New York Times,* April 18, p. 37.

Tran, C. (1997). Domestic violence among Vietnamese refugee women: Prevalence, abuse characteristics, psychiatric symptoms, and psychological factors (Doctoral dissertation, Boston University, 1997). *Dissertation Abstracts International, 57,* 7237.

Tran, M. (2000). Poll finds paradox among Vietnamese in Orange County. *The Los Angeles Times,* April 20. Available: http://www.latimes.com/cgi-bin/ print.cgi.

Tran, T. (1959). *Vietnam.* New York: Frederick A. Preager.

Uphoff, R. (1992). The criminal defense lawyer: Zealous advocate, double agent, or beleaguered dealer? *Criminal Law Bulletin, 28,* 418–456.

U.S. Census Bureau (1993). *We the Americans: Asians.* Washington, D.C.: U.S. Government Printing Office.

———. (2000). *From the Mideast to the Pacific: A Profile of the Nation's Asian Foreign-Born Population.* Washington, D.C.: U.S. Department of Commerce.

———. (2002). *The Asian Population: 2000.* Washington, D.C.: U.S. Department of Commerce.

U.S. Department of Justice. (1984). *Attorney General's Task Force on Family Violence: Final Report.* Washington, D.C.: U.S. Government Printing Office.

———. (1999). *Annual Admission of Immigrants. Immigration and Naturalization Services.* Available: http://www.ins.usdoj.gov/graphics/publicaffairs/newsrels/98Legal.pdf.

Vu, M. (1971). *Co Luat Viet Nam Luoc Khao (Survey of Traditional Vietnamese Law).* Saigon, Vietnam. (Published by the author himself).

Walby, S. (1989). Theorizing patriarchy. *Sociology, 23,* 213–234.

Walker, L. (1979). *The Battered Women.* New York: Harper & Row.

Walsh, K. (1995). The mandatory arrest law: Police reaction. *Pace Law Review, 16,* 97–108.

Wanless, M. (1996). Mandatory arrest: A step toward eradicating domestic violence, but is it enough? *University of Illinois Law Review, 2,* 533–586.

Websdale, N. (1995). An ethnographic assessment of the policing of domestic violence in rural eastern Kentucky. *Social Justice, 22,* 102–122.

Yoshihama, M. (1999). Domestic violence against women of Japanese descent in Los Angeles: Two methods of estimating prevalence. *Violence Against Women, 5,* 869–897.

Zalman, M. (1992). The court's response to police intervention in domestic violence. In E. Buzawa & C. Buzawa (Eds.), *Domestic Violence: The Changing Criminal Justice Response* (pp. 79–109). Westport, CT: Auburn House.

Zhou, M. & Bankston, III, C. (1998). *Growing Up American: How Vietnamese Children Adapt to Life in the U.S.* New York: Russell Sage Foundation.

Zinn, M. B. & Dill, B. (1994). Difference and domination. In M. B. Zinn & B. Dill (Eds.), *Women of Color in the U.S. Society* (pp. 3–12). Philadelphia: Temple University Press.

LEGAL CASE

State v. Oliver, 70 N.C. 60, 1874.

INDEX

ABA Model Code of Professional Responsibility, 81
Abused women: characteristics, 6; desire to drop charge, 114; diverse expectations, 8, 124; diverse experiences, 9; experiences with criminal justice interventions, 11; opposition to arrest, 47
Allen, Shannon, 116
American common law, husband's right, 120
American jurisprudence, husband's right, 120
Anti-immigrant sentiment, effect of, 36
Arrest policies: consequences, 118; effects, 4, 113, 117; implementation, 49–50; mandatory arrest, 4, 47, 71, 130; zero-tolerance policy, 130. *See also* Women's arrest
Assimilation, experience of Vietnamese immigrants, 128

Bail: purpose, 78–79; for women offenders in domestic violence cases, 79. *See also* Women offenders
Battered women's advocates, roles and contributions 4, 114
Battered women's movement, 114, 121

Batterers' treatment programs, 4, 116; effects, 4
Belknap, Joanne, 123
Boat people, 18
Buddhism, 19–20

Campbell, Rebecca, 132
Child custody, effects of criminal justice interventions, 106
Chin, Ko-Lin, 103
Chivalrous treatments, 79
Collectivism: effects on abused women's help-seeking decision, 123; effects on family relationships, 107–108
Confucianism, 19–20
Corcoran, Jacqueline, 116
Court delays, 63, 84
Court Interpreters Act of 1978, 59
Court interventions, effects, 96
Court-mandated treatment, 4, 115, 116
Court's culture and biases, 82–84
Criminal justice interventions: criminal justice indifference, 120; effectiveness, 4, 94–98, 113, 121; effects on family relationships, 102–108; financial costs, 109–111; gender-blind policy, 119; impact on women's safety, 95; tradi-

tional judicial responses, 50, 114; unintended consequences, 5

Criminal justice process: barriers to participation, 57; lack of understanding, 61

Criminal justice responses. *See* Criminal justice interventions

Criminal justice system: organizational goals, 118; practices of criminal justice agencies, 11; traditional goals, 115

Criminalization of family violence, 115; consequences, 117

Culture: cultural constraint, 118; cultural isolation, 37

Deportation of aliens, 39, 54. *See also* Illegal Immigration Reform and Responsibility Act of 1996

Deterrence, 93, 115; effectiveness, 98–99; theory, 124

Diversion program, for domestic violence cases, 2

Divorce: approach to domestic violence, 117; consequence of criminal justice interventions, 105

Domestic violence: women's experiences, 11, 27–34; women's response, 11

Domestic violence law: effectiveness, 121; issues in enforcement, 4

Domestic violence policies: effects, 113; narrow vision, 114. *See also* Criminal justice interventions

Dual arrests, 119. *See also* Women's arrest

Economic dependency, 35–36, 121; absolute dependency, 122; issues in conceptualization, 122; relative dependency, 122

Economic isolation, 35–36, 117

Emotional abuse, 7, 28, 74; consequence of criminal justice interventions, 103–105

English common law, husband's right, 120

Enhanced penalty, effects, 117

Erez, Edna, 123

Family breakups, consequence of criminal justice interventions, 103, 106

Feminist: research methods, 131; scholarship on women's experiences, 9; standpoint approach, 8, 13; theories, 9

Feminist-oriented therapy approach, 116

Feminist-oriented victim services, 117

Figueria-McDonough, Josefina, 80

Five Cardinal Virtues, 20

Four Virtues, 22, 27

Gender bias, 119

Gender practices, 11

Gender roles, changing views, 30, 32

Germain, Adrienne, 105

Gonzales, Felipe, 10

Grassroots activists, in battered women's movement, 4

Harding, Sandra, 10

Heise, Lori, 105

Heterosexuality, in gender ideology, 117

Housing assistance, for battered women, 68

Humanitarian Operation (HO) program, 19

Ideology of marriage, 117

Ideology of women's empowerment, 121

Illegal Immigration Reform and Responsibility Act of 1996, 39, 54

Immediate protection, by criminal justice interventions, 94

Immigrant family life: changes in family life, 23–25, 41; experiences with resettlement, 6, 23; men's downward mobility, 24–25, 41; men's jealousy, 31; role reversal, 24, 27–30; shift in family dynamics, 24, 29

Immigrants: jobs, 32; resettlement experience, 6; undocumented immigrants, 6

Immigration Act of 1965, 7

Immigration laws, effects on domestic violence, 12

Immigration Marriage Fraud Amendment (IMFA), 38

Immigration status, effects on women's help-seeking behavior, 38–39

Intimate violence. *See* Domestic violence

Judicial process: judicial indifference, 5, 50; victims' cooperation, 5

Lamphere, Louis, 10
Language barriers: problems caused by translation, 82; problems in communications with the police, 58–61, 76; problems with legal counsel, 86; women's special needs, 118
Legal advocacy, for abused women, 116
Legal services, for abused women, 67
Lewis, Ruth, 101
Lin, Keh-Ming, 31
Little Saigon, 25, 127–128

Manning, Peter, 11
Masuda, Minoru, 31
Matrix of domination, 10, 123
Miller, Susan, 85
Minneapolis Experiment, 102
Minority communities, effects on abused women's help-seeking behavior, 123
Mississippi Supreme Court, ruling on wife beating, 120
Mutual combat, 119. *See* also Women's arrest

No-contact bond, 2, 15
No-drop-charge policies 4, 5, 51, 62; effects, 117
North Carolina Supreme Court, ruling on wife beating, 120

Orderly Departure Program (ODP), 19

Patriarchy, 9
Penalty enhancement, in domestic violence cases, 115
Perryman, Derrelyn, 116
Personal protection order (PPO). *See* Restraining order
Physical abuse, forms, 28–29; attack strategies, 33; injuries, 33–34
Pitanguy, Jacqueline, 105

Police attitudes, 47
Police interventions: domestic violence cases, 47–50, 114; effects, 96
Police referrals, 64
Pro-arrest policies, 47; assumption, 102; purpose, 115
Probation, domestic violence cases, 87
Prosecution: consequences, 118; effectiveness, 99, 113; mandatory prosecution, 4; no-drop-charge policies, 115; obstacles to prosecution, 50; prosecution decision, 80; prosecutor-filing-charge policies, 51; prosecutors' indifference, 62; women's desire to drop charges, 50, 52–54
Prosecutorial innovations, 115–116
Psychological abuse, 7. *See also* Emotional abuse
Public assistance, 67; impacts, 67–68
Punishment package, domestic violence cases, 87, 116, 130
Punitive treatment, 115

Quasi-judicial remedies, 114

Racial discrimination, effect on women's help-seeking behavior, 123
Racism, effects on gender relationships, 13
Radford, Jill, 123
Restraining order: effectiveness, 97–98, 101, 113; limited use, 55–57; obtaining, 55, 130–131; terminating, 56, 98; unintended consequences, 106; violation, 56–57, 98; for women offenders, 88
Rhetoric of empowerment, 121
Rimonte, Nilda, 27
Romulus, 120
ROVR (Resettlement Opportunities for Vietnamese Returnees) program, 1, 42, 90

Separation: consequences of restraining order, 106; effects on women's housing status, 111
Short-term prevention, 94
Smith, Dorothy, 9
Social control model, 116

Social isolation, 35
Social power, 11, 12
Spouse abuse, dynamics, 29
Stanko, Elizabeth, 123
Stark, Evan, 5
Stephenson, Margaret, 116
Structural inequality, effects on women's empowerment, 120
Support services, for abused women, 63
Symbolic interactionism, 8, 13

Taoism, 19–20
Tazuma, Laurie, 31
Three Obediences, 22, 27
Translation assistance, 59; problems, 60. *See also* Language barriers
Tu Luc Van Doan, 23

Victim advocate, 121
Victim assistance program, 116
Victim services, 64–66, 117; bilingual services, 65; health-care services, 65; services for Vietnamese immigrants, 128–130; services for women offenders, 87
Victim-witness program, 116
Vietnam syndrome, 24
Vietnam War, effects on Vietnamese immigration, 17
Vietnamese Amerasians, 19; experience of racial prejudice, 34
Vietnamese Americans. *See* Vietnamese immigrants
Vietnamese culture: changes, 25, 128; religious outlooks, 19. *See also* Little Saigon
Vietnamese family traditions, 20–23, 39
Vietnamese gender norms, 25
Vietnamese immigrant women: barriers to seeking help, 35; resettlement experiences, 6; seeking help with the personal support network, 34; seeking help from the criminal justice system, 39
Vietnamese immigrants: attitudes toward acculturation, 128; attitudes toward interracial marriages, 34; attitudes toward intimate violence, 46, 51, 137; intimate violence report, 46; population, 17, 18, 25, 46, 129; resettlement experience, 128
Vietnamese immigration, 19, 72
Vietnamese social practices and traditions, 20

Welfare policies, effects on domestic violence, 12
Women offenders: bail status, 78–79; convictions and sentences, 87; court delays, 84; custody status, 89; language barriers, 86; legal counsel, 80, 85–86; plea bargaining, 80–82; prosecution, 80. *See also* Bail
Women's arrest, 71, 76; dual arrest, 119
Women's choice, 120
Women's cultural image, 11
Women's disempowerment, 117; consequence of criminal justice interventions, 118
Women's empowerment, 98–100, 120–124; theory, 121
Women's powerlessness, in plea bargaining, 80. *See also* Women offenders
Women's safety, 94
Women's shelters, in Vietnamese communities, 128–130
Women's status, in Vietnamese traditional culture, 20–23

Zavella, Patricia, 10

ABOUT THE AUTHOR

HOAN N. BUI is Assistant Professor in the Department of Sociology at the University of Tennessee, Knoxville.

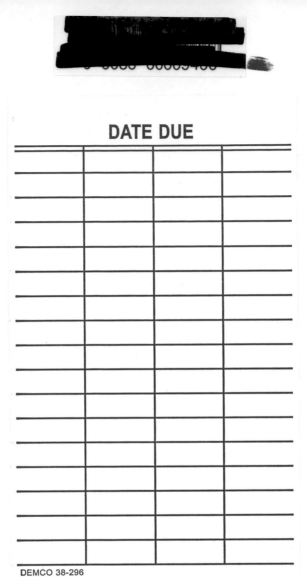

DATE DUE